Florida State Parks

Travel to all the Florida State Parks

This book belongs to ______________________

Call this number if found _________________

My Nature Book Adventures

www.mynaturebookadventures.com
11th Edition - updated 2022

ISBN 978-1-956162-07-3

https://www.floridastateparks.org/parks-and-trails

https://mynaturebookadventures.com/

What you will find inside

The **FLORIDA** State Parks Adventure Book is part planner, part journal, and 100% your adventure! Created to include dedicated space for you to plan your journey and share your experience. Check out each of the Parks and cross them off your MUST DO exploration list. Then look back at the experiences with your family and friends. Plan your adventures, then share all of the fun! Decorate your pages YOUR way.

Find your next adventure and share your treasured memories!

We have organized each park in alphabetical order, making it easy to find the park you are looking for. Each map has a pin to match the location of the destination to be used with the table of contents, identifying the page number you can find each location. Use the table of contents as your KEY to the map inside.

Spend your time surrounded in nature, taking in all of the unique geological features, and unusual ecosystems within the FLORIDA State Parks. Write about the special moments from each destination inside. You are creating your own special keepsake and making cherished lifelong memories. So what are you waiting for. It's time to explore!

Florida

Inside your book you will find...

ON THE LEFT SIDE OF EACH 2 PAGE SPREAD, YOU HAVE

A place to plan the details of your trip.

A would you return area

A section for reservation information, including refund policy, reserved dates, address, check-in and check-out times, website, phone, wifi information, and even a place for your confirmation number.

Plus an area to show how far you are traveling.

A fun color-in of the transportation modes you used during your adventures in the park.

A space to attach your favorite postcard, picture, drawing, stamp and ticket stub.

THE RIGHT SIDE INCLUDES PARK INFORMATION AND GIVES YOU A PLACE TO SHARE THE SPECIAL MOMENTS ABOUT YOUR JOURNEY

Park Information

The county the park is located in

The year the park was established

The location and contact information of the park

Special Moments

Include why you went

Who went with you

When you went

What you did

The souvenir you brought home

What you saw

What you learned

An unforgettable moment

A laughable moment

A surprising moment

An unforeseeable moment

A QR code for the most up to date park information available

A fun color-in of the weather you experienced during your adventures

Make it all about YOU and your journey!

Also inside is an adventure checklist to make your adventures even more memorable.

We want you to spend every moment of your trip enjoying every bit of the FLORIDA State Parks!

FLORIDA

Adventure Begins

TABLE OF CONTENTS

FLORIDA COUNTY MAP

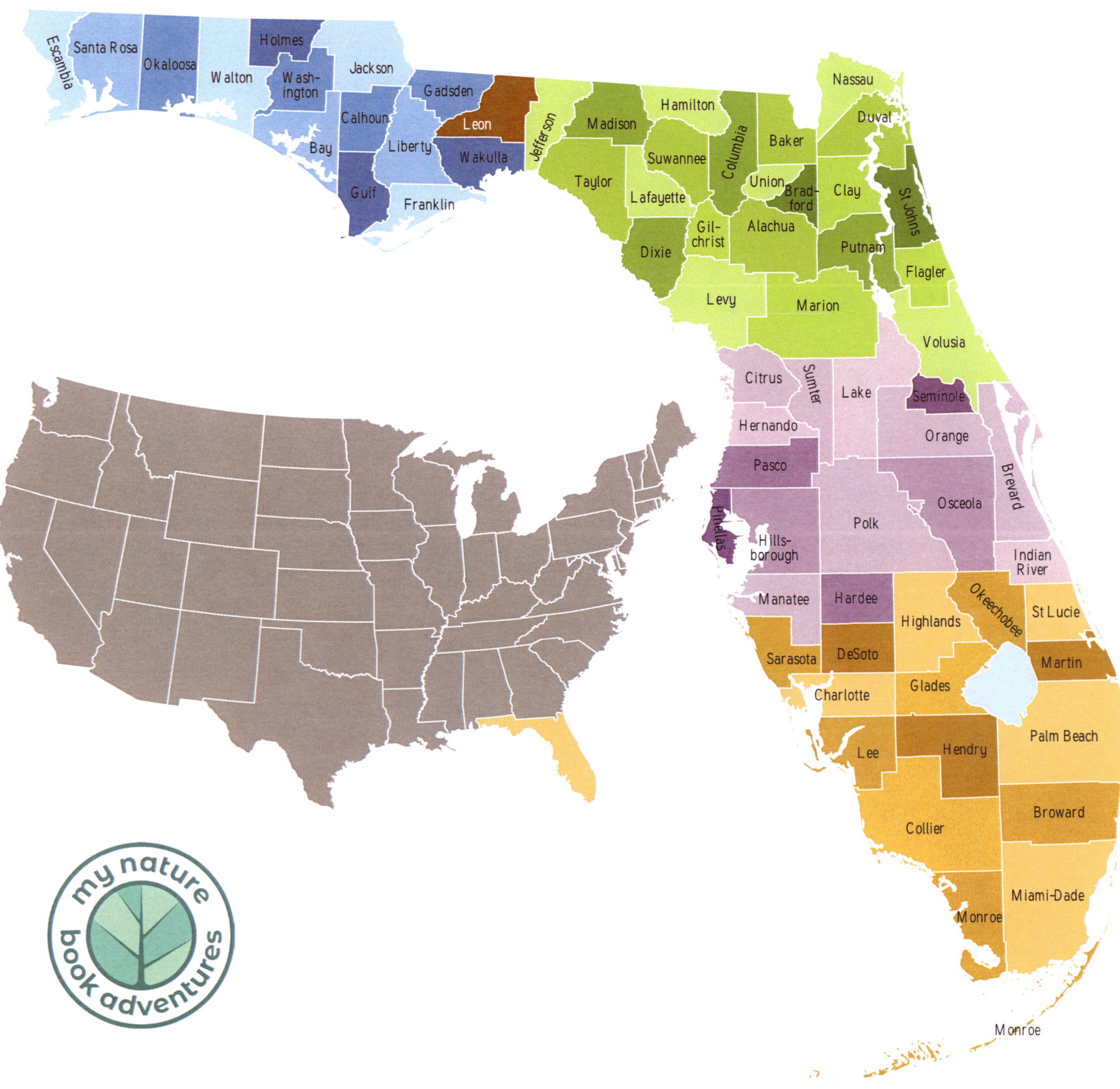

my nature book adventures

Mark the places on the map that you have been to.
Be creative use a sticker or just put a dot to mark your journey.

TABLE OF CONTENTS

What You Will Find At The Parks

Beach Sunset

Website: https://www.floridastateparks.org

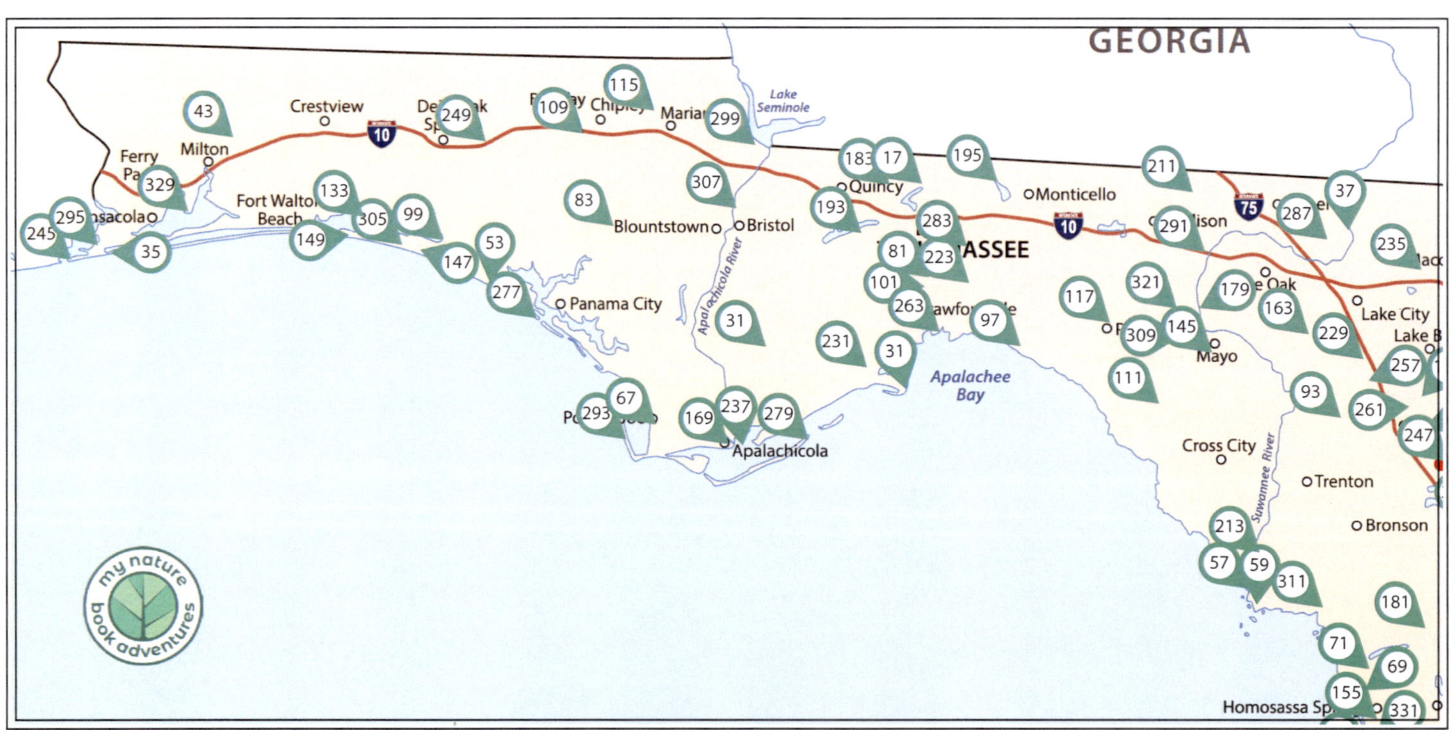

TABLE OF CONTENTS

WHAT YOU WILL FIND AT THE PARKS

America's largest spring sits untouched within Silver Springs State Park

Website: https://www.floridastateparks.org

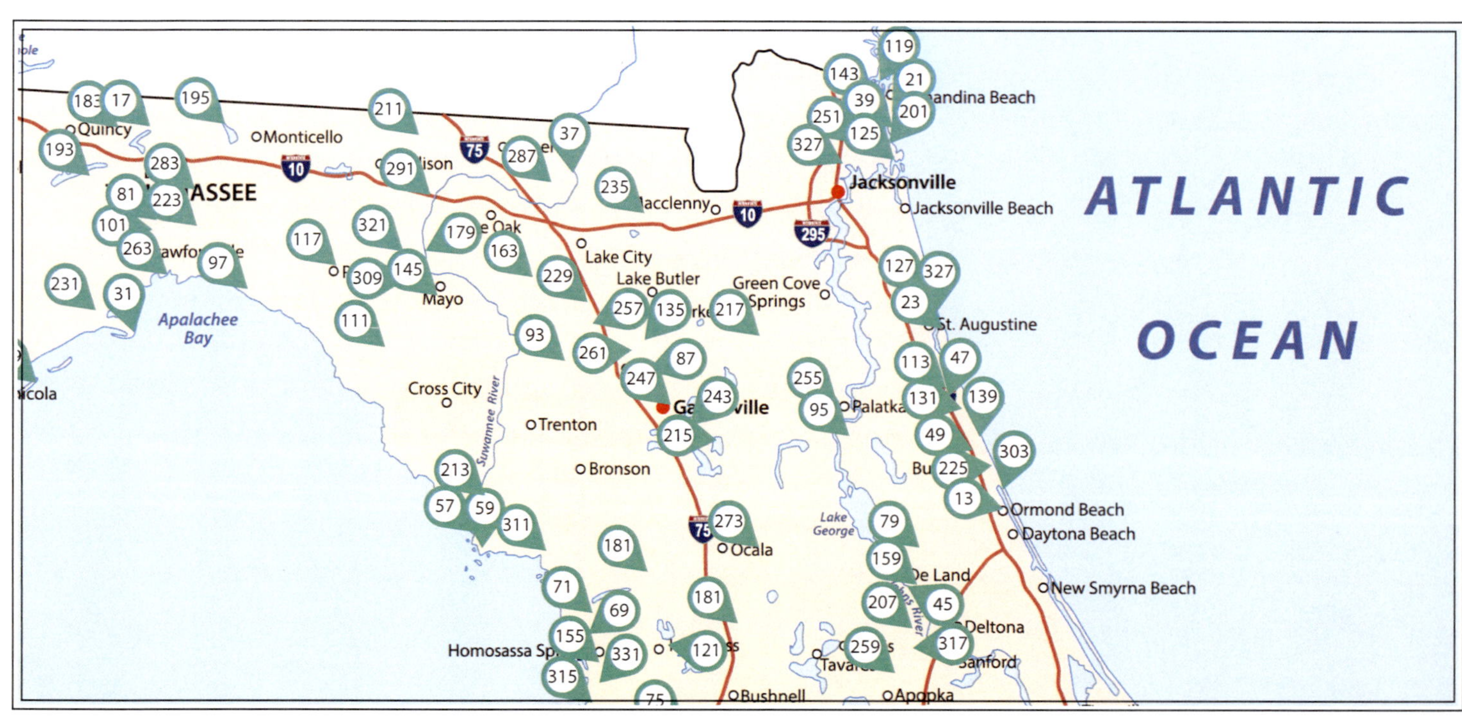

TABLE OF CONTENTS

FLORIDA STATE MAP

Mark the places on the map that you have been to.
Be creative use a sticker or just put a dot to mark your journey.

Table of Contents

What You Will Find At The Parks

Manatee at Blue Springs State Park

Website: https://www.floridastateparks.org

TABLE OF CONTENTS

FLORIDA STATE MAP

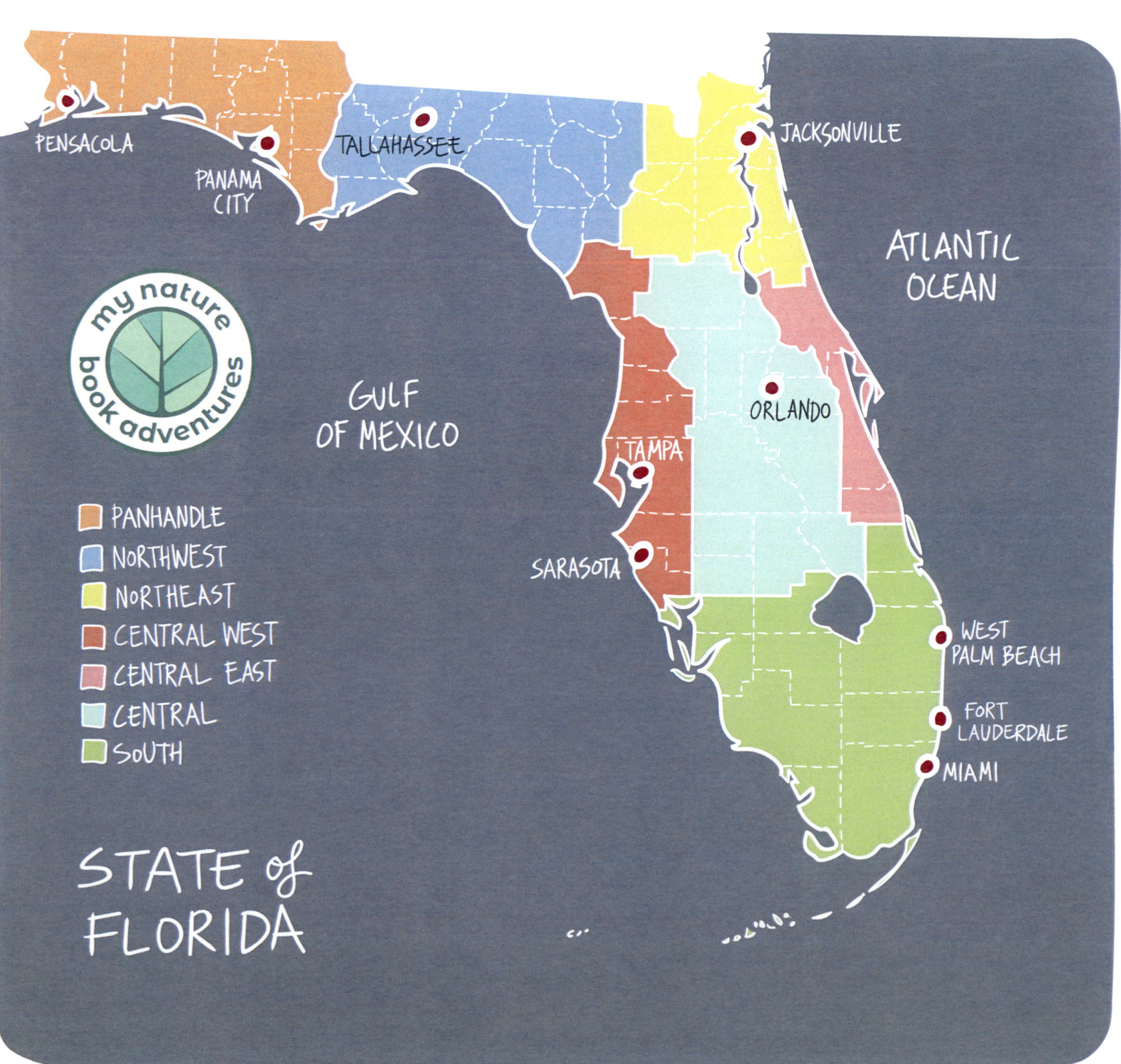

Mark the places on the map that you have been to.
Be creative use a sticker or just put a dot to mark your journey.

Adventure List

- [ ] Go on a nature scavenger hunt
- [ ] Perfect your bird calls
- [ ] Have a breakfast picnic
- [ ] Go horseback riding
- [ ] Snap a selfie at a park entrance sign
- [ ] Help Someone become a Jr Ranger
- [ ] Go RVing
- [ ] Take a ranger-led tour
- [ ] Splash in a waterfall
- [ ] Stop at scenic overlooks
- [ ] Hunt for fossils
- [ ] Look for EarthCache sites
- [ ] Canoe along a river
- [ ] Go on a photography walk
- [ ] Take a nature hike
- [ ] Hunt for animal tracks
- [ ] Go kayaking
- [ ] Try rock climbing
- [ ] Visit a nature center
- [ ] Watch the sunset
- [ ] Ride a bike
- [ ] Try a night sky program
- [ ] Go geocaching
- [ ] Pitch a tent
- [ ] Photograph wildflowers
- [ ] Cast a fishing line
- [ ] Take a boat cruise across a lake
- [ ] Enjoy a scenic drive
- [ ] Snap lots of photos
- [ ] Smell the fresh air
- [ ] Arrive early for wildlife watching
- [ ] Scramble over rocks
- [ ] Eat a picnic at a scenic spot
- [ ] Go on a night hike
- [ ] Ride a historic train
- [ ] Hike to the top of a mountain
- [ ] Try a cell phone audio tour
- [ ] Enjoy a tidepool walk
- [ ] Go on a full moon ranger hike
- [ ] Go on a cave tour
- [ ] Go stargazing
- [ ] Adhere to Leave No Trace principles
- [ ] Play in the water

Plan Your Trip:

☐ Trip Plan Completed

☐ Day Trip ☐ Overnight Stay

Reservations required: ☐y ☐n

Date reservations made: ________

Refund Policy: ☐y ☐n Site/Room #: ____

Confirmation #: ________

Miles to travel: ________

Time traveling: ________

Dog friendly?: ☐y ☐n

Destination Information:

Places we discovered along the way

Places to stop and see along the way

Would you go again?: ☐y ☐n Open all year?: ☐y ☐n

Activities Accomplished:

- ☐ Archery
- ☐ Biking
- ☐ Birding
- ☐ Boating
- ☐ Camping
- ☐ Caving
- ☐ Geocaching
- ☐ Fishing
- ☐ Hiking
- ☐ Horseback Riding
- ☐ Hunting
- ☐ Off-Roading
- ☐ Paddle Boarding
- ☐ Photography
- ☐ Picnicking
- ☐ Rock Climbing
- ☐ Shooting Range
- ☐ Snowshoeing
- ☐ Stargazing
- ☐ Swimming
- ☐ Tennis
- ☐ Walking
- ☐ Wildlife Watching
- ☐ ________
- ☐ ________
- ☐ ________
- ☐ ________
- ☐ ________

Traveled by:

☐ ☐ ☐ ☐ ☐ ☐ ☐ ☐ ☐ ☐ ☐ ☐

Add your favorite ticket stub, postcard, photo, stamp or drawing here

N E S W NOT ALL THOSE WHO WANDER ARE LOST

Addison Blockhouse Historic State Park

County: Volusia
2099 N Beach Street, Ormond Beach, Fl 32174 | 386-676-4050

Website: https://www.floridastateparks.org/addison-blockhouse
Email: FSP.Feedback@FloridaDEP.gov

Water Body: Tomoka River

Size: 134.51 acres 54.43 ha
Established: 1939

Ruins of a 19th-century plantation owned by John Addison

Star Rating ☆☆☆☆☆

What souvenir did you bring home?... Decal Magnet

My favorite thing about this place is...

Why I went ...

Who I went with ...

When I went ...

What I did...

What I saw...

What I learned...

An unforgettable moment...

A laughable moment...

A surprising moment...

An unforeseeable moment...

Snapped a selfie | Location...

Took a park sign selfie? - Y | N

The weather was ...

My List

- ☐
- ☐
- ☐
- ☐
- ☐
- ☐
- ☐
- ☐
- ☐
- ☐
- ☐
- ☐

Plan Your Trip:

☐ Trip Plan Completed

☐ Day Trip ☐ Overnight Stay

Reservations required: ☐y ☐n

Date reservations made: ____________

Refund Policy: ☐y ☐n Site/Room #: ____

Confirmation #: ____________

Miles to travel: ____________

Time traveling: ____________

Dog friendly?: ☐y ☐n

Destination Information:

Places we discovered along the way

Places to stop and see along the way

Would you go again?: ☐y ☐n

Open all year?: ☐y ☐n

Activities Accomplished:

☐ Archery
☐ Biking
☐ Birding
☐ Boating
☐ Camping
☐ Caving
☐ Geocaching
☐ Fishing
☐ Hiking
☐ Horseback Riding
☐ Hunting
☐ Off-Roading
☐ Paddle Boarding
☐ Photography
☐ Picnicking
☐ Rock Climbing
☐ Shooting Range
☐ Snowshoeing
☐ Stargazing
☐ Swimming
☐ Tennis
☐ Walking
☐ Wildlife Watching
☐ ____________
☐ ____________
☐ ____________
☐ ____________
☐ ____________

Traveled by:

☐ ☐ ☐ ☐ ☐ ☐ ☐ ☐ ☐ ☐ ☐ ☐

Add your favorite ticket stub, postcard, photo, stamp or drawing here

N E S W
NOT ALL THOSE WHO WANDER ARE LOST

Alafia River State Park

County: Hillsborough
14326 S. County Road 39, Lithia FL 33547 | 813-672-5320

Website: https://www.floridastateparks.org/Alafia
Email: FSP.Feedback@FloridaDEP.gov

Water Body: Alafia River

Size: 6,312 acres 2,556 ha
Established: 1996

Former phosphorus strip mine unremediated

Star Rating ☆☆☆☆☆

What souvenir did you bring home?... Decal Magnet

My favorite thing about this place is...

Why I went ...

Who I went with ...

When I went ...

What I did...

What I saw...

What I learned...

An unforgettable moment...

A laughable moment...

A surprising moment...

An unforeseeable moment...

My List

- ☐
- ☐
- ☐
- ☐
- ☐
- ☐
- ☐
- ☐
- ☐
- ☐
- ☐
- ☐

Snapped a selfie | Location...

Took a park sign selfie? - Y | N

The weather was ...

Plan Your Trip:

☐ Trip Plan Completed

☐ Day Trip ☐ Overnight Stay

Reservations required: ☐y ☐n

Date reservations made: ______

Refund Policy: ☐y ☐n Site/Room #: ______

Confirmation #: ______

Miles to travel: ______

Time traveling: ______

Dog friendly?: ☐y ☐n

Destination Information:

______

______

Places we discovered along the way

______

______

______

Places to stop and see along the way

______

______

Activities Accomplished:

Would you go again?: ☐y ☐n Open all year?: ☐y ☐n

☐ Archery
☐ Biking
☐ Birding
☐ Boating
☐ Camping
☐ Caving
☐ Geocaching
☐ Fishing
☐ Hiking
☐ Horseback Riding
☐ Hunting
☐ Off-Roading
☐ Paddle Boarding
☐ Photography
☐ Picnicking
☐ Rock Climbing
☐ Shooting Range
☐ Snowshoeing
☐ Stargazing
☐ Swimming
☐ Tennis
☐ Walking
☐ Wildlife Watching
☐ ______
☐ ______
☐ ______
☐ ______
☐ ______

Traveled by:

☐ ☐ ☐ ☐ ☐ ☐ ☐ ☐ ☐ ☐ ☐ ☐

Add your favorite ticket stub, postcard, photo, stamp or drawing here

N E S W NOT ALL THOSE WHO WANDER ARE LOST

Alfred B. Maclay Gardens State Park

County: Leon
3540 Thomasville Road, Tallahassee FL 32309 | 850-487-4556

Website: **https://www.floridastateparks.org/maclaygardens**
Email: **FSP.Feedback@FloridaDEP.gov**

Water Body: Lake Hall

Size: 1,180 acres
Established: 1954

Originally named Killearn Gardens State Park

Star Rating ☆☆☆☆☆

What souvenir did you bring home?... Decal Magnet

My favorite thing about this place is...

Why I went ...

Who I went with ...

When I went ...

What I did...

What I saw...

What I learned...

An unforgettable moment...

A laughable moment...

A surprising moment...

An unforeseeable moment...

My List

- ☐
- ☐
- ☐
- ☐
- ☐
- ☐
- ☐
- ☐
- ☐
- ☐
- ☐
- ☐

Snapped a selfie | Location...

Took a park sign selfie? - y | n

The weather was ...

Plan Your Trip:

☐ Trip Plan Completed

☐ Day Trip ☐ Overnight Stay

Reservations required: ☐y ☐n

Date reservations made: ______

Refund Policy: ☐y ☐n Site/Room #: ______

Confirmation #: ______

Miles to travel: ______

Time traveling: ______

Dog friendly?: ☐y ☐n

Destination Information:

______

______

Places we discovered along the way

______

______

______

Places to stop and see along the way

______

______

Would you go again?: ☐y ☐n

Open all year?: ☐y ☐n

Activities Accomplished:

☐ Archery
☐ Biking
☐ Birding
☐ Boating
☐ Camping
☐ Caving
☐ Geocaching
☐ Fishing
☐ Hiking
☐ Horseback Riding
☐ Hunting
☐ Off-Roading
☐ Paddle Boarding
☐ Photography
☐ Picnicking
☐ Rock Climbing
☐ Shooting Range
☐ Snowshoeing
☐ Stargazing
☐ Swimming
☐ Tennis
☐ Walking
☐ Wildlife Watching
☐ ______
☐ ______
☐ ______
☐ ______
☐ ______

Traveled by:

☐ ☐ ☐ ☐ ☐ ☐ ☐ ☐ ☐ ☐ ☐ ☐

Add your favorite ticket stub, postcard, photo, stamp or drawing here

N E S W NOT ALL THOSE WHO WANDER ARE LOST

Allen David Broussard Catfish Creek Preserve State Park

County: Polk
4335 Firetower Road, Haines City FL 33844 | 863-696-1112

Website: https://www.floridastateparks.org/catfish-creek
Email: FSP.Feedback@FloridaDEP.gov

Water Body: unnamed ponds

Size: 8,065 acres
Established: 1991

Home to rare scrub habitat for wildlife

Star Rating ☆☆☆☆☆

What souvenir did you bring home?... Decal Magnet

My favorite thing about this place is...

Why I went ...

Who I went with ...

When I went ...

What I did...

What I saw...

What I learned...

An unforgettable moment...

A laughable moment...

A surprising moment...

An unforeseeable moment...

My List

- ☐
- ☐
- ☐
- ☐
- ☐
- ☐
- ☐
- ☐
- ☐
- ☐
- ☐
- ☐

 Snapped a selfie | Location...

 Took a park sign selfie? - Y | N

The weather was ... 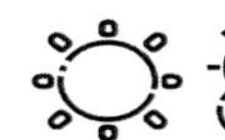     

Plan Your Trip:

☐ Trip Plan Completed

☐ Day Trip ☐ Overnight Stay

Reservations required: ☐y ☐n

Date reservations made: ______

Refund Policy: ☐y ☐n Site/Room #: ______

Confirmation #: ______

Miles to travel: ______

Time traveling: ______

Dog friendly?: ☐y ☐n

Destination Information:

______

______

Places we discovered along the way

______

______

______

Places to stop and see along the way

______

______

Would you go again?: ☐y ☐n Open all year?: ☐y ☐n

Activities Accomplished:

☐ Archery
☐ Biking
☐ Birding
☐ Boating
☐ Camping
☐ Caving
☐ Geocaching
☐ Fishing
☐ Hiking
☐ Horseback Riding
☐ Hunting
☐ Off-Roading
☐ Paddle Boarding
☐ Photography
☐ Picnicking
☐ Rock Climbing
☐ Shooting Range
☐ Snowshoeing
☐ Stargazing
☐ Swimming
☐ Tennis
☐ Walking
☐ Wildlife Watching
☐ ______
☐ ______
☐ ______
☐ ______
☐ ______

Traveled by:

☐ ☐ ☐ ☐ ☐ ☐ ☐ ☐ ☐ ☐ ☐ ☐

Add your favorite ticket stub, postcard, photo, stamp or drawing here

N W E S NOT ALL THOSE WHO WANDER ARE LOST

Amelia Island State Park

County: Nassau
State Road A1A North, Jacksonville FL 32226 | 904-251-2320

Website: https://www.floridastateparks.org/amelia-island
Email: FSP.Feedback@FloridaDEP.gov

Water Body: Nassau Sound - Atlantic Ocean

Size: 230 acres
Established: 1983

Horseback riding is permitted on the beach

Star Rating ☆☆☆☆☆

What souvenir did you bring home?... Decal Magnet

My favorite thing about this place is...

Why I went ...

Who I went with ...

When I went ...

What I did...

What I saw...

What I learned...

An unforgettable moment...

A laughable moment...

A surprising moment...

An unforeseeable moment...

Snapped a selfie | Location...

Took a park sign selfie? - Y | N

My List

- ☐
- ☐
- ☐
- ☐
- ☐
- ☐
- ☐
- ☐
- ☐
- ☐
- ☐
- ☐

The weather was ...

Plan Your Trip:

☐ Trip Plan Completed

☐ Day Trip ☐ Overnight Stay

Reservations required: ☐y ☐n

Date reservations made: ____________

Refund Policy: ☐y ☐n Site/Room #: ____

Confirmation #: ____________

Miles to travel: ____________

Time traveling: ____________

Dog friendly?: ☐y ☐n

Destination Information:

____

____

Places we discovered along the way

____

____

____

Places to stop and see along the way

____

____

Would you go again?: ☐y ☐n

Open all year?: ☐y ☐n

Activities Accomplished:

☐ Archery
☐ Biking
☐ Birding
☐ Boating
☐ Camping
☐ Caving
☐ Geocaching
☐ Fishing
☐ Hiking
☐ Horseback Riding
☐ Hunting
☐ Off-Roading
☐ Paddle Boarding
☐ Photography
☐ Picnicking
☐ Rock Climbing
☐ Shooting Range
☐ Snowshoeing
☐ Stargazing
☐ Swimming
☐ Tennis
☐ Walking
☐ Wildlife Watching
☐ ____________
☐ ____________
☐ ____________
☐ ____________
☐ ____________

Traveled by:

☐ ☐ ☐ ☐ ☐ ☐ ☐ ☐ ☐ ☐ ☐ ☐

Add your favorite ticket stub, postcard, photo, stamp or drawing here

N
W E
S
NOT ALL THOSE WHO WANDER ARE LOST

Anastasia State Park

County: St. Johns
300 Anastasia Park Road, St. Augustine FL 32080 | 904-461-2033

Website: https://www.floridastateparks.org/anastasia
Email: FSP.Feedback@FloridaDEP.gov

Water Body: Atlantic Ocean

Size: 1,600 acres
Established: 1949

Hurricane Dora connected Anastasia Island and Conch Island in 1964

Star Rating ☆☆☆☆☆

What souvenir did you bring home?... Decal Magnet

My favorite thing about this place is...

Why I went ...

Who I went with ...

When I went ...

What I did...

What I saw...

What I learned...

An unforgettable moment...

A laughable moment...

A surprising moment...

An unforeseeable moment...

My List

- ☐
- ☐
- ☐
- ☐
- ☐
- ☐
- ☐
- ☐
- ☐
- ☐
- ☐
- ☐

 Snapped a selfie | Location...

 Took a park sign selfie? - Y | N

The weather was ...

PLAN YOUR TRIP:

☐ Trip Plan Completed

☐ Day Trip ☐ Overnight Stay

Reservations required: ☐y ☐n

Date reservations made: ____

Refund Policy: ☐y ☐n Site/Room #: ____

Confirmation #: ____

Miles to travel: ____

Time traveling: ____

Dog friendly?: ☐y ☐n

DESTINATION INFORMATION:

PLACES WE DISCOVERED ALONG THE WAY

PLACES TO STOP AND SEE ALONG THE WAY

Activities Accomplished:

Would you go again?: ☐y ☐n

Open all year?: ☐y ☐n

☐ Archery	☐ Fishing	☐ Picnicking	☐ Walking
☐ Biking	☐ Hiking	☐ Rock Climbing	☐ Wildlife Watching
☐ Birding	☐ Horseback Riding	☐ Shooting Range	☐ ____
☐ Boating	☐ Hunting	☐ Snowshoeing	☐ ____
☐ Camping	☐ Off-Roading	☐ Stargazing	☐ ____
☐ Caving	☐ Paddle Boarding	☐ Swimming	☐ ____
☐ Geocaching	☐ Photography	☐ Tennis	☐ ____

Traveled by:

☐ ☐ ☐ ☐ ☐ ☐ ☐ ☐ ☐ ☐ ☐ ☐

Add your favorite ticket stub, postcard, photo, stamp or drawing here

N W E S NOT ALL THOSE WHO WANDER ARE LOST

Anclote Key Preserve State Park

County: Pasco

Offshore, Tarpon Springs FL 34689, N 2810.020 W 08250.687 | 727-241-6106

Website: https://www.floridastateparks.org/Anclote-Key
Email: FSP.Feedback@FloridaDEP.gov

Water Body: Gulf of Mexico

Size: 403 acres
Established: 1997

Accessible only by ferry or boat

Star Rating ☆☆☆☆☆

What souvenir did you bring home?... Decal Magnet

My favorite thing about this place is...

Why I went ...

Who I went with ...

When I went ...

What I did...

What I saw...

What I learned...

An unforgettable moment...

A laughable moment...

A surprising moment...

An unforeseeable moment...

My List

- ☐
- ☐
- ☐
- ☐
- ☐
- ☐
- ☐
- ☐
- ☐
- ☐
- ☐
- ☐

 Snapped a selfie | Location...

 Took a park sign selfie? - Y | N

The weather was ...      

Plan Your Trip:

☐ Trip Plan Completed

☐ Day Trip ☐ Overnight Stay

Reservations required: ☐y ☐n

Date reservations made: ____________

Refund Policy: ☐y ☐n Site/Room #: ______

Confirmation #: ____________

Miles to travel: ____________

Time traveling: ____________

Dog friendly?: ☐y ☐n

Destination Information:

____

____

Places we discovered along the way

____

____

____

Places to stop and see along the way

____

____

Would you go again?: ☐y ☐n

Open all year?: ☐y ☐n

Activities Accomplished:

☐ Archery	☐ Fishing	☐ Picnicking	☐ Walking
☐ Biking	☐ Hiking	☐ Rock Climbing	☐ Wildlife Watching
☐ Birding	☐ Horseback Riding	☐ Shooting Range	☐ ________
☐ Boating	☐ Hunting	☐ Snowshoeing	☐ ________
☐ Camping	☐ Off-Roading	☐ Stargazing	☐ ________
☐ Caving	☐ Paddle Boarding	☐ Swimming	☐ ________
☐ Geocaching	☐ Photography	☐ Tennis	☐ ________

Traveled by:

☐ ☐ ☐ ☐ ☐ ☐ ☐ ☐ ☐ ☐ ☐ ☐

Add your favorite ticket stub, postcard, photo, stamp or drawing here

N E S W NOT ALL THOSE WHO WANDER ARE LOST

Avalon State Park

County: St. Lucie

State Road A1A North, North Hutchinson Island FL 34949 | 772-468-4007

Website: https://www.floridastateparks.org/parks-and-trails/avalon-state-park
Email: FSP.Feedback@FloridaDEP.gov

Water Body: Atlantic Ocean

Size: 650 acres
Established: 1987

Used for frogman training during World War II

Star Rating
☆☆☆☆☆

What souvenir did you bring home?... Decal Magnet ____________________

My favorite thing about this place is... ____________________

Why I went ... ____________________

Who I went with ... ____________________

When I went ... ____________________

What I did... ____________________

What I saw... ____________________

What I learned... ____________________

An unforgettable moment... ____________________

A laughable moment... ____________________

A surprising moment... ____________________

An unforeseeable moment... ____________________

Snapped a selfie | Location... ____________________

Took a park sign selfie? - Y | N

The weather was ...

My List

- ☐ ____________________
- ☐ ____________________
- ☐ ____________________
- ☐ ____________________
- ☐ ____________________
- ☐ ____________________
- ☐ ____________________
- ☐ ____________________
- ☐ ____________________
- ☐ ____________________
- ☐ ____________________
- ☐ ____________________

Plan Your Trip:

☐ Trip Plan Completed

☐ Day Trip ☐ Overnight Stay

Reservations required: ☐y ☐n

Date reservations made: ____________

Refund Policy: ☐y ☐n Site/Room #: ______

Confirmation #: ____________

Miles to travel: ____________

Time traveling: ____________

Dog friendly?: ☐y ☐n

Destination Information:

____

____

Places we discovered along the way

____

____

____

Places to stop and see along the way

____

____

Activities Accomplished:

Would you go again?: ☐y ☐n

Open all year?: ☐y ☐n

- ☐ Archery
- ☐ Biking
- ☐ Birding
- ☐ Boating
- ☐ Camping
- ☐ Caving
- ☐ Geocaching
- ☐ Fishing
- ☐ Hiking
- ☐ Horseback Riding
- ☐ Hunting
- ☐ Off-Roading
- ☐ Paddle Boarding
- ☐ Photography
- ☐ Picnicking
- ☐ Rock Climbing
- ☐ Shooting Range
- ☐ Snowshoeing
- ☐ Stargazing
- ☐ Swimming
- ☐ Tennis
- ☐ Walking
- ☐ Wildlife Watching
- ☐ ____________
- ☐ ____________
- ☐ ____________
- ☐ ____________
- ☐ ____________

Traveled by:

☐ ☐ ☐ ☐ ☐ ☐ ☐ ☐ ☐ ☐ ☐ ☐

Add your favorite ticket stub, postcard, photo, stamp or drawing here

N W E S NOT ALL THOSE WHO WANDER ARE LOST

Bahia Honda State Park

County: Monroe

36850 Overseas Highway, Big Pine Key FL 33043 | 305-872-2353

Website: https://www.floridastateparks.org/BahiaHonda
Email: info@bahiahondapark.com

Water Body: Atlantic Ocean - Gulf of Mexico

Size: 524 acres
Established: 1961

An island in the lower Florida Keys

Star Rating ☆☆☆☆☆

What souvenir did you bring home?... Decal Magnet ______

My favorite thing about this place is... ______

______

Why I went ... ______

Who I went with ... ______

When I went ... ______

______

What I did... ______

What I saw... ______

______

______

What I learned... ______

______

______

An unforgettable moment... ______

______

______

______

A laughable moment... ______

______

______

A surprising moment... ______

______

______

______

An unforeseeable moment... ______

______

______

Snapped a selfie | Location... ______

Took a park sign selfie? - Y | N

The weather was ...

My List

- ☐ ______
- ☐ ______
- ☐ ______
- ☐ ______
- ☐ ______
- ☐ ______
- ☐ ______
- ☐ ______
- ☐ ______
- ☐ ______
- ☐ ______
- ☐ ______

PLAN YOUR TRIP:

☐ Trip Plan Completed

☐ Day Trip ☐ Overnight Stay

Reservations required: ☐y ☐n

Date reservations made: ______

Refund Policy: ☐y ☐n Site/Room #: ______

Confirmation #: ______

Miles to travel: ______

Time traveling: ______

Dog friendly?: ☐y ☐n

DESTINATION INFORMATION:

PLACES WE DISCOVERED ALONG THE WAY

PLACES TO STOP AND SEE ALONG THE WAY

Would you go again?: ☐y ☐n Open all year?: ☐y ☐n

Activities Accomplished:

☐ Archery	☐ Fishing	☐ Picnicking	☐ Walking
☐ Biking	☐ Hiking	☐ Rock Climbing	☐ Wildlife Watching
☐ Birding	☐ Horseback Riding	☐ Shooting Range	☐ ______
☐ Boating	☐ Hunting	☐ Snowshoeing	☐ ______
☐ Camping	☐ Off-Roading	☐ Stargazing	☐ ______
☐ Caving	☐ Paddle Boarding	☐ Swimming	☐ ______
☐ Geocaching	☐ Photography	☐ Tennis	☐ ______

Traveled by:

☐ ☐ ☐ ☐ ☐ ☐ ☐ ☐ ☐ ☐ ☐ ☐

Add your favorite ticket stub, postcard, photo, stamp or drawing here

N E S W NOT ALL THOSE WHO WANDER ARE LOST

BALD POINT STATE PARK

County: Franklin
146 Box Cut Road, Alligator Point FL 32346 | 850-349-9146

Website: **https://www.floridastateparks.org/parks-and-trails/bald-point-state-park**
Email: **FSP.Feedback@FloridaDEP.gov**

Water Body: Gulf of Mexico

Size: 4,065 acres
Established: 1999

Amphibious landing exercises held during World War II

Star Rating ☆☆☆☆☆

What souvenir did you bring home?... Decal Magnet

My favorite thing about this place is...

Why I went ...

Who I went with ...

When I went ...

What I did...

What I saw...

What I learned...

An unforgettable moment...

A laughable moment...

A surprising moment...

An unforeseeable moment...

MY LIST

- ☐
- ☐
- ☐
- ☐
- ☐
- ☐
- ☐
- ☐
- ☐
- ☐
- ☐
- ☐

 Snapped a selfie | Location...

 Took a park sign selfie? - Y | N

The weather was ... 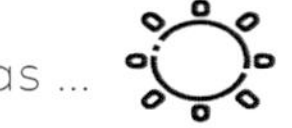     

Plan Your Trip:

Destination Information:

☐ Trip Plan Completed

☐ Day Trip ☐ Overnight Stay

Reservations required: ☐y ☐n

Date reservations made: ______

Refund Policy: ☐y ☐n Site/Room #: ______

Confirmation #: ______

Miles to travel: ______

Time traveling: ______

Dog friendly?: ☐y ☐n

Places we discovered along the way

Places to stop and see along the way

Activities Accomplished:

Would you go again?: ☐y ☐n Open all year?: ☐y ☐n

☐ Archery
☐ Biking
☐ Birding
☐ Boating
☐ Camping
☐ Caving
☐ Geocaching
☐ Fishing
☐ Hiking
☐ Horseback Riding
☐ Hunting
☐ Off-Roading
☐ Paddle Boarding
☐ Photography
☐ Picnicking
☐ Rock Climbing
☐ Shooting Range
☐ Snowshoeing
☐ Stargazing
☐ Swimming
☐ Tennis
☐ Walking
☐ Wildlife Watching
☐ ______
☐ ______
☐ ______
☐ ______
☐ ______

Traveled by:

☐ ☐ ☐ ☐ ☐ ☐ ☐ ☐ ☐ ☐ ☐ ☐

Add your favorite ticket stub, postcard, photo, stamp or drawing here

N
NOT ALL THOSE WHO
W E
WANDER ARE LOST
S

The Barnacle Historic State Park

County: Miami-Dade
3485 Main Highway, Miami FL 33133 | 305-442-6866

Website: https://www.floridastateparks.org/parks-and-trails/barnacle-historic-state-park
Email: FSP.Feedback@FloridaDEP.gov

Water Body: Biscayne Bay

Size: 5 acres
Established: 1973

Oldest house in Coconut Grove; built in 1891

Star Rating ☆☆☆☆☆

What souvenir did you bring home?... Decal Magnet ______

My favorite thing about this place is... ______

______

Why I went ... ______

Who I went with ... ______

When I went ... ______

______

What I did... ______

What I saw... ______

______

______

What I learned... ______

______

______

An unforgettable moment... ______

______

______

______

A laughable moment... ______

______

______

A surprising moment... ______

______

______

______

An unforeseeable moment... ______

______

______

Snapped a selfie | Location... ______

Took a park sign selfie? - Y | N

The weather was ...

My List

- ☐ ______
- ☐ ______
- ☐ ______
- ☐ ______
- ☐ ______
- ☐ ______
- ☐ ______
- ☐ ______
- ☐ ______
- ☐ ______
- ☐ ______
- ☐ ______

Plan Your Trip:

☐ Trip Plan Completed

☐ Day Trip ☐ Overnight Stay

Reservations required: ☐y ☐n

Date reservations made: ______

Refund Policy: ☐y ☐n Site/Room #: ______

Confirmation #: ______

Miles to travel: ______

Time traveling: ______

Dog friendly?: ☐y ☐n

Destination Information:

______

______

Places we discovered along the way

______

______

______

Places to stop and see along the way

______

______

Activities Accomplished:

Would you go again?: ☐y ☐n

Open all year?: ☐y ☐n

- ☐ Archery
- ☐ Biking
- ☐ Birding
- ☐ Boating
- ☐ Camping
- ☐ Caving
- ☐ Geocaching
- ☐ Fishing
- ☐ Hiking
- ☐ Horseback Riding
- ☐ Hunting
- ☐ Off-Roading
- ☐ Paddle Boarding
- ☐ Photography
- ☐ Picnicking
- ☐ Rock Climbing
- ☐ Shooting Range
- ☐ Snowshoeing
- ☐ Stargazing
- ☐ Swimming
- ☐ Tennis
- ☐ Walking
- ☐ Wildlife Watching
- ☐ ______
- ☐ ______
- ☐ ______
- ☐ ______
- ☐ ______

Traveled by:

☐ ☐ ☐ ☐ ☐ ☐ ☐ ☐ ☐ ☐ ☐ ☐

Add your favorite ticket stub, postcard, photo, stamp or drawing here

N W E S NOT ALL THOSE WHO WANDER ARE LOST

Big Lagoon State Park

County: Escambia
12301 Gulf Beach Highway, Pensacola FL 32507 | 850-492-1595

Website: https://www.floridastateparks.org/parks-and-trails/big-lagoon-state-park
Email: FSP.Feedback@FloridaDEP.gov

Water Body: Big Lagoon

Size: 705 acres
Established: 1977

Start of the Great Florida Birding Trail

Star Rating ☆☆☆☆☆

What souvenir did you bring home?... Decal Magnet

My favorite thing about this place is... ______

Why I went ... ______

Who I went with ... ______

When I went ... ______

What I did... ______

What I saw... ______

What I learned... ______

An unforgettable moment... ______

A laughable moment... ______

A surprising moment... ______

An unforeseeable moment... ______

Snapped a selfie | Location... ______

Took a park sign selfie? - Y | N

The weather was ...

My List

- ☐ ______
- ☐ ______
- ☐ ______
- ☐ ______
- ☐ ______
- ☐ ______
- ☐ ______
- ☐ ______
- ☐ ______
- ☐ ______
- ☐ ______
- ☐ ______

PLAN YOUR TRIP:

☐ Trip Plan Completed

☐ Day Trip ☐ Overnight Stay

Reservations required: ☐y ☐n

Date reservations made: ____________

Refund Policy: ☐y ☐n Site/Room #: ____

Confirmation #: ____________

Miles to travel: ____________

Time traveling: ____________

Dog friendly?: ☐y ☐n

DESTINATION INFORMATION:

PLACES WE DISCOVERED ALONG THE WAY

PLACES TO STOP AND SEE ALONG THE WAY

Would you go again?: ☐y ☐n

Open all year?: ☐y ☐n

Activities Accomplished:

☐ Archery
☐ Biking
☐ Birding
☐ Boating
☐ Camping
☐ Caving
☐ Geocaching
☐ Fishing
☐ Hiking
☐ Horseback Riding
☐ Hunting
☐ Off-Roading
☐ Paddle Boarding
☐ Photography
☐ Picnicking
☐ Rock Climbing
☐ Shooting Range
☐ Snowshoeing
☐ Stargazing
☐ Swimming
☐ Tennis
☐ Walking
☐ Wildlife Watching
☐ ____________
☐ ____________
☐ ____________
☐ ____________
☐ ____________

Traveled by:

☐ ☐ ☐ ☐ ☐ ☐ ☐ ☐ ☐ ☐ ☐ ☐

Add your favorite ticket stub, postcard, photo, stamp or drawing here

Big Shoals State Park

County: Hamilton

Little Shoals Entrance: 11330 S.E. County Road 135, or Big Shoals Entrance: 18738 Southeast 94th St., White Springs FL 32096 | 386-397-4331

Website: https://www.floridastateparks.org/parks-and-trails/big-shoals-state-park
Email: FSP.Feedback@FloridaDEP.gov

Water Body: Suwannee River

Size: 3,772 acres
Established: 1989

Largest whitewater Class III rapids in Florida

Star Rating ☆☆☆☆☆

What souvenir did you bring home?... Decal Magnet

My favorite thing about this place is...

Why I went ...

Who I went with ...

When I went ...

What I did...

What I saw...

What I learned...

An unforgettable moment...

A laughable moment...

A surprising moment...

An unforeseeable moment...

My List

- ☐
- ☐
- ☐
- ☐
- ☐
- ☐
- ☐
- ☐
- ☐
- ☐
- ☐
- ☐

Snapped a selfie | Location...

Took a park sign selfie? - Y | N

The weather was ...

Plan Your Trip:

☐ Trip Plan Completed

☐ Day Trip ☐ Overnight Stay

Reservations required: ☐y ☐n

Date reservations made: ______

Refund Policy: ☐y ☐n Site/Room #: ______

Confirmation #: ______

Miles to travel: ______

Time traveling: ______

Dog friendly?: ☐y ☐n

Destination Information:

______

______

Places we discovered along the way

______

______

______

Places to stop and see along the way

______

______

Activities Accomplished:

Would you go again?: ☐y ☐n Open all year?: ☐y ☐n

☐ Archery	☐ Fishing	☐ Picnicking	☐ Walking
☐ Biking	☐ Hiking	☐ Rock Climbing	☐ Wildlife Watching
☐ Birding	☐ Horseback Riding	☐ Shooting Range	☐ ______
☐ Boating	☐ Hunting	☐ Snowshoeing	☐ ______
☐ Camping	☐ Off-Roading	☐ Stargazing	☐ ______
☐ Caving	☐ Paddle Boarding	☐ Swimming	☐ ______
☐ Geocaching	☐ Photography	☐ Tennis	☐ ______

Traveled by:

☐ ☐ ☐ ☐ ☐ ☐ ☐ ☐ ☐ ☐ ☐ ☐

Add your favorite ticket stub, postcard, photo, stamp or drawing here

N W E S NOT ALL THOSE WHO WANDER ARE LOST

Big Talbot Island State Park

County: Duval
State Road A1A North, Jacksonville FL 32226 | 904-251-2320

Website: https://www.floridastateparks.org/parks-and-trails/big-talbot-island-state-park
Email: FSP.Feedback@FloridaDEP.gov

Water Body: Atlantic Ocean

Size: 1,600 acres
Established: 1949

Part of Talbot Islands State Parks

Star Rating ☆☆☆☆☆

What souvenir did you bring home?... Decal Magnet

My favorite thing about this place is... ____________

Why I went ... ____________

Who I went with ... ____________

When I went ... ____________

What I did... ____________

What I saw... ____________

What I learned... ____________

An unforgettable moment... ____________

A laughable moment... ____________

A surprising moment... ____________

An unforeseeable moment... ____________

My List

- ☐
- ☐
- ☐
- ☐
- ☐
- ☐
- ☐
- ☐
- ☐
- ☐
- ☐
- ☐

Snapped a selfie | Location... ____________

Took a park sign selfie? - Y | N

The weather was ...

PLAN YOUR TRIP:

☐ Trip Plan Completed

☐ Day Trip ☐ Overnight Stay

Reservations required: ☐y ☐n

Date reservations made: __________

Refund Policy: ☐y ☐n Site/Room #: ______

Confirmation #: __________

Miles to travel: __________

Time traveling: __________

Dog friendly?: ☐y ☐n

DESTINATION INFORMATION:

PLACES WE DISCOVERED ALONG THE WAY

PLACES TO STOP AND SEE ALONG THE WAY

Activities Accomplished:

Would you go again?: ☐y ☐n

Open all year?: ☐y ☐n

- ☐ Archery
- ☐ Biking
- ☐ Birding
- ☐ Boating
- ☐ Camping
- ☐ Caving
- ☐ Geocaching
- ☐ Fishing
- ☐ Hiking
- ☐ Horseback Riding
- ☐ Hunting
- ☐ Off-Roading
- ☐ Paddle Boarding
- ☐ Photography
- ☐ Picnicking
- ☐ Rock Climbing
- ☐ Shooting Range
- ☐ Snowshoeing
- ☐ Stargazing
- ☐ Swimming
- ☐ Tennis
- ☐ Walking
- ☐ Wildlife Watching
- ☐ __________
- ☐ __________
- ☐ __________
- ☐ __________
- ☐ __________

Traveled by:

☐ ☐ ☐ ☐ ☐ ☐ ☐ ☐ ☐ ☐ ☐ ☐

Add your favorite ticket stub, postcard, photo, stamp or drawing here

N E S W NOT ALL THOSE WHO WANDER ARE LOST

Bill Baggs Cape Florida State Park

County: Miami-Dade
1200 South Crandon Blvd, Key Biscayne, FL 33149 | 786-582-2673

Website: https://www.floridastateparks.org/parks-and-trails/bill-baggs-cape-florida-state-park
Email: FSP.Feedback@FloridaDEP.gov

Water Body: Atlantic Ocean

Size: 400 acres
Established: 1967

Home to the Cape Florida Light on Key Biscayne

Star Rating ☆☆☆☆☆

What souvenir did you bring home?... Decal Magnet

My favorite thing about this place is...

Why I went ...

Who I went with ...

When I went ...

What I did...

What I saw...

What I learned...

An unforgettable moment...

A laughable moment...

A surprising moment...

An unforeseeable moment...

Snapped a selfie | Location...

Took a park sign selfie? - Y | N

The weather was ...

My List

- ☐
- ☐
- ☐
- ☐
- ☐
- ☐
- ☐
- ☐
- ☐
- ☐
- ☐
- ☐

Plan Your Trip:

☐ Trip Plan Completed

☐ Day Trip ☐ Overnight Stay

Reservations required: ☐y ☐n

Date reservations made: ____________

Refund Policy: ☐y ☐n Site/Room #: ____

Confirmation #: ____________

Miles to travel: ____________

Time traveling: ____________

Dog friendly?: ☐y ☐n

Destination Information:

Places we discovered along the way

Places to stop and see along the way

Would you go again?: ☐y ☐n Open all year?: ☐y ☐n

Activities Accomplished:

☐ Archery	☐ Fishing	☐ Picnicking	☐ Walking
☐ Biking	☐ Hiking	☐ Rock Climbing	☐ Wildlife Watching
☐ Birding	☐ Horseback Riding	☐ Shooting Range	☐ ________
☐ Boating	☐ Hunting	☐ Snowshoeing	☐ ________
☐ Camping	☐ Off-Roading	☐ Stargazing	☐ ________
☐ Caving	☐ Paddle Boarding	☐ Swimming	☐ ________
☐ Geocaching	☐ Photography	☐ Tennis	☐ ________

Traveled by:

☐ ☐ ☐ ☐ ☐ ☐ ☐ ☐ ☐ ☐ ☐ ☐

Add your favorite ticket stub, postcard, photo, stamp or drawing here

N
NOT ALL THOSE WHO WANDER ARE LOST
W E
S

Blackwater River State Park

County: Santa Rosa
7720 Deaton Bridge Road, Milton FL 32564 | 850-983-5363

Website: https://www.floridastateparks.org/parks-and-trails/blackwater-river-state-park
Email: FSP.Feedback@FloridaDEP.gov

Water Body: Blackwater River

Size: 590 acres
Established: 1967

Home to 1982 Florida Champion Atlantic white cedar tree

Star Rating ☆☆☆☆☆

What souvenir did you bring home?... Decal Magnet

My favorite thing about this place is...

Why I went ...

Who I went with ...

When I went ...

What I did...

What I saw...

What I learned...

An unforgettable moment...

A laughable moment...

A surprising moment...

An unforeseeable moment...

My List

- ☐
- ☐
- ☐
- ☐
- ☐
- ☐
- ☐
- ☐
- ☐
- ☐
- ☐
- ☐

Snapped a selfie | Location...

Took a park sign selfie? - Y | N

The weather was ...

Plan Your Trip:

☐ Trip Plan Completed

☐ Day Trip ☐ Overnight Stay

Reservations required: ☐y ☐n

Date reservations made: ______

Refund Policy: ☐y ☐n Site/Room #: ______

Confirmation #: ______

Miles to travel: ______

Time traveling: ______

Dog friendly?: ☐y ☐n

Destination Information:

______

______

Places we discovered along the way

______

______

______

Places to stop and see along the way

______

______

Would you go again?: ☐y ☐n

Open all year?: ☐y ☐n

Activities Accomplished:

☐ Archery
☐ Biking
☐ Birding
☐ Boating
☐ Camping
☐ Caving
☐ Geocaching
☐ Fishing
☐ Hiking
☐ Horseback Riding
☐ Hunting
☐ Off-Roading
☐ Paddle Boarding
☐ Photography
☐ Picnicking
☐ Rock Climbing
☐ Shooting Range
☐ Snowshoeing
☐ Stargazing
☐ Swimming
☐ Tennis
☐ Walking
☐ Wildlife Watching
☐ ______
☐ ______
☐ ______
☐ ______
☐ ______

Traveled by:

☐ ☐ ☐ ☐ ☐ ☐ ☐ ☐ ☐ ☐ ☐ ☐

Add your favorite ticket stub, postcard, photo, stamp or drawing here

N W E S NOT ALL THOSE WHO WANDER ARE LOST

Blue Spring State Park

County: Volusia
2100 W. French Ave., Orange City FL 32763 | 386-775-3663

Website: https://www.floridastateparks.org/parks-and-trails/blue-spring-state-park
Email: FSP.Feedback@FloridaDEP.gov

Water Body: St. Johns River

Size: 2,600 acres
Established: 1972

Largest spring on the St. Johns River and a designated manatee refuge

Star Rating
☆☆☆☆☆

What souvenir did you bring home?... Decal Magnet

My favorite thing about this place is...

Why I went ...

Who I went with ...

When I went ...

What I did...

What I saw...

What I learned...

An unforgettable moment...

A laughable moment...

A surprising moment...

An unforeseeable moment...

My List

- ☐
- ☐
- ☐
- ☐
- ☐
- ☐
- ☐
- ☐
- ☐
- ☐
- ☐
- ☐

Snapped a selfie | Location...

Took a park sign selfie? - Y | N

The weather was ...

Plan Your Trip:

☐ Trip Plan Completed

☐ Day Trip ☐ Overnight Stay

Reservations required: ☐y ☐n

Date reservations made: ________

Refund Policy: ☐y ☐n Site/Room #: ____

Confirmation #: ________

Miles to travel: ________

Time traveling: ________

Dog friendly?: ☐y ☐n

Destination Information:

____

____

Places we discovered along the way

____

____

____

Places to stop and see along the way

____

____

Would you go again?: ☐y ☐n Open all year?: ☐y ☐n

Activities Accomplished:

- ☐ Archery
- ☐ Biking
- ☐ Birding
- ☐ Boating
- ☐ Camping
- ☐ Caving
- ☐ Geocaching
- ☐ Fishing
- ☐ Hiking
- ☐ Horseback Riding
- ☐ Hunting
- ☐ Off-Roading
- ☐ Paddle Boarding
- ☐ Photography
- ☐ Picnicking
- ☐ Rock Climbing
- ☐ Shooting Range
- ☐ Snowshoeing
- ☐ Stargazing
- ☐ Swimming
- ☐ Tennis
- ☐ Walking
- ☐ Wildlife Watching
- ☐ ________
- ☐ ________
- ☐ ________
- ☐ ________
- ☐ ________

Traveled by:

☐ ☐ ☐ ☐ ☐ ☐ ☐ ☐ ☐ ☐ ☐ ☐

Add your favorite ticket stub, postcard, photo, stamp or drawing here

N W E S NOT ALL THOSE WHO WANDER ARE LOST

Bulow Creek State Park

County: Volusia

3351 Old Dixie Highway, Ormond Beach FL 32174 | 386-676-4050

Website: https://www.floridastateparks.org/parks-and-trails/bulow-creek-state-park
Email: FSP.Feedback@FloridaDEP.gov

Water Body: Bulow Creek

Size: 5,600 acres
Established: 1981

400-year-old Fairfield oak and 11 plantation sites

Star Rating ☆☆☆☆☆

What souvenir did you bring home?... Decal Magnet

My favorite thing about this place is...

Why I went ...

Who I went with ...

When I went ...

What I did...

What I saw...

What I learned...

An unforgettable moment...

A laughable moment...

A surprising moment...

An unforeseeable moment...

My List

- ☐
- ☐
- ☐
- ☐
- ☐
- ☐
- ☐
- ☐
- ☐
- ☐
- ☐
- ☐

Snapped a selfie | Location...

Took a park sign selfie? - Y | N

The weather was ...

Plan Your Trip:

☐ Trip Plan Completed

☐ Day Trip ☐ Overnight Stay

Reservations required: ☐y ☐n

Date reservations made: ______

Refund Policy: ☐y ☐n Site/Room #: ______

Confirmation #: ______

Miles to travel: ______

Time traveling: ______

Dog friendly?: ☐y ☐n

Destination Information:

Places we discovered along the way

Places to stop and see along the way

Would you go again?: ☐y ☐n Open all year?: ☐y ☐n

Activities Accomplished:

- ☐ Archery
- ☐ Biking
- ☐ Birding
- ☐ Boating
- ☐ Camping
- ☐ Caving
- ☐ Geocaching
- ☐ Fishing
- ☐ Hiking
- ☐ Horseback Riding
- ☐ Hunting
- ☐ Off-Roading
- ☐ Paddle Boarding
- ☐ Photography
- ☐ Picnicking
- ☐ Rock Climbing
- ☐ Shooting Range
- ☐ Snowshoeing
- ☐ Stargazing
- ☐ Swimming
- ☐ Tennis
- ☐ Walking
- ☐ Wildlife Watching
- ☐ ______
- ☐ ______
- ☐ ______
- ☐ ______
- ☐ ______

Traveled by:

☐ ☐ ☐ ☐ ☐ ☐ ☐ ☐ ☐ ☐ ☐ ☐

Add your favorite ticket stub, postcard, photo, stamp or drawing here

N NOT ALL THOSE WHO WANDER ARE LOST E S W

BULOW PLANTATION RUINS HISTORIC STATE PARK

County: Flagler
3501 Old Kings Road, Flagler Beach FL 32136 | 386-517-2084

Website: https://www.floridastateparks.org/parks-and-trails/bulow-plantation-ruins-historic-state-park
Email: FSP.Feedback@FloridaDEP.gov

Water Body: Bulow Creek

Size: 150 acres
Established: 1945

Extensive stone ruins

Star Rating ☆☆☆☆☆

What souvenir did you bring home?... Decal Magnet

My favorite thing about this place is...

Why I went ...

Who I went with ...

When I went ...

What I did...

What I saw...

What I learned...

An unforgettable moment...

A laughable moment...

A surprising moment...

An unforeseeable moment...

MY LIST

- ☐
- ☐
- ☐
- ☐
- ☐
- ☐
- ☐
- ☐
- ☐
- ☐
- ☐
- ☐

Snapped a selfie | Location...

Took a park sign selfie? - Y | N

The weather was ...

PLAN YOUR TRIP:

☐ Trip Plan Completed

☐ Day Trip ☐ Overnight Stay

Reservations required: ☐y ☐n

Date reservations made: ____

Refund Policy: ☐y ☐n Site/Room #: ____

Confirmation #: ____

Miles to travel: ____

Time traveling: ____

Dog friendly?: ☐y ☐n

DESTINATION INFORMATION:

PLACES WE DISCOVERED ALONG THE WAY

PLACES TO STOP AND SEE ALONG THE WAY

Would you go again?: ☐y ☐n Open all year?: ☐y ☐n

Activities Accomplished:

☐ Archery
☐ Biking
☐ Birding
☐ Boating
☐ Camping
☐ Caving
☐ Geocaching
☐ Fishing
☐ Hiking
☐ Horseback Riding
☐ Hunting
☐ Off-Roading
☐ Paddle Boarding
☐ Photography
☐ Picnicking
☐ Rock Climbing
☐ Shooting Range
☐ Snowshoeing
☐ Stargazing
☐ Swimming
☐ Tennis
☐ Walking
☐ Wildlife Watching
☐ ____
☐ ____
☐ ____
☐ ____
☐ ____

Traveled by:

☐ ☐ ☐ ☐ ☐ ☐ ☐ ☐ ☐ ☐ ☐ ☐

Add your favorite ticket stub, postcard, photo, stamp or drawing here

N
NOT ALL THOSE WHO WANDER ARE LOST
W E
S

Caladesi Island State Park

County: Pinellas
Offshore Island, Dunedin FL 34698 | 727-469-5918

Website: https://www.floridastateparks.org/parks-and-trails/caladesi-island-state-park
Email: FSP.Feedback@FloridaDEP.gov

Water Body: Gulf of Mexico

Size: 2,450 acres
Established: 1966

Ferry available, 108-slip marina

Star Rating ☆☆☆☆☆

What souvenir did you bring home?... Decal Magnet

My favorite thing about this place is...

Why I went ...

Who I went with ...

When I went ...

What I did...

What I saw...

What I learned...

An unforgettable moment...

A laughable moment...

A surprising moment...

An unforeseeable moment...

My List

- ☐
- ☐
- ☐
- ☐
- ☐
- ☐
- ☐
- ☐
- ☐
- ☐
- ☐
- ☐

 Snapped a selfie | Location...

 Took a park sign selfie? - Y | N

The weather was ...       

Plan Your Trip:

☐ Trip Plan Completed

☐ Day Trip ☐ Overnight Stay

Reservations required: ☐y ☐n

Date reservations made: ______

Refund Policy: ☐y ☐n Site/Room #: ______

Confirmation #: ______

Miles to travel: ______

Time traveling: ______

Dog friendly?: ☐y ☐n

Destination Information:

______

______

Places we discovered along the way

______

______

______

Places to stop and see along the way

______

______

Would you go again?: ☐y ☐n

Open all year?: ☐y ☐n

Activities Accomplished:

☐ Archery
☐ Biking
☐ Birding
☐ Boating
☐ Camping
☐ Caving
☐ Geocaching
☐ Fishing
☐ Hiking
☐ Horseback Riding
☐ Hunting
☐ Off-Roading
☐ Paddle Boarding
☐ Photography
☐ Picnicking
☐ Rock Climbing
☐ Shooting Range
☐ Snowshoeing
☐ Stargazing
☐ Swimming
☐ Tennis
☐ Walking
☐ Wildlife Watching
☐ ______
☐ ______
☐ ______
☐ ______
☐ ______

Traveled by:

☐ ☐ ☐ ☐ ☐ ☐ ☐ ☐ ☐ ☐ ☐ ☐

Add your favorite ticket stub, postcard, photo, stamp or drawing here

N E S W NOT ALL THOSE WHO WANDER ARE LOST

Camp Helen State Park

County: Bay

23937 Panama City Beach Parkway, Panama City Beach FL 32413 | 850-233-5059

Website: https://www.floridastateparks.org/parks-and-trails/camp-helen-state-park
Email: FSP.Feedback@FloridaDEP.gov

Water Body: Lake Powell - Gulf of Mexico

Size: 185 acres
Established: 1996

Day use park formerly used as private resort

Star Rating ☆☆☆☆☆

What souvenir did you bring home?... Decal Magnet

My favorite thing about this place is...

Why I went ...

Who I went with ...

When I went ...

What I did...

What I saw...

What I learned...

An unforgettable moment...

A laughable moment...

A surprising moment...

An unforeseeable moment...

My List

- ☐
- ☐
- ☐
- ☐
- ☐
- ☐
- ☐
- ☐
- ☐
- ☐
- ☐
- ☐

Snapped a selfie | Location...

Took a park sign selfie? - Y | N

The weather was ...

Plan Your Trip:

☐ Trip Plan Completed

☐ Day Trip ☐ Overnight Stay

Reservations required: ☐y ☐n

Date reservations made: ______

Refund Policy: ☐y ☐n Site/Room #: ______

Confirmation #: ______

Miles to travel: ______

Time traveling: ______

Dog friendly?: ☐y ☐n

Destination Information:

______

______

Places we discovered along the way

______

______

______

Places to stop and see along the way

______

______

Would you go again?: ☐y ☐n

Open all year?: ☐y ☐n

Activities Accomplished:

- ☐ Archery
- ☐ Biking
- ☐ Birding
- ☐ Boating
- ☐ Camping
- ☐ Caving
- ☐ Geocaching
- ☐ Fishing
- ☐ Hiking
- ☐ Horseback Riding
- ☐ Hunting
- ☐ Off-Roading
- ☐ Paddle Boarding
- ☐ Photography
- ☐ Picnicking
- ☐ Rock Climbing
- ☐ Shooting Range
- ☐ Snowshoeing
- ☐ Stargazing
- ☐ Swimming
- ☐ Tennis
- ☐ Walking
- ☐ Wildlife Watching
- ☐ ______
- ☐ ______
- ☐ ______
- ☐ ______
- ☐ ______

Traveled by:

☐ ☐ ☐ ☐ ☐ ☐ ☐ ☐ ☐ ☐ ☐ ☐

Add your favorite ticket stub, postcard, photo, stamp or drawing here

N W E S NOT ALL THOSE WHO WANDER ARE LOST

Cayo Costa State Park

County: Lee

4 Nautical Miles West of Pine Island, Cayo Costa FL 33922, 26.685789, -82.245381 | 941-964-0375

Website: https://www.floridastateparks.org/CayoCosta
Email: FSP.Feedback@FloridaDEP.gov

Water Body: Gulf of Mexico

Size: 2,426 acres
Established: 1976

Accessible only by ferry or boat - primitive cabins

Star Rating ☆☆☆☆☆

What souvenir did you bring home?... Decal Magnet

My favorite thing about this place is...

Why I went ...

Who I went with ...

When I went ...

What I did...

What I saw...

What I learned...

An unforgettable moment...

A laughable moment...

A surprising moment...

An unforeseeable moment...

My List

- ☐
- ☐
- ☐
- ☐
- ☐
- ☐
- ☐
- ☐
- ☐
- ☐
- ☐
- ☐

Snapped a selfie | Location...

Took a park sign selfie? - Y | N

The weather was ...

Plan Your Trip:

- ☐ Trip Plan Completed
- ☐ Day Trip ☐ Overnight Stay

Reservations required: ☐y ☐n

Date reservations made: ____________

Refund Policy: ☐y ☐n Site/Room #: ______

Confirmation #: ____________

Miles to travel: ____________

Time traveling: ____________

Dog friendly?: ☐y ☐n

Destination Information:

Places we discovered along the way

Places to stop and see along the way

Would you go again?: ☐y ☐n Open all year?: ☐y ☐n

Activities Accomplished:

- ☐ Archery
- ☐ Biking
- ☐ Birding
- ☐ Boating
- ☐ Camping
- ☐ Caving
- ☐ Geocaching
- ☐ Fishing
- ☐ Hiking
- ☐ Horseback Riding
- ☐ Hunting
- ☐ Off-Roading
- ☐ Paddle Boarding
- ☐ Photography
- ☐ Picnicking
- ☐ Rock Climbing
- ☐ Shooting Range
- ☐ Snowshoeing
- ☐ Stargazing
- ☐ Swimming
- ☐ Tennis
- ☐ Walking
- ☐ Wildlife Watching
- ☐ ____________
- ☐ ____________
- ☐ ____________
- ☐ ____________
- ☐ ____________

Traveled by:

☐ ☐ ☐ ☐ ☐ ☐ ☐ ☐ ☐ ☐ ☐ ☐

Add your favorite ticket stub, postcard, photo, stamp or drawing here

N E S W NOT ALL THOSE WHO WANDER ARE LOST

Cedar Key Scrub State Reserve

County: Levy
29.204539, -82.987923, Cedar Key FL 32625 | 352-543-5567

Website: https://www.floridastateparks.org/parks-and-trails/cedar-key-scrub-state-reserve
Email: FSP.Feedback@FloridaDEP.gov

Water Body: Gulf of Mexico

Size: 5,028 acres
Established: 1978

Very limited facilities

Star Rating
☆☆☆☆☆

What souvenir did you bring home?... Decal Magnet

My favorite thing about this place is...

Why I went ...

Who I went with ...

When I went ...

What I did...

What I saw...

What I learned...

An unforgettable moment...

A laughable moment...

A surprising moment...

An unforeseeable moment...

My List

- ☐
- ☐
- ☐
- ☐
- ☐
- ☐
- ☐
- ☐
- ☐
- ☐
- ☐
- ☐

 Snapped a selfie | Location...

 Took a park sign selfie? - y | n

The weather was ...       

Plan Your Trip:

☐ Trip Plan Completed

☐ Day Trip ☐ Overnight Stay

Reservations required: ☐y ☐n

Date reservations made: ____________

Refund Policy: ☐y ☐n Site/Room #: ______

Confirmation #: ____________

Miles to travel: ____________

Time traveling: ____________

Dog friendly?: ☐y ☐n

Destination Information:

____

____

Places we discovered along the way

____

____

____

Places to stop and see along the way

____

____

Activities Accomplished:

Would you go again?: ☐y ☐n Open all year?: ☐y ☐n

- ☐ Archery
- ☐ Biking
- ☐ Birding
- ☐ Boating
- ☐ Camping
- ☐ Caving
- ☐ Geocaching
- ☐ Fishing
- ☐ Hiking
- ☐ Horseback Riding
- ☐ Hunting
- ☐ Off-Roading
- ☐ Paddle Boarding
- ☐ Photography
- ☐ Picnicking
- ☐ Rock Climbing
- ☐ Shooting Range
- ☐ Snowshoeing
- ☐ Stargazing
- ☐ Swimming
- ☐ Tennis
- ☐ Walking
- ☐ Wildlife Watching
- ☐ ____________
- ☐ ____________
- ☐ ____________
- ☐ ____________
- ☐ ____________

Traveled by:

☐ ☐ ☐ ☐ ☐ ☐ ☐ ☐ ☐ ☐ ☐ ☐

Add your favorite ticket stub, postcard, photo, stamp or drawing here

N W E S NOT ALL THOSE WHO WANDER ARE LOST

Cedar Key Museum State Park

County: Levy
12231 S.W. 166th Court, Cedar Key FL 32625 | 352-543-5350

Website: https://www.floridastateparks.org/parks-and-trails/cedar-key-museum-state-park
Email: FSP.Feedback@FloridaDEP.gov

Water Body: Gulf of Mexico

Size: 19 acres
Established: 1960

The St. Clair Whitman house depicts life in Cedar Key circa 1920

Star Rating ☆☆☆☆☆

What souvenir did you bring home?... Decal Magnet

My favorite thing about this place is...

Why I went ...

Who I went with ...

When I went ...

What I did...

What I saw...

What I learned...

An unforgettable moment...

A laughable moment...

A surprising moment...

An unforeseeable moment...

My List

- ☐
- ☐
- ☐
- ☐
- ☐
- ☐
- ☐
- ☐
- ☐
- ☐
- ☐
- ☐

Snapped a selfie | Location...

Took a park sign selfie? - Y | N

The weather was ...

Plan Your Trip:

☐ Trip Plan Completed

☐ Day Trip ☐ Overnight Stay

Reservations required: ☐y ☐n

Date reservations made: ______

Refund Policy: ☐y ☐n Site/Room #: ______

Confirmation #: ______

Miles to travel: ______

Time traveling: ______

Dog friendly?: ☐y ☐n

Destination Information:

______

______

Places we discovered along the way

______

______

______

Places to stop and see along the way

______

______

Activities Accomplished:

Would you go again?: ☐y ☐n

Open all year?: ☐y ☐n

- ☐ Archery
- ☐ Biking
- ☐ Birding
- ☐ Boating
- ☐ Camping
- ☐ Caving
- ☐ Geocaching
- ☐ Fishing
- ☐ Hiking
- ☐ Horseback Riding
- ☐ Hunting
- ☐ Off-Roading
- ☐ Paddle Boarding
- ☐ Photography
- ☐ Picnicking
- ☐ Rock Climbing
- ☐ Shooting Range
- ☐ Snowshoeing
- ☐ Stargazing
- ☐ Swimming
- ☐ Tennis
- ☐ Walking
- ☐ Wildlife Watching
- ☐ ______
- ☐ ______
- ☐ ______
- ☐ ______
- ☐ ______

Traveled by:

☐ ☐ ☐ ☐ ☐ ☐ ☐ ☐ ☐ ☐ ☐ ☐

Add your favorite ticket stub, postcard, photo, stamp or drawing here

N W E S NOT ALL THOSE WHO WANDER ARE LOST

Charlotte Harbor Preserve State Park

County: Charlotte
12301 Burnt Store Road, Punta Gorda FL 33955 | 941-575-5816

Website: https://www.floridastateparks.org/parks-and-trails/charlotte-harbor-preserve-state-park
Email: FSP.Feedback@FloridaDEP.gov

Water Body: Gasparilla Pass - Charlotte Harbor

Size: 42,518 acres
Established: 1978

Very limited facilities

Star Rating ☆☆☆☆☆

What souvenir did you bring home?... Decal Magnet

My favorite thing about this place is...

Why I went ...

Who I went with ...

When I went ...

What I did...

What I saw...

What I learned...

An unforgettable moment...

A laughable moment...

A surprising moment...

An unforeseeable moment...

Snapped a selfie | Location...

Took a park sign selfie? - y | n

The weather was ...

My List

- ☐
- ☐
- ☐
- ☐
- ☐
- ☐
- ☐
- ☐
- ☐
- ☐
- ☐
- ☐

Plan Your Trip:

☐ Trip Plan Completed

☐ Day Trip ☐ Overnight Stay

Reservations required: ☐y ☐n

Date reservations made: ____________

Refund Policy: ☐y ☐n Site/Room #: ______

Confirmation #: ____________

Miles to travel: ____________

Time traveling: ____________

Dog friendly?: ☐y ☐n

Destination Information:

Places we discovered along the way

Places to stop and see along the way

Activities Accomplished:

Would you go again?: ☐y ☐n Open all year?: ☐y ☐n

- ☐ Archery
- ☐ Biking
- ☐ Birding
- ☐ Boating
- ☐ Camping
- ☐ Caving
- ☐ Geocaching
- ☐ Fishing
- ☐ Hiking
- ☐ Horseback Riding
- ☐ Hunting
- ☐ Off-Roading
- ☐ Paddle Boarding
- ☐ Photography
- ☐ Picnicking
- ☐ Rock Climbing
- ☐ Shooting Range
- ☐ Snowshoeing
- ☐ Stargazing
- ☐ Swimming
- ☐ Tennis
- ☐ Walking
- ☐ Wildlife Watching
- ☐ ____________
- ☐ ____________
- ☐ ____________
- ☐ ____________
- ☐ ____________

Traveled by:

☐ ☐ ☐ ☐ ☐ ☐ ☐ ☐ ☐ ☐ ☐ ☐

Add your favorite ticket stub, postcard, photo, stamp or drawing here

N NOT ALL THOSE WHO E WANDER ARE LOST S W

Collier-Seminole State Park

County: Collier
20200 Tamiami Trail E., Naples FL 34114 | 239-394-3397

Website: https://www.floridastateparks.org/parks-and-trails/collier-seminole-state-park
Email: FSP.Feedback@FloridaDEP.gov

Water Body: Gulf of Mexico

Size: 6,430 acres
Established: 1947

National Historic Mechanical Engineering Landmark, the Bay City Walking Dredge used to build the Tamiami Trail through the Everglades

What souvenir did you bring home?... Decal Magnet ______

Star Rating ☆☆☆☆☆

My favorite thing about this place is... ______

Why I went ... ______

Who I went with ... ______

When I went ... ______

What I did... ______

What I saw... ______

What I learned... ______

An unforgettable moment... ______

A laughable moment... ______

A surprising moment... ______

An unforeseeable moment... ______

Snapped a selfie | Location... ______

Took a park sign selfie? - Y | N

The weather was ...

My List

- ☐ ______
- ☐ ______
- ☐ ______
- ☐ ______
- ☐ ______
- ☐ ______
- ☐ ______
- ☐ ______
- ☐ ______
- ☐ ______
- ☐ ______
- ☐ ______

Plan Your Trip:

☐ Trip Plan Completed

☐ Day Trip ☐ Overnight Stay

Reservations required: ☐y ☐n

Date reservations made: ______

Refund Policy: ☐y ☐n Site/Room #: ______

Confirmation #: ______

Miles to travel: ______

Time traveling: ______

Dog friendly?: ☐y ☐n

Destination Information:

______

______

Places we discovered along the way

______

______

______

Places to stop and see along the way

______

______

Activities Accomplished:

Would you go again?: ☐y ☐n Open all year?: ☐y ☐n

- ☐ Archery
- ☐ Biking
- ☐ Birding
- ☐ Boating
- ☐ Camping
- ☐ Caving
- ☐ Geocaching
- ☐ Fishing
- ☐ Hiking
- ☐ Horseback Riding
- ☐ Hunting
- ☐ Off-Roading
- ☐ Paddle Boarding
- ☐ Photography
- ☐ Picnicking
- ☐ Rock Climbing
- ☐ Shooting Range
- ☐ Snowshoeing
- ☐ Stargazing
- ☐ Swimming
- ☐ Tennis
- ☐ Walking
- ☐ Wildlife Watching
- ☐ ______
- ☐ ______
- ☐ ______
- ☐ ______
- ☐ ______

Traveled by:

☐ ☐ ☐ ☐ ☐ ☐ ☐ ☐ ☐ ☐ ☐ ☐

Add your favorite ticket stub, postcard, photo, stamp or drawing here

N E S W NOT ALL THOSE WHO WANDER ARE LOST

Colt Creek State Park

County: Polk
16000 State Road 471, Lakeland FL 33809 | 863-815-6761

Website: https://www.floridastateparks.org/parks-and-trails/colt-creek-state-park
Email: FSP.Feedback@FloridaDEP.gov

Water Body: several small lakes and creeks

Size: 5,067 acres
Established: 2007

Part of the Green Swamp Wilderness Preserve

Star Rating ☆☆☆☆☆

What souvenir did you bring home?... Decal Magnet

My favorite thing about this place is...

Why I went ...

Who I went with ...

When I went ...

What I did...

What I saw...

What I learned...

An unforgettable moment...

A laughable moment...

A surprising moment...

An unforeseeable moment...

My List

- ☐
- ☐
- ☐
- ☐
- ☐
- ☐
- ☐
- ☐
- ☐
- ☐
- ☐
- ☐

Snapped a selfie | Location...

Took a park sign selfie? - Y | N

The weather was ...

Plan Your Trip:

☐ Trip Plan Completed

☐ Day Trip ☐ Overnight Stay

Reservations required: ☐y ☐n

Date reservations made: ____________

Refund Policy: ☐y ☐n Site/Room #: ______

Confirmation #: ____________

Miles to travel: ____________

Time traveling: ____________

Dog friendly?: ☐y ☐n

Destination Information:

____

____

Places we discovered along the way

____

____

____

Places to stop and see along the way

____

____

Would you go again?: ☐y ☐n

Open all year?: ☐y ☐n

Activities Accomplished:

☐ Archery
☐ Biking
☐ Birding
☐ Boating
☐ Camping
☐ Caving
☐ Geocaching
☐ Fishing
☐ Hiking
☐ Horseback Riding
☐ Hunting
☐ Off-Roading
☐ Paddle Boarding
☐ Photography
☐ Picnicking
☐ Rock Climbing
☐ Shooting Range
☐ Snowshoeing
☐ Stargazing
☐ Swimming
☐ Tennis
☐ Walking
☐ Wildlife Watching
☐ ____________
☐ ____________
☐ ____________
☐ ____________
☐ ____________

Traveled by:

☐ ☐ ☐ ☐ ☐ ☐ ☐ ☐ ☐ ☐ ☐ ☐

Add your favorite ticket stub, postcard, photo, stamp or drawing here

Constitution Convention Museum State Park

County: Gulf
200 Allen Memorial Way, Port St. Joe FL 32456 | 850-229-8029

Website: https://www.floridastateparks.org/index.php/parks-and-trails/constitution-convention-museum-state-park
Email: FSP.Feedback@FloridaDEP.gov

Water Body: none, but near St. Joseph Bay

Size: 13 acres
Established: 1956

Site where first Florida Constitution was drafted in 1838

Star Rating ☆☆☆☆☆

What souvenir did you bring home?... Decal Magnet

My favorite thing about this place is...

Why I went ...

Who I went with ...

When I went ...

What I did...

What I saw...

What I learned...

An unforgettable moment...

A laughable moment...

A surprising moment...

An unforeseeable moment...

My List

- ☐
- ☐
- ☐
- ☐
- ☐
- ☐
- ☐
- ☐
- ☐
- ☐
- ☐
- ☐

Snapped a selfie | Location...

Took a park sign selfie? - y | n

The weather was ...

Plan Your Trip:

☐ Trip Plan Completed

☐ Day Trip ☐ Overnight Stay

Reservations required: ☐y ☐n

Date reservations made: ______

Refund Policy: ☐y ☐n Site/Room #: ______

Confirmation #: ______

Miles to travel: ______

Time traveling: ______

Dog friendly?: ☐y ☐n

Destination Information:

______

______

Places we discovered along the way

______

______

______

Places to stop and see along the way

______

______

Would you go again?: ☐y ☐n Open all year?: ☐y ☐n

Activities Accomplished:

- ☐ Archery
- ☐ Biking
- ☐ Birding
- ☐ Boating
- ☐ Camping
- ☐ Caving
- ☐ Geocaching
- ☐ Fishing
- ☐ Hiking
- ☐ Horseback Riding
- ☐ Hunting
- ☐ Off-Roading
- ☐ Paddle Boarding
- ☐ Photography
- ☐ Picnicking
- ☐ Rock Climbing
- ☐ Shooting Range
- ☐ Snowshoeing
- ☐ Stargazing
- ☐ Swimming
- ☐ Tennis
- ☐ Walking
- ☐ Wildlife Watching
- ☐ ______
- ☐ ______
- ☐ ______
- ☐ ______
- ☐ ______

Traveled by:

☐ ☐ ☐ ☐ ☐ ☐ ☐ ☐ ☐ ☐ ☐ ☐

Add your favorite ticket stub, postcard, photo, stamp or drawing here

N E S W NOT ALL THOSE WHO WANDER ARE LOST

Crystal River Archaeological State Park

County: Citrus
3400 N. Museum Point, Crystal River FL 34428 | 352-795-3817

Website: https://www.floridastateparks.org/parks-and-trails/crystal-river-archaeological-state-park
Email: FSP.Feedback@FloridaDEP.gov

Water Body: Crystal River

Size: 61 acres
Established: 1965

National Historic Landmark and one of the oldest continuously occupied pre-Columbian sites in Florida

Star Rating ☆☆☆☆☆

What souvenir did you bring home?... Decal Magnet

My favorite thing about this place is... ______

Why I went ... ______

Who I went with ... ______

When I went ... ______

What I did... ______

What I saw... ______

What I learned... ______

An unforgettable moment... ______

A laughable moment... ______

A surprising moment... ______

An unforeseeable moment... ______

My List

- ☐ ______
- ☐ ______
- ☐ ______
- ☐ ______
- ☐ ______
- ☐ ______
- ☐ ______
- ☐ ______
- ☐ ______
- ☐ ______
- ☐ ______
- ☐ ______

Snapped a selfie | Location... ______

Took a park sign selfie? - Y | N

The weather was ...

Plan Your Trip:

☐ Trip Plan Completed

☐ Day Trip ☐ Overnight Stay

Reservations required: ☐y ☐n

Date reservations made: ______

Refund Policy: ☐y ☐n Site/Room #: ______

Confirmation #: ______

Miles to travel: ______

Time traveling: ______

Dog friendly?: ☐y ☐n

Destination Information:

______

______

Places we discovered along the way

______

______

______

Places to stop and see along the way

______

______

Activities Accomplished:

Would you go again?: ☐y ☐n Open all year?: ☐y ☐n

☐ Archery
☐ Biking
☐ Birding
☐ Boating
☐ Camping
☐ Caving
☐ Geocaching
☐ Fishing
☐ Hiking
☐ Horseback Riding
☐ Hunting
☐ Off-Roading
☐ Paddle Boarding
☐ Photography
☐ Picnicking
☐ Rock Climbing
☐ Shooting Range
☐ Snowshoeing
☐ Stargazing
☐ Swimming
☐ Tennis
☐ Walking
☐ Wildlife Watching
☐ ______
☐ ______
☐ ______
☐ ______
☐ ______

Traveled by:

☐ ☐ ☐ ☐ ☐ ☐ ☐ ☐ ☐ ☐ ☐ ☐

Add your favorite ticket stub, postcard, photo, stamp or drawing here

Crystal River Preserve State Park

County: Citrus

3266 N. Sailboat Ave., Crystal River FL 34428 | 352-795-3817

Website: https://www.floridastateparks.org/parks-and-trails/crystal-river-preserve-state-park
Email: FSP.Feedback@FloridaDEP.gov

Water Body: Crystal River

Size: 30,000 acres
Established: 2004

Rare spring-fed estuary

Star Rating ☆☆☆☆☆

What souvenir did you bring home?... Decal Magnet

My favorite thing about this place is...

Why I went ...

Who I went with ...

When I went ...

What I did...

What I saw...

What I learned...

An unforgettable moment...

A laughable moment...

A surprising moment...

An unforeseeable moment...

My List

- ☐
- ☐
- ☐
- ☐
- ☐
- ☐
- ☐
- ☐
- ☐
- ☐
- ☐
- ☐

Snapped a selfie | Location...

Took a park sign selfie? - Y | N

The weather was ...

Plan Your Trip:

☐ Trip Plan Completed

☐ Day Trip ☐ Overnight Stay

Reservations required: ☐y ☐n

Date reservations made: ______

Refund Policy: ☐y ☐n Site/Room #: ______

Confirmation #: ______

Miles to travel: ______

Time traveling: ______

Dog friendly?: ☐y ☐n

Destination Information:

______

______

Places we discovered along the way

______

______

______

Places to stop and see along the way

______

______

Activities Accomplished:

Would you go again?: ☐y ☐n

Open all year?: ☐y ☐n

☐ Archery
☐ Biking
☐ Birding
☐ Boating
☐ Camping
☐ Caving
☐ Geocaching
☐ Fishing
☐ Hiking
☐ Horseback Riding
☐ Hunting
☐ Off-Roading
☐ Paddle Boarding
☐ Photography
☐ Picnicking
☐ Rock Climbing
☐ Shooting Range
☐ Snowshoeing
☐ Stargazing
☐ Swimming
☐ Tennis
☐ Walking
☐ Wildlife Watching
☐ ______
☐ ______
☐ ______
☐ ______
☐ ______

Traveled by:

☐ ☐ ☐ ☐ ☐ ☐ ☐ ☐ ☐ ☐ ☐ ☐

Add your favorite ticket stub, postcard, photo, stamp or drawing here

N W E S NOT ALL THOSE WHO WANDER ARE LOST

Curry Hammock State Park

County: Monroe
56200 Overseas Highway, Marathon FL 33050 | 305-289-2690

Website: https://www.floridastateparks.org/parks-and-trails/curry-hammock-state-park
Email: FSP.Feedback@FloridaDEP.gov

Water Body: Atlantic Ocean - Gulf of Mexico

Size: 1,000 acres
Established: 1991

Named for a Miami teacher whose family owned key land

Star Rating ☆☆☆☆☆

What souvenir did you bring home?... Decal Magnet

My favorite thing about this place is...

Why I went ...

Who I went with ...

When I went ...

What I did...

What I saw...

What I learned...

An unforgettable moment...

A laughable moment...

A surprising moment...

An unforeseeable moment...

Snapped a selfie | Location...

Took a park sign selfie? - Y | N

The weather was ...

My List

- ☐
- ☐
- ☐
- ☐
- ☐
- ☐
- ☐
- ☐
- ☐
- ☐
- ☐
- ☐

Plan Your Trip:

☐ Trip Plan Completed

☐ Day Trip ☐ Overnight Stay

Reservations required: ☐y ☐n

Date reservations made: ____________

Refund Policy: ☐y ☐n Site/Room #: ____

Confirmation #: ____________

Miles to travel: ____________

Time traveling: ____________

Dog friendly?: ☐y ☐n

Destination Information:

____

____

Places we discovered along the way

____

____

____

Places to stop and see along the way

____

____

Would you go again?: ☐y ☐n Open all year?: ☐y ☐n

Activities Accomplished:

- ☐ Archery
- ☐ Biking
- ☐ Birding
- ☐ Boating
- ☐ Camping
- ☐ Caving
- ☐ Geocaching
- ☐ Fishing
- ☐ Hiking
- ☐ Horseback Riding
- ☐ Hunting
- ☐ Off-Roading
- ☐ Paddle Boarding
- ☐ Photography
- ☐ Picnicking
- ☐ Rock Climbing
- ☐ Shooting Range
- ☐ Snowshoeing
- ☐ Stargazing
- ☐ Swimming
- ☐ Tennis
- ☐ Walking
- ☐ Wildlife Watching
- ☐ ____________
- ☐ ____________
- ☐ ____________
- ☐ ____________
- ☐ ____________

Traveled by:

☐ ☐ ☐ ☐ ☐ ☐ ☐ ☐ ☐ ☐ ☐ ☐

Add your favorite ticket stub, postcard, photo, stamp or drawing here

N E S W NOT ALL THOSE WHO WANDER ARE LOST

DADE BATTLEFIELD HISTORIC STATE PARK

County: Sumter
7200 Battlefield Parkway, Bushnell FL 33513 | 352-793-4781

Website: https://www.floridastateparks.org/index.php/parks-and-trails/dade-battlefield-historic-state-park
Email: FSP.Feedback@FloridaDEP.gov

Water Body: none

Size: 80 acres
Established: 1921

Second Seminole War battle where 105 of 108 troops were massacred by 180 Native Americans

Star Rating
☆☆☆☆☆

What souvenir did you bring home?... Decal Magnet

My favorite thing about this place is...

Why I went ...

Who I went with ...

When I went ...

What I did...

What I saw...

What I learned...

An unforgettable moment...

A laughable moment...

A surprising moment...

An unforeseeable moment...

MY LIST

- ☐
- ☐
- ☐
- ☐
- ☐
- ☐
- ☐
- ☐
- ☐
- ☐
- ☐
- ☐

Snapped a selfie | Location...

Took a park sign selfie? - Y | N

The weather was ...

Plan Your Trip:

Destination Information:

☐ Trip Plan Completed

☐ Day Trip ☐ Overnight Stay

Reservations required: ☐y ☐n

Date reservations made: ______

Refund Policy: ☐y ☐n Site/Room #: ______

Confirmation #: ______

Miles to travel: ______

Time traveling: ______

Dog friendly?: ☐y ☐n

Places we discovered along the way

Places to stop and see along the way

Activities Accomplished:

Would you go again?: ☐y ☐n

Open all year?: ☐y ☐n

☐ Archery
☐ Biking
☐ Birding
☐ Boating
☐ Camping
☐ Caving
☐ Geocaching
☐ Fishing
☐ Hiking
☐ Horseback Riding
☐ Hunting
☐ Off-Roading
☐ Paddle Boarding
☐ Photography
☐ Picnicking
☐ Rock Climbing
☐ Shooting Range
☐ Snowshoeing
☐ Stargazing
☐ Swimming
☐ Tennis
☐ Walking
☐ Wildlife Watching
☐ ______
☐ ______
☐ ______
☐ ______
☐ ______

Traveled by:

☐ ☐ ☐ ☐ ☐ ☐ ☐ ☐ ☐ ☐ ☐ ☐

Add your favorite ticket stub, postcard, photo, stamp or drawing here

N W E S NOT ALL THOSE WHO WANDER ARE LOST

Dagny Johnson Key Largo Hammock Botanical State Park

County: Monroe
County Road 905, Mile Marker 106, Key Largo FL 33037 | 305-676-3777

Website: https://www.floridastateparks.org/parks-and-trails/dagny-johnson-key-largo-hammock-botanical-state-park
Email: FSP.Feedback@FloridaDEP.gov

Water Body: Atlantic Ocean

Size: 2,421 acres
Established: 1982

Park's name changed in 2001 to honor park activist

Star Rating ☆☆☆☆☆

What souvenir did you bring home?... Decal Magnet

My favorite thing about this place is...

Why I went ...

Who I went with ...

When I went ...

What I did...

What I saw...

What I learned...

An unforgettable moment...

A laughable moment...

A surprising moment...

An unforeseeable moment...

My List

- ☐
- ☐
- ☐
- ☐
- ☐
- ☐
- ☐
- ☐
- ☐
- ☐
- ☐
- ☐

Snapped a selfie | Location...

Took a park sign selfie? - Y | N

The weather was ...

Plan Your Trip:

☐ Trip Plan Completed

☐ Day Trip ☐ Overnight Stay

Reservations required: ☐y ☐n

Date reservations made: ____________

Refund Policy: ☐y ☐n Site/Room #: ______

Confirmation #: ____________

Miles to travel: ____________

Time traveling: ____________

Dog friendly?: ☐y ☐n

Destination Information:

Places we discovered along the way

Places to stop and see along the way

Activities Accomplished:

Would you go again?: ☐y ☐n

Open all year?: ☐y ☐n

- ☐ Archery
- ☐ Biking
- ☐ Birding
- ☐ Boating
- ☐ Camping
- ☐ Caving
- ☐ Geocaching
- ☐ Fishing
- ☐ Hiking
- ☐ Horseback Riding
- ☐ Hunting
- ☐ Off-Roading
- ☐ Paddle Boarding
- ☐ Photography
- ☐ Picnicking
- ☐ Rock Climbing
- ☐ Shooting Range
- ☐ Snowshoeing
- ☐ Stargazing
- ☐ Swimming
- ☐ Tennis
- ☐ Walking
- ☐ Wildlife Watching
- ☐ ____________
- ☐ ____________
- ☐ ____________
- ☐ ____________
- ☐ ____________

Traveled by:

☐ ☐ ☐ ☐ ☐ ☐ ☐ ☐ ☐ ☐ ☐ ☐

Add your favorite ticket stub, postcard, photo, stamp or drawing here

N
NOT ALL THOSE WHO WANDER ARE LOST
W E
S

De Leon Springs State Park

County: Volusia

601 Ponce de Leon Blvd., De Leon Springs FL 32130 | 386-985-4212

Website: https://www.floridastateparks.org/parks-and-trails/de-leon-springs-state-park
Email: FSP.Feedback@FloridaDEP.gov

Water Body: Crystal River

Size: 600 acres
Established: 1982

"Old Methuselah" is a 500-year-old bald cypress; previously a private park with Jungle Cruise; 19 million gallons 72 million liters of 72 ¬∞F 22 ¬∞C water daily

Star Rating ☆☆☆☆☆

What souvenir did you bring home?... Decal Magnet

My favorite thing about this place is...

Why I went ...

Who I went with ...

When I went ...

What I did...

What I saw...

What I learned...

An unforgettable moment...

A laughable moment...

A surprising moment...

An unforeseeable moment...

My List

- ☐
- ☐
- ☐
- ☐
- ☐
- ☐
- ☐
- ☐
- ☐
- ☐
- ☐
- ☐

Snapped a selfie | Location...

Took a park sign selfie? - Y | N

The weather was ...

Plan Your Trip:

☐ Trip Plan Completed

☐ Day Trip ☐ Overnight Stay

Reservations required: ☐y ☐n

Date reservations made: ____________

Refund Policy: ☐y ☐n Site/Room #: ______

Confirmation #: ____________

Miles to travel: ____________

Time traveling: ____________

Dog friendly?: ☐y ☐n

Destination Information:

Places we discovered along the way

Places to stop and see along the way

Would you go again?: ☐y ☐n Open all year?: ☐y ☐n

Activities Accomplished:

☐ Archery
☐ Biking
☐ Birding
☐ Boating
☐ Camping
☐ Caving
☐ Geocaching
☐ Fishing
☐ Hiking
☐ Horseback Riding
☐ Hunting
☐ Off-Roading
☐ Paddle Boarding
☐ Photography
☐ Picnicking
☐ Rock Climbing
☐ Shooting Range
☐ Snowshoeing
☐ Stargazing
☐ Swimming
☐ Tennis
☐ Walking
☐ Wildlife Watching
☐ ____________
☐ ____________
☐ ____________
☐ ____________
☐ ____________

Traveled by:

☐ ☐ ☐ ☐ ☐ ☐ ☐ ☐ ☐ ☐ ☐ ☐

Add your favorite ticket stub, postcard, photo, stamp or drawing here

DeSoto Site Historic State Park

County: Leon
1001 Desoto Park Dr, Tallahassee, FL 32301 | 850-245-6444

Website: https://www.exploresouthernhistory.com/fldesoto1.html
Email:

Water Body: none

Size: 5 acres
Established: 2003

Site of Hernando de Soto 1539 encampment and Gov. John W. Martin House

What souvenir did you bring home?... Decal Magnet

Star Rating ☆☆☆☆☆

My favorite thing about this place is...

Why I went ...

Who I went with ...

When I went ...

What I did...

What I saw...

What I learned...

An unforgettable moment...

A laughable moment...

A surprising moment...

An unforeseeable moment...

Snapped a selfie | Location...

Took a park sign selfie? - Y | N

The weather was ...

My List

- ☐
- ☐
- ☐
- ☐
- ☐
- ☐
- ☐
- ☐
- ☐
- ☐
- ☐
- ☐

Plan Your Trip:

☐ Trip Plan Completed

☐ Day Trip ☐ Overnight Stay

Reservations required: ☐y ☐n

Date reservations made: ____________

Refund Policy: ☐y ☐n Site/Room #: ____

Confirmation #: ____________

Miles to travel: ____________

Time traveling: ____________

Dog friendly?: ☐y ☐n

Destination Information:

____

____

Places we discovered along the way

____

____

____

Places to stop and see along the way

____

____

Would you go again?: ☐y ☐n

Open all year?: ☐y ☐n

Activities Accomplished:

☐ Archery
☐ Biking
☐ Birding
☐ Boating
☐ Camping
☐ Caving
☐ Geocaching
☐ Fishing
☐ Hiking
☐ Horseback Riding
☐ Hunting
☐ Off-Roading
☐ Paddle Boarding
☐ Photography
☐ Picnicking
☐ Rock Climbing
☐ Shooting Range
☐ Snowshoeing
☐ Stargazing
☐ Swimming
☐ Tennis
☐ Walking
☐ Wildlife Watching
☐ ____________
☐ ____________
☐ ____________
☐ ____________
☐ ____________

Traveled by:

☐ ☐ ☐ ☐ ☐ ☐ ☐ ☐ ☐ ☐ ☐ ☐

Add your favorite ticket stub, postcard, photo, stamp or drawing here

N W E S
NOT ALL THOSE WHO WANDER ARE LOST

Deer Lake State Park

County: Walton
6350 E. County Road 30-A, Santa Rosa FL 32459 | 850-267-8300

Website: https://www.floridastateparks.org/parks-and-trails/deer-lake-state-park
Email: FSP.Feedback@FloridaDEP.gov

Water Body: Gulf of Mexico - Deer Lake

Size: 1,995 acres
Established: 1996

Very rare freshwater lake among coastal dunes

What souvenir did you bring home?... Decal Magnet

Star Rating ☆☆☆☆☆

My favorite thing about this place is...

Why I went ...

Who I went with ...

When I went ...

What I did...

What I saw...

What I learned...

An unforgettable moment...

A laughable moment...

A surprising moment...

An unforeseeable moment...

My List

- ☐
- ☐
- ☐
- ☐
- ☐
- ☐
- ☐
- ☐
- ☐
- ☐
- ☐
- ☐

Snapped a selfie | Location...

Took a park sign selfie? - Y | N

The weather was ...

Plan Your Trip:

☐ Trip Plan Completed

☐ Day Trip ☐ Overnight Stay

Reservations required: ☐y ☐n

Date reservations made: ______

Refund Policy: ☐y ☐n Site/Room #: ______

Confirmation #: ______

Miles to travel: ______

Time traveling: ______

Dog friendly?: ☐y ☐n

Destination Information:

Places we discovered along the way

Places to stop and see along the way

Would you go again?: ☐y ☐n

Open all year?: ☐y ☐n

Activities Accomplished:

☐ Archery
☐ Biking
☐ Birding
☐ Boating
☐ Camping
☐ Caving
☐ Geocaching
☐ Fishing
☐ Hiking
☐ Horseback Riding
☐ Hunting
☐ Off-Roading
☐ Paddle Boarding
☐ Photography
☐ Picnicking
☐ Rock Climbing
☐ Shooting Range
☐ Snowshoeing
☐ Stargazing
☐ Swimming
☐ Tennis
☐ Walking
☐ Wildlife Watching
☐ ______
☐ ______
☐ ______
☐ ______
☐ ______

Traveled by:

☐ ☐ ☐ ☐ ☐ ☐ ☐ ☐ ☐ ☐ ☐ ☐

Add your favorite ticket stub, postcard, photo, stamp or drawing here

N W E S NOT ALL THOSE WHO WANDER ARE LOST

Delnor-Wiggins Pass State Park

County: Collier
11135 Gulfshore Drive, Naples FL 34108 | 239-597-6196

Website: https://www.floridastateparks.org/index.php/parks-and-trails/delnor-wiggins-pass-state-park
Email: FSP.Feedback@FloridaDEP.gov

Water Body: Cocohatchee River - Gulf of Mexico

Size: 166 acres
Established: 1981

Barrier island with white sugar sand beach

Star Rating ☆☆☆☆☆

What souvenir did you bring home?... Decal Magnet

My favorite thing about this place is...

Why I went ...

Who I went with ...

When I went ...

What I did...

What I saw...

What I learned...

An unforgettable moment...

A laughable moment...

A surprising moment...

An unforeseeable moment...

Snapped a selfie | Location...

Took a park sign selfie? - Y | N

The weather was ...

My List

- ☐
- ☐
- ☐
- ☐
- ☐
- ☐
- ☐
- ☐
- ☐
- ☐
- ☐
- ☐

PLAN YOUR TRIP:

☐ Trip Plan Completed

☐ Day Trip ☐ Overnight Stay

Reservations required: ☐y ☐n

Date reservations made: ____________

Refund Policy: ☐y ☐n Site/Room #: ____

Confirmation #: ____________

Miles to travel: ____________

Time traveling: ____________

Dog friendly?: ☐y ☐n

DESTINATION INFORMATION:

PLACES WE DISCOVERED ALONG THE WAY

PLACES TO STOP AND SEE ALONG THE WAY

Activities Accomplished:

Would you go again?: ☐y ☐n Open all year?: ☐y ☐n

- ☐ Archery
- ☐ Biking
- ☐ Birding
- ☐ Boating
- ☐ Camping
- ☐ Caving
- ☐ Geocaching
- ☐ Fishing
- ☐ Hiking
- ☐ Horseback Riding
- ☐ Hunting
- ☐ Off-Roading
- ☐ Paddle Boarding
- ☐ Photography
- ☐ Picnicking
- ☐ Rock Climbing
- ☐ Shooting Range
- ☐ Snowshoeing
- ☐ Stargazing
- ☐ Swimming
- ☐ Tennis
- ☐ Walking
- ☐ Wildlife Watching
- ☐ ____________
- ☐ ____________
- ☐ ____________
- ☐ ____________
- ☐ ____________

Traveled by:

☐ ☐ ☐ ☐ ☐ ☐ ☐ ☐ ☐ ☐ ☐ ☐

Add your favorite ticket stub, postcard, photo, stamp or drawing here

N
NOT ALL THOSE WHO WANDER ARE LOST
W E S

DEVIL'S MILLHOPPER GEOLOGICAL STATE PARK

County: Alachua
4732 Millhopper Road, Gainesville FL 32653 | 352-955-2008

Website: https://www.floridastateparks.org/parks-and-trails/devils-millhopper-geological-state-park
Email: FSP.Feedback@FloridaDEP.gov

Water Body: sinkhole pond

Size: 67 acres
Established: 1974

120-foot 36.6 m deep, 500-foot 152.4 m wide sinkhole accessed by 232 step stairway

Star Rating ☆☆☆☆☆

What souvenir did you bring home?... Decal Magnet

My favorite thing about this place is...

Why I went ...

Who I went with ...

When I went ...

What I did...

What I saw...

What I learned...

An unforgettable moment...

A laughable moment...

A surprising moment...

An unforeseeable moment...

MY LIST

- ☐
- ☐
- ☐
- ☐
- ☐
- ☐
- ☐
- ☐
- ☐
- ☐
- ☐
- ☐

Snapped a selfie | Location...

Took a park sign selfie? - Y | N

The weather was ...

Plan Your Trip:

☐ Trip Plan Completed

☐ Day Trip ☐ Overnight Stay

Reservations required: ☐y ☐n

Date reservations made: ______

Refund Policy: ☐y ☐n Site/Room #: ______

Confirmation #: ______

Miles to travel: ______

Time traveling: ______

Dog friendly?: ☐y ☐n

Destination Information:

______

______

Places we discovered along the way

______

______

______

Places to stop and see along the way

______

______

Activities Accomplished:

Would you go again?: ☐y ☐n Open all year?: ☐y ☐n

- ☐ Archery
- ☐ Biking
- ☐ Birding
- ☐ Boating
- ☐ Camping
- ☐ Caving
- ☐ Geocaching
- ☐ Fishing
- ☐ Hiking
- ☐ Horseback Riding
- ☐ Hunting
- ☐ Off-Roading
- ☐ Paddle Boarding
- ☐ Photography
- ☐ Picnicking
- ☐ Rock Climbing
- ☐ Shooting Range
- ☐ Snowshoeing
- ☐ Stargazing
- ☐ Swimming
- ☐ Tennis
- ☐ Walking
- ☐ Wildlife Watching
- ☐ ______
- ☐ ______
- ☐ ______
- ☐ ______
- ☐ ______

Traveled by:

☐ ☐ ☐ ☐ ☐ ☐ ☐ ☐ ☐ ☐ ☐ ☐

Add your favorite ticket stub, postcard, photo, stamp or drawing here

N E S W NOT ALL THOSE WHO WANDER ARE LOST

Don Pedro Island State Park

County: Charlotte
8450 Placida Road, Cape Haze FL 33946 | 941-964-0375

Website: https://www.floridastateparks.org/parks-and-trails/don-pedro-island-state-park
Email: FSP.Feedback@FloridaDEP.gov

Water Body: Gulf of Mexico

Size: 230 acres
Established: 1985

Barrier island accessible only by boat or ferry

Star Rating ☆☆☆☆☆

What souvenir did you bring home?... Decal Magnet

My favorite thing about this place is...

Why I went ...

Who I went with ...

When I went ...

What I did...

What I saw...

What I learned...

An unforgettable moment...

A laughable moment...

A surprising moment...

An unforeseeable moment...

My List

- ☐
- ☐
- ☐
- ☐
- ☐
- ☐
- ☐
- ☐
- ☐
- ☐
- ☐
- ☐

 Snapped a selfie | Location...

 Took a park sign selfie? - Y | N

The weather was ... 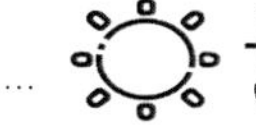     

PLAN YOUR TRIP:

☐ Trip Plan Completed

☐ Day Trip ☐ Overnight Stay

Reservations required: ☐y ☐n

Date reservations made: ____________

Refund Policy: ☐y ☐n Site/Room #: ______

Confirmation #: ____________

Miles to travel: ____________

Time traveling: ____________

Dog friendly?: ☐y ☐n

DESTINATION INFORMATION:

____

____

PLACES WE DISCOVERED ALONG THE WAY

____

____

____

PLACES TO STOP AND SEE ALONG THE WAY

____

____

Would you go again?: ☐y ☐n

Open all year?: ☐y ☐n

Activities Accomplished:

☐ Archery
☐ Biking
☐ Birding
☐ Boating
☐ Camping
☐ Caving
☐ Geocaching
☐ Fishing
☐ Hiking
☐ Horseback Riding
☐ Hunting
☐ Off-Roading
☐ Paddle Boarding
☐ Photography
☐ Picnicking
☐ Rock Climbing
☐ Shooting Range
☐ Snowshoeing
☐ Stargazing
☐ Swimming
☐ Tennis
☐ Walking
☐ Wildlife Watching
☐ ____________
☐ ____________
☐ ____________
☐ ____________
☐ ____________

Traveled by:

☐ ☐ ☐ ☐ ☐ ☐ ☐ ☐ ☐ ☐ ☐ ☐

Add your favorite ticket stub, postcard, photo, stamp or drawing here

DR. VON D. MIZELL-EULA JOHNSON STATE PARK

***County:* Broward**
6503 N. Ocean Drive, Dania Beach FL 33004 | 954-923-2833

Website: https://www.floridastateparks.org/mizell
Email: FSP.Feedback@FloridaDEP.gov

Water Body: Atlantic Ocean

Size: 310 acres
Established: 1973

Formerly known as John U Loyd State Park

Star Rating ☆☆☆☆☆

What souvenir did you bring home?... Decal Magnet

My favorite thing about this place is...

Why I went ...

Who I went with ...

When I went ...

What I did...

What I saw...

What I learned...

An unforgettable moment...

A laughable moment...

A surprising moment...

An unforeseeable moment...

MY LIST

- ☐
- ☐
- ☐
- ☐
- ☐
- ☐
- ☐
- ☐
- ☐
- ☐
- ☐
- ☐

Snapped a selfie | Location...

Took a park sign selfie? - Y | N

The weather was ... °F

Plan Your Trip:

☐ Trip Plan Completed

☐ Day Trip ☐ Overnight Stay

Reservations required: ☐y ☐n

Date reservations made: ____________

Refund Policy: ☐y ☐n Site/Room #: ______

Confirmation #: ____________

Miles to travel: ____________

Time traveling: ____________

Dog friendly?: ☐y ☐n

Destination Information:

____

____

Places we discovered along the way

____

____

____

Places to stop and see along the way

____

____

Activities Accomplished:

Would you go again?: ☐y ☐n Open all year?: ☐y ☐n

- ☐ Archery
- ☐ Biking
- ☐ Birding
- ☐ Boating
- ☐ Camping
- ☐ Caving
- ☐ Geocaching
- ☐ Fishing
- ☐ Hiking
- ☐ Horseback Riding
- ☐ Hunting
- ☐ Off-Roading
- ☐ Paddle Boarding
- ☐ Photography
- ☐ Picnicking
- ☐ Rock Climbing
- ☐ Shooting Range
- ☐ Snowshoeing
- ☐ Stargazing
- ☐ Swimming
- ☐ Tennis
- ☐ Walking
- ☐ Wildlife Watching
- ☐ ____________
- ☐ ____________
- ☐ ____________
- ☐ ____________
- ☐ ____________

Traveled by:

☐ ☐ ☐ ☐ ☐ ☐ ☐ ☐ ☐ ☐ ☐ ☐

Add your favorite ticket stub, postcard, photo, stamp or drawing here

N W E S NOT ALL THOSE WHO WANDER ARE LOST

Dudley Farm Historic State Park

County: Alachua
18730 W. Newberry Road, Newberry FL 32669 | 352-472-1142

Website: https://www.floridastateparks.org/parks-and-trails/dudley-farm-historic-state-park
Email: FSP.Feedback@FloridaDEP.gov

Water Body: none

Size: 325 acres
Established: 1989

Shows agricultural development in Florida from the 1850s through the mid-1940s

Star Rating ☆☆☆☆☆

What souvenir did you bring home?... Decal Magnet

My favorite thing about this place is... ______

Why I went ... ______

Who I went with ... ______

When I went ... ______

What I did... ______

What I saw... ______

What I learned... ______

An unforgettable moment... ______

A laughable moment... ______

A surprising moment... ______

An unforeseeable moment... ______

My List

- ☐
- ☐
- ☐
- ☐
- ☐
- ☐
- ☐
- ☐
- ☐
- ☐
- ☐
- ☐

Snapped a selfie | Location... ______

Took a park sign selfie? - Y | N

The weather was ...

Plan Your Trip:

☐ Trip Plan Completed

☐ Day Trip ☐ Overnight Stay

Reservations required: ☐y ☐n

Date reservations made: ____________

Refund Policy: ☐y ☐n Site/Room #: ______

Confirmation #: ____________

Miles to travel: ____________

Time traveling: ____________

Dog friendly?: ☐y ☐n

Destination Information:

____

____

Places we discovered along the way

____

____

____

Places to stop and see along the way

____

____

Activities Accomplished:

Would you go again?: ☐y ☐n Open all year?: ☐y ☐n

- ☐ Archery
- ☐ Biking
- ☐ Birding
- ☐ Boating
- ☐ Camping
- ☐ Caving
- ☐ Geocaching
- ☐ Fishing
- ☐ Hiking
- ☐ Horseback Riding
- ☐ Hunting
- ☐ Off-Roading
- ☐ Paddle Boarding
- ☐ Photography
- ☐ Picnicking
- ☐ Rock Climbing
- ☐ Shooting Range
- ☐ Snowshoeing
- ☐ Stargazing
- ☐ Swimming
- ☐ Tennis
- ☐ Walking
- ☐ Wildlife Watching
- ☐ ____________
- ☐ ____________
- ☐ ____________
- ☐ ____________
- ☐ ____________

Traveled by:

☐ ☐ ☐ ☐ ☐ ☐ ☐ ☐ ☐ ☐ ☐ ☐

Add your favorite ticket stub, postcard, photo, stamp or drawing here

N E S W NOT ALL THOSE WHO WANDER ARE LOST

Dunns Creek State Park

County: Putnam
320 Sisco Road, Pomona Park FL 32181 | 386-329-3721

Website: https://www.floridastateparks.org/dunnscreek
Email: FSP.Feedback@FloridaDEP.gov

Water Body: St. Johns River - Dunns Creek

Size: 6,000 acres
Established: 2001

Steamboat stop during the 1920s

Star Rating ☆☆☆☆☆

What souvenir did you bring home?... Decal Magnet

My favorite thing about this place is...

Why I went ...

Who I went with ...

When I went ...

What I did...

What I saw...

What I learned...

An unforgettable moment...

A laughable moment...

A surprising moment...

An unforeseeable moment...

Snapped a selfie | Location...

Took a park sign selfie? - Y | N

The weather was ...

My List

- ☐
- ☐
- ☐
- ☐
- ☐
- ☐
- ☐
- ☐
- ☐
- ☐
- ☐
- ☐

Plan Your Trip:

☐ Trip Plan Completed

☐ Day Trip ☐ Overnight Stay

Reservations required: ☐y ☐n

Date reservations made: ______

Refund Policy: ☐y ☐n Site/Room #: ______

Confirmation #: ______

Miles to travel: ______

Time traveling: ______

Dog friendly?: ☐y ☐n

Destination Information:

______

______

Places we discovered along the way

______

______

______

Places to stop and see along the way

______

______

Would you go again?: ☐y ☐n

Open all year?: ☐y ☐n

Activities Accomplished:

☐ Archery	☐ Fishing	☐ Picnicking	☐ Walking
☐ Biking	☐ Hiking	☐ Rock Climbing	☐ Wildlife Watching
☐ Birding	☐ Horseback Riding	☐ Shooting Range	☐ ______
☐ Boating	☐ Hunting	☐ Snowshoeing	☐ ______
☐ Camping	☐ Off-Roading	☐ Stargazing	☐ ______
☐ Caving	☐ Paddle Boarding	☐ Swimming	☐ ______
☐ Geocaching	☐ Photography	☐ Tennis	☐ ______

Traveled by:

☐ ☐ ☐ ☐ ☐ ☐ ☐ ☐ ☐ ☐ ☐ ☐

Add your favorite ticket stub, postcard, photo, stamp or drawing here

N E S W NOT ALL THOSE WHO WANDER ARE LOST

Econfina River State Park

County: Taylor
4741 Econfina River Road, Lamont FL 32336 | 850-487-7989

Website: https://www.floridastateparks.org/parks-and-trails/econfina-river-state-park
Email: FSP.Feedback@FloridaDEP.gov

Water Body: Econfina River

Size: 4,543 acres
Established: 1989

Confederate deserters camped here and assisted Union blockade ships during the Civil War

Star Rating ☆☆☆☆☆

What souvenir did you bring home?... Decal Magnet ______

My favorite thing about this place is... ______

Why I went ... ______

Who I went with ... ______

When I went ... ______

What I did... ______

What I saw... ______

What I learned... ______

An unforgettable moment... ______

A laughable moment... ______

A surprising moment... ______

An unforeseeable moment... ______

My List

- ☐ ______
- ☐ ______
- ☐ ______
- ☐ ______
- ☐ ______
- ☐ ______
- ☐ ______
- ☐ ______
- ☐ ______
- ☐ ______
- ☐ ______
- ☐ ______

 Snapped a selfie | Location... ______

 Took a park sign selfie? - Y | N

The weather was ... 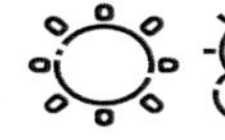     

Plan Your Trip:

☐ Trip Plan Completed

☐ Day Trip ☐ Overnight Stay

Reservations required: ☐y ☐n

Date reservations made: ____________

Refund Policy: ☐y ☐n Site/Room #: ______

Confirmation #: ____________

Miles to travel: ____________

Time traveling: ____________

Dog friendly?: ☐y ☐n

Destination Information:

____

____

Places we discovered along the way

____

____

____

Places to stop and see along the way

____

____

Activities Accomplished:

Would you go again?: ☐y ☐n Open all year?: ☐y ☐n

- ☐ Archery
- ☐ Biking
- ☐ Birding
- ☐ Boating
- ☐ Camping
- ☐ Caving
- ☐ Geocaching
- ☐ Fishing
- ☐ Hiking
- ☐ Horseback Riding
- ☐ Hunting
- ☐ Off-Roading
- ☐ Paddle Boarding
- ☐ Photography
- ☐ Picnicking
- ☐ Rock Climbing
- ☐ Shooting Range
- ☐ Snowshoeing
- ☐ Stargazing
- ☐ Swimming
- ☐ Tennis
- ☐ Walking
- ☐ Wildlife Watching
- ☐ ____________
- ☐ ____________
- ☐ ____________
- ☐ ____________
- ☐ ____________

Traveled by:

☐ ☐ ☐ ☐ ☐ ☐ ☐ ☐ ☐ ☐ ☐ ☐

Add your favorite ticket stub, postcard, photo, stamp or drawing here

N E S W NOT ALL THOSE WHO WANDER ARE LOST

Eden Gardens State Park

County: Walton

181 Eden Gardens Road, Santa Rosa Beach FL 32459 | 850-267-8320

Website: https://www.floridastateparks.org/parks-and-trails/eden-gardens-state-park
Email: FSP.Feedback@FloridaDEP.gov

Water Body: Tucker Bayou

Size: 163 acres
Established: 1968

Restored plantation house with Louis XVI style furniture

Star Rating ☆☆☆☆☆

What souvenir did you bring home?... Decal Magnet

My favorite thing about this place is...

Why I went ...

Who I went with ...

When I went ...

What I did...

What I saw...

What I learned...

An unforgettable moment...

A laughable moment...

A surprising moment...

An unforeseeable moment...

Snapped a selfie | Location...

Took a park sign selfie? - Y | N

The weather was ...

My List

- ☐
- ☐
- ☐
- ☐
- ☐
- ☐
- ☐
- ☐
- ☐
- ☐
- ☐
- ☐

Plan Your Trip:

☐ Trip Plan Completed

☐ Day Trip ☐ Overnight Stay

Reservations required: ☐y ☐n

Date reservations made: ____________

Refund Policy: ☐y ☐n Site/Room #: ______

Confirmation #: ____________

Miles to travel: ____________

Time traveling: ____________

Dog friendly?: ☐y ☐n

Destination Information:

Places we discovered along the way

Places to stop and see along the way

Activities Accomplished:

Would you go again?: ☐y ☐n

Open all year?: ☐y ☐n

- ☐ Archery
- ☐ Biking
- ☐ Birding
- ☐ Boating
- ☐ Camping
- ☐ Caving
- ☐ Geocaching
- ☐ Fishing
- ☐ Hiking
- ☐ Horseback Riding
- ☐ Hunting
- ☐ Off-Roading
- ☐ Paddle Boarding
- ☐ Photography
- ☐ Picnicking
- ☐ Rock Climbing
- ☐ Shooting Range
- ☐ Snowshoeing
- ☐ Stargazing
- ☐ Swimming
- ☐ Tennis
- ☐ Walking
- ☐ Wildlife Watching
- ☐ ____________
- ☐ ____________
- ☐ ____________
- ☐ ____________
- ☐ ____________

Traveled by:

☐ ☐ ☐ ☐ ☐ ☐ ☐ ☐ ☐ ☐ ☐ ☐

Add your favorite ticket stub, postcard, photo, stamp or drawing here

N
NOT ALL THOSE WHO WANDER ARE LOST
W E
S

Edward Ball Wakulla Springs State Park

County: Wakulla
465 Wakulla Park Drive, Wakulla Springs FL 32327 | 850-561-7276

Website: https://www.floridastateparks.org/WakullaSprings
Email: FSP.Feedback@FloridaDEP.gov

Water Body: Wakulla River

Size: 6,000 acres
Established: 1968

One of the largest and deepest freshwater springs in the world

Star Rating ☆☆☆☆☆

What souvenir did you bring home?... Decal Magnet ______

My favorite thing about this place is... ______

Why I went ... ______

Who I went with ... ______

When I went ... ______

What I did... ______

What I saw... ______

What I learned... ______

An unforgettable moment... ______

A laughable moment... ______

A surprising moment... ______

An unforeseeable moment... ______

My List

- ☐ ______
- ☐ ______
- ☐ ______
- ☐ ______
- ☐ ______
- ☐ ______
- ☐ ______
- ☐ ______
- ☐ ______
- ☐ ______
- ☐ ______
- ☐ ______

Snapped a selfie | Location... ______

Took a park sign selfie? - Y | N

The weather was ...

Plan Your Trip:

☐ Trip Plan Completed

☐ Day Trip ☐ Overnight Stay

Reservations required: ☐y ☐n

Date reservations made: ____

Refund Policy: ☐y ☐n Site/Room #: ____

Confirmation #: ____

Miles to travel: ____

Time traveling: ____

Dog friendly?: ☐y ☐n

Destination Information:

Places we discovered along the way

Places to stop and see along the way

Would you go again?: ☐y ☐n Open all year?: ☐y ☐n

Activities Accomplished:

☐ Archery	☐ Fishing	☐ Picnicking	☐ Walking
☐ Biking	☐ Hiking	☐ Rock Climbing	☐ Wildlife Watching
☐ Birding	☐ Horseback Riding	☐ Shooting Range	☐ ____
☐ Boating	☐ Hunting	☐ Snowshoeing	☐ ____
☐ Camping	☐ Off-Roading	☐ Stargazing	☐ ____
☐ Caving	☐ Paddle Boarding	☐ Swimming	☐ ____
☐ Geocaching	☐ Photography	☐ Tennis	☐ ____

Traveled by:

☐ ☐ ☐ ☐ ☐ ☐ ☐ ☐ ☐ ☐ ☐ ☐

Add your favorite ticket stub, postcard, photo, stamp or drawing here

Egmont Key State Park

County: Hillsborough
4905 34th St. South, #5000, St. Petersburg FL 33711 | 727-644-6235

Website: https://www.floridastateparks.org/parks-and-trails/egmont-key-state-park
Email: FSP.Feedback@FloridaDEP.gov

Water Body: Tampa Bay

Size: 328 acres
Established: 1974

The ruins of Fort Dade and Egmont Key Light are inside the park

Star Rating ☆☆☆☆☆

What souvenir did you bring home?... Decal Magnet ____________

My favorite thing about this place is... ____________

Why I went ... ____________

Who I went with ... ____________

When I went ... ____________

What I did... ____________

What I saw... ____________

What I learned... ____________

An unforgettable moment... ____________

A laughable moment... ____________

A surprising moment... ____________

An unforeseeable moment... ____________

Snapped a selfie | Location... ____________

Took a park sign selfie? - Y | N

My List

- ☐ ____________
- ☐ ____________
- ☐ ____________
- ☐ ____________
- ☐ ____________
- ☐ ____________
- ☐ ____________
- ☐ ____________
- ☐ ____________
- ☐ ____________
- ☐ ____________
- ☐ ____________

The weather was ... F

PLAN YOUR TRIP:

☐ Trip Plan Completed

☐ Day Trip ☐ Overnight Stay

Reservations required: ☐y ☐n

Date reservations made: __________

Refund Policy: ☐y ☐n Site/Room #: _____

Confirmation #: __________

Miles to travel: __________

Time traveling: __________

Dog friendly?: ☐y ☐n

DESTINATION INFORMATION:

PLACES WE DISCOVERED ALONG THE WAY

PLACES TO STOP AND SEE ALONG THE WAY

Activities Accomplished:

Would you go again?: ☐y ☐n

Open all year?: ☐y ☐n

☐ Archery	☐ Fishing	☐ Picnicking	☐ Walking
☐ Biking	☐ Hiking	☐ Rock Climbing	☐ Wildlife Watching
☐ Birding	☐ Horseback Riding	☐ Shooting Range	☐ ________
☐ Boating	☐ Hunting	☐ Snowshoeing	☐ ________
☐ Camping	☐ Off-Roading	☐ Stargazing	☐ ________
☐ Caving	☐ Paddle Boarding	☐ Swimming	☐ ________
☐ Geocaching	☐ Photography	☐ Tennis	☐ ________

Traveled by:

☐ ☐ ☐ ☐ ☐ ☐ ☐ ☐ ☐ ☐ ☐ ☐

Add your favorite ticket stub, postcard, photo, stamp or drawing here

N W E S NOT ALL THOSE WHO WANDER ARE LOST

Estero Bay Preserve State Park

County: Lee
4940 Broadway West, Estero FL 33928 | 239-992-0311

Website: https://www.floridastateparks.org/parks-and-trails/estero-bay-preserve-state-park
Email: FSP.Feedback@FloridaDEP.gov

Water Body: Estero Bay

Size: 10,000 acres
Established: 1974

The first aquatic nature preserve established in Florida

Star Rating ☆☆☆☆☆

What souvenir did you bring home?... Decal Magnet

My favorite thing about this place is...

Why I went ...

Who I went with ...

When I went ...

What I did...

What I saw...

What I learned...

An unforgettable moment...

A laughable moment...

A surprising moment...

An unforeseeable moment...

My List

- ☐
- ☐
- ☐
- ☐
- ☐
- ☐
- ☐
- ☐
- ☐
- ☐
- ☐
- ☐

Snapped a selfie | Location...

Took a park sign selfie? - Y | N

The weather was ...

PLAN YOUR TRIP:

☐ Trip Plan Completed

☐ Day Trip ☐ Overnight Stay

Reservations required: ☐y ☐n

Date reservations made: ____________

Refund Policy: ☐y ☐n Site/Room #: ______

Confirmation #: ____________

Miles to travel: ____________

Time traveling: ____________

Dog friendly?: ☐y ☐n

DESTINATION INFORMATION:

PLACES WE DISCOVERED ALONG THE WAY

PLACES TO STOP AND SEE ALONG THE WAY

Activities Accomplished:

Would you go again?: ☐y ☐n

Open all year?: ☐y ☐n

☐ Archery
☐ Biking
☐ Birding
☐ Boating
☐ Camping
☐ Caving
☐ Geocaching
☐ Fishing
☐ Hiking
☐ Horseback Riding
☐ Hunting
☐ Off-Roading
☐ Paddle Boarding
☐ Photography
☐ Picnicking
☐ Rock Climbing
☐ Shooting Range
☐ Snowshoeing
☐ Stargazing
☐ Swimming
☐ Tennis
☐ Walking
☐ Wildlife Watching
☐ ____________
☐ ____________
☐ ____________
☐ ____________
☐ ____________

Traveled by:

☐ ☐ ☐ ☐ ☐ ☐ ☐ ☐ ☐ ☐ ☐ ☐

Add your favorite ticket stub, postcard, photo, stamp or drawing here

N W E S NOT ALL THOSE WHO WANDER ARE LOST

Fakahatchee Strand Preserve State Park

County: Collier

137 Coastline Drive, Copeland FL 34137 | 239-695-4593

Website: **https://www.floridastateparks.org/parks-and-trails/fakahatchee-strand-preserve-state-park**
Email: FSP.Feedback@FloridaDEP.gov

Water Body: none

Size: 75,000 acres
Established: 1975

Part of the Big Cypress National Preserve in the Everglades

Star Rating ☆☆☆☆☆

What souvenir did you bring home?... Decal Magnet

My favorite thing about this place is...

Why I went ...

Who I went with ...

When I went ...

What I did...

What I saw...

What I learned...

An unforgettable moment...

A laughable moment...

A surprising moment...

An unforeseeable moment...

Snapped a selfie | Location...

Took a park sign selfie? - Y | N

The weather was ...

My List

- ☐
- ☐
- ☐
- ☐
- ☐
- ☐
- ☐
- ☐
- ☐
- ☐
- ☐
- ☐

Plan Your Trip:

☐ Trip Plan Completed

☐ Day Trip ☐ Overnight Stay

Reservations required: ☐y ☐n

Date reservations made: ____________

Refund Policy: ☐y ☐n Site/Room #: ______

Confirmation #: ____________

Miles to travel: ____________

Time traveling: ____________

Dog friendly?: ☐y ☐n

Destination Information:

____

____

Places we discovered along the way

____

____

____

Places to stop and see along the way

____

____

Would you go again?: ☐y ☐n Open all year?: ☐y ☐n

Activities Accomplished:

☐ Archery
☐ Biking
☐ Birding
☐ Boating
☐ Camping
☐ Caving
☐ Geocaching
☐ Fishing
☐ Hiking
☐ Horseback Riding
☐ Hunting
☐ Off-Roading
☐ Paddle Boarding
☐ Photography
☐ Picnicking
☐ Rock Climbing
☐ Shooting Range
☐ Snowshoeing
☐ Stargazing
☐ Swimming
☐ Tennis
☐ Walking
☐ Wildlife Watching
☐ ____________
☐ ____________
☐ ____________
☐ ____________
☐ ____________

Traveled by:

☐ ☐ ☐ ☐ ☐ ☐ ☐ ☐ ☐ ☐ ☐ ☐

Add your favorite ticket stub, postcard, photo, stamp or drawing here

N E S W
NOT ALL THOSE WHO WANDER ARE LOST

Falling Waters State Park

County: Washington
1130 State Park Road, Chipley FL 32428 | 850-638-6130

Website: https://www.floridastateparks.org/parks-and-trails/falling-waters-state-park
Email: FSP.Feedback@FloridaDEP.gov

Water Body: 2-acre pond

Size: 171 acres
Established: 1962

Contains a 73-foot 22.3 m waterfall, tallest in Florida

Star Rating ☆☆☆☆☆

What souvenir did you bring home?... Decal Magnet ____

My favorite thing about this place is... ____

Why I went ... ____

Who I went with ... ____

When I went ... ____

What I did... ____

What I saw... ____

What I learned... ____

An unforgettable moment... ____

A laughable moment... ____

A surprising moment... ____

An unforeseeable moment... ____

My List

- ☐ ____
- ☐ ____
- ☐ ____
- ☐ ____
- ☐ ____
- ☐ ____
- ☐ ____
- ☐ ____
- ☐ ____
- ☐ ____
- ☐ ____
- ☐ ____

 Snapped a selfie | Location... ____

 Took a park sign selfie? - Y | N

The weather was ...  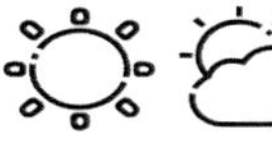     

Plan Your Trip:

☐ Trip Plan Completed

☐ Day Trip ☐ Overnight Stay

Reservations required: ☐y ☐n

Date reservations made: ________

Refund Policy: ☐y ☐n Site/Room #: ____

Confirmation #: ________

Miles to travel: ________

Time traveling: ________

Dog friendly?: ☐y ☐n

Destination Information:

____

____

Places we discovered along the way

____

____

____

Places to stop and see along the way

____

____

Activities Accomplished:

Would you go again?: ☐y ☐n

Open all year?: ☐y ☐n

☐ Archery	☐ Fishing	☐ Picnicking	☐ Walking
☐ Biking	☐ Hiking	☐ Rock Climbing	☐ Wildlife Watching
☐ Birding	☐ Horseback Riding	☐ Shooting Range	☐ ________
☐ Boating	☐ Hunting	☐ Snowshoeing	☐ ________
☐ Camping	☐ Off-Roading	☐ Stargazing	☐ ________
☐ Caving	☐ Paddle Boarding	☐ Swimming	☐ ________
☐ Geocaching	☐ Photography	☐ Tennis	☐ ________

Traveled by:

☐ ☐ ☐ ☐ ☐ ☐ ☐ ☐ ☐ ☐ ☐ ☐

Add your favorite ticket stub, postcard, photo, stamp or drawing here

N E S W NOT ALL THOSE WHO WANDER ARE LOST

Fanning Springs State Park

County: Gilchrist
18020 N.W. Highway 19, Fanning Springs FL 32693 | 352-463-3420

Website: https://www.floridastateparks.org/parks-and-trails/fanning-springs-state-park
Email: FSP.Feedback@FloridaDEP.gov

Water Body: Fanning Springs - Suwannee River

Size: 1,427 acres
Established: 1997

A first magnitude spring purchased by the state in 1993

Star Rating ☆☆☆☆☆

What souvenir did you bring home?... Decal Magnet

My favorite thing about this place is...

Why I went ...

Who I went with ...

When I went ...

What I did...

What I saw...

What I learned...

An unforgettable moment...

A laughable moment...

A surprising moment...

An unforeseeable moment...

Snapped a selfie | Location...

Took a park sign selfie? - Y | N

The weather was ...

My List

- ☐
- ☐
- ☐
- ☐
- ☐
- ☐
- ☐
- ☐
- ☐
- ☐
- ☐
- ☐

Plan Your Trip:

☐ Trip Plan Completed

☐ Day Trip ☐ Overnight Stay

Reservations required: ☐y ☐n

Date reservations made: ____________

Refund Policy: ☐y ☐n Site/Room #: ______

Confirmation #: ____________

Miles to travel: ____________

Time traveling: ____________

Dog friendly?: ☐y ☐n

Destination Information:

Places we discovered along the way

Places to stop and see along the way

Would you go again?: ☐y ☐n

Open all year?: ☐y ☐n

Activities Accomplished:

- ☐ Archery
- ☐ Biking
- ☐ Birding
- ☐ Boating
- ☐ Camping
- ☐ Caving
- ☐ Geocaching
- ☐ Fishing
- ☐ Hiking
- ☐ Horseback Riding
- ☐ Hunting
- ☐ Off-Roading
- ☐ Paddle Boarding
- ☐ Photography
- ☐ Picnicking
- ☐ Rock Climbing
- ☐ Shooting Range
- ☐ Snowshoeing
- ☐ Stargazing
- ☐ Swimming
- ☐ Tennis
- ☐ Walking
- ☐ Wildlife Watching
- ☐ ____________
- ☐ ____________
- ☐ ____________
- ☐ ____________
- ☐ ____________

Traveled by:

☐ ☐ ☐ ☐ ☐ ☐ ☐ ☐ ☐ ☐ ☐ ☐

Add your favorite ticket stub, postcard, photo, stamp or drawing here

N E S W NOT ALL THOSE WHO WANDER ARE LOST

Faver-Dykes State Park

County: St. Johns
1000 Faver-Dykes Road, St. Augustine FL 32086 | 904-794-0997

Website: https://www.floridastateparks.org/parks-and-trails/faver-dykes-state-park
Email: FSP.Feedback@FloridaDEP.gov

Water Body: Pellicer Creek

Size: 6,045 acres
Established: 1950

A wilderness area

Star Rating ☆☆☆☆☆

What souvenir did you bring home?... Decal Magnet

My favorite thing about this place is...

Why I went ...

Who I went with ...

When I went ...

What I did...

What I saw...

What I learned...

An unforgettable moment...

A laughable moment...

A surprising moment...

An unforeseeable moment...

My List

- ☐
- ☐
- ☐
- ☐
- ☐
- ☐
- ☐
- ☐
- ☐
- ☐
- ☐
- ☐

Snapped a selfie | Location...

Took a park sign selfie? - Y | N

The weather was ...

Plan Your Trip:

☐ Trip Plan Completed

☐ Day Trip ☐ Overnight Stay

Reservations required: ☐y ☐n

Date reservations made: ____________

Refund Policy: ☐y ☐n Site/Room #: ______

Confirmation #: ____________

Miles to travel: ____________

Time traveling: ____________

Dog friendly?: ☐y ☐n

Destination Information:

____

____

Places we discovered along the way

____

____

____

Places to stop and see along the way

____

____

Would you go again?: ☐y ☐n

Open all year?: ☐y ☐n

Activities Accomplished:

- ☐ Archery
- ☐ Biking
- ☐ Birding
- ☐ Boating
- ☐ Camping
- ☐ Caving
- ☐ Geocaching
- ☐ Fishing
- ☐ Hiking
- ☐ Horseback Riding
- ☐ Hunting
- ☐ Off-Roading
- ☐ Paddle Boarding
- ☐ Photography
- ☐ Picnicking
- ☐ Rock Climbing
- ☐ Shooting Range
- ☐ Snowshoeing
- ☐ Stargazing
- ☐ Swimming
- ☐ Tennis
- ☐ Walking
- ☐ Wildlife Watching
- ☐ ____________
- ☐ ____________
- ☐ ____________
- ☐ ____________
- ☐ ____________

Traveled by:

☐ ☐ ☐ ☐ ☐ ☐ ☐ ☐ ☐ ☐ ☐ ☐

Add your favorite ticket stub, postcard, photo, stamp or drawing here

N E S W NOT ALL THOSE WHO WANDER ARE LOST

Florida Caverns State Park

County: Jackson
3345 Caverns Road, Marianna FL 32446 | 850-482-1228

Website: https://www.floridastateparks.org/parks-and-trails/florida-caverns-state-park
Email: FSP.Feedback@FloridaDEP.gov

Water Body: Chipola River

Size: 1,300 acres
Established: 1942

The only Florida state park with public cave tours

Star Rating
☆☆☆☆☆

What souvenir did you bring home?... Decal Magnet

My favorite thing about this place is...

Why I went ...

Who I went with ...

When I went ...

What I did...

What I saw...

What I learned...

An unforgettable moment...

A laughable moment...

A surprising moment...

An unforeseeable moment...

My List

- ☐
- ☐
- ☐
- ☐
- ☐
- ☐
- ☐
- ☐
- ☐
- ☐
- ☐
- ☐

Snapped a selfie | Location...

Took a park sign selfie? - Y | N

The weather was ...

Plan Your Trip:

☐ Trip Plan Completed

☐ Day Trip ☐ Overnight Stay

Reservations required: ☐y ☐n

Date reservations made: ______

Refund Policy: ☐y ☐n Site/Room #: ______

Confirmation #: ______

Miles to travel: ______

Time traveling: ______

Dog friendly?: ☐y ☐n

Destination Information:

______

______

Places we discovered along the way

______

______

______

Places to stop and see along the way

______

______

Activities Accomplished:

Would you go again?: ☐y ☐n Open all year?: ☐y ☐n

- ☐ Archery
- ☐ Biking
- ☐ Birding
- ☐ Boating
- ☐ Camping
- ☐ Caving
- ☐ Geocaching
- ☐ Fishing
- ☐ Hiking
- ☐ Horseback Riding
- ☐ Hunting
- ☐ Off-Roading
- ☐ Paddle Boarding
- ☐ Photography
- ☐ Picnicking
- ☐ Rock Climbing
- ☐ Shooting Range
- ☐ Snowshoeing
- ☐ Stargazing
- ☐ Swimming
- ☐ Tennis
- ☐ Walking
- ☐ Wildlife Watching
- ☐ ______
- ☐ ______
- ☐ ______
- ☐ ______
- ☐ ______

Traveled by:

☐ ☐ ☐ ☐ ☐ ☐ ☐ ☐ ☐ ☐ ☐ ☐

Add your favorite ticket stub, postcard, photo, stamp or drawing here

NOT ALL THOSE WHO WANDER ARE LOST

Forest Capital Museum State Park

County: Taylor
204 Forest Park Drive, Perry FL 32348 | 850-584-3227

Website: https://www.floridastateparks.org/parks-and-trails/forest-capital-museum-state-park
Email: FSP.Feedback@FloridaDEP.gov

Water Body: none

Size: 14 acres
Established: 1967

Includes a late 1800s Florida cracker homestead

Star Rating ☆☆☆☆☆

What souvenir did you bring home?... Decal Magnet

My favorite thing about this place is...

Why I went ...

Who I went with ...

When I went ...

What I did...

What I saw...

What I learned...

An unforgettable moment...

A laughable moment...

A surprising moment...

An unforeseeable moment...

Snapped a selfie | Location...

Took a park sign selfie? - Y | N

The weather was ...

My List

- ☐
- ☐
- ☐
- ☐
- ☐
- ☐
- ☐
- ☐
- ☐
- ☐
- ☐
- ☐

Plan Your Trip:

☐ Trip Plan Completed

☐ Day Trip ☐ Overnight Stay

Reservations required: ☐y ☐n

Date reservations made: ______

Refund Policy: ☐y ☐n Site/Room #: ______

Confirmation #: ______

Miles to travel: ______

Time traveling: ______

Dog friendly?: ☐y ☐n

Destination Information:

______

______

Places we discovered along the way

______

______

______

Places to stop and see along the way

______

______

Would you go again?: ☐y ☐n Open all year?: ☐y ☐n

Activities Accomplished:

☐ Archery
☐ Biking
☐ Birding
☐ Boating
☐ Camping
☐ Caving
☐ Geocaching
☐ Fishing
☐ Hiking
☐ Horseback Riding
☐ Hunting
☐ Off-Roading
☐ Paddle Boarding
☐ Photography
☐ Picnicking
☐ Rock Climbing
☐ Shooting Range
☐ Snowshoeing
☐ Stargazing
☐ Swimming
☐ Tennis
☐ Walking
☐ Wildlife Watching
☐ ______
☐ ______
☐ ______
☐ ______
☐ ______

Traveled by:

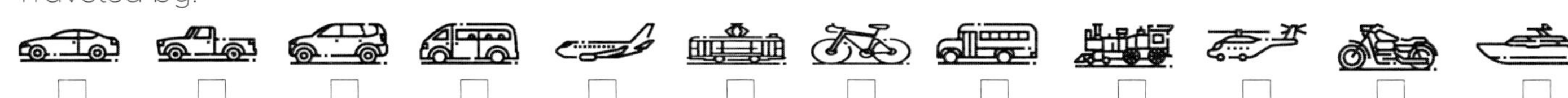

☐ ☐ ☐ ☐ ☐ ☐ ☐ ☐ ☐ ☐ ☐ ☐

Add your favorite ticket stub, postcard, photo, stamp or drawing here

Fort Clinch State Park

County: Nassau
2601 Atlantic Ave., Fernandina Beach FL 32034 | 904-277-7274

Website: https://www.floridastateparks.org/fortclinch
Email: FSP.Feedback@FloridaDEP.gov

Water Body: Amelia River

Size: 1,427 acres
Established: 1935

Construction of Fort Clinch began in 1847

Star Rating ☆☆☆☆☆

What souvenir did you bring home?... Decal Magnet ________

My favorite thing about this place is... ________

Why I went ... ________

Who I went with ... ________

When I went ... ________

What I did... ________

What I saw... ________

What I learned... ________

An unforgettable moment... ________

A laughable moment... ________

A surprising moment... ________

An unforeseeable moment... ________

Snapped a selfie | Location... ________

Took a park sign selfie? - Y | N

The weather was ... °F

My List

- ☐ ________
- ☐ ________
- ☐ ________
- ☐ ________
- ☐ ________
- ☐ ________
- ☐ ________
- ☐ ________
- ☐ ________
- ☐ ________
- ☐ ________
- ☐ ________

Plan Your Trip:

☐ Trip Plan Completed

☐ Day Trip ☐ Overnight Stay

Reservations required: ☐y ☐n

Date reservations made: ______

Refund Policy: ☐y ☐n Site/Room #: ______

Confirmation #: ______

Miles to travel: ______

Time traveling: ______

Dog friendly?: ☐y ☐n

Destination Information:

______

______

Places we discovered along the way

______

______

______

Places to stop and see along the way

______

______

Activities Accomplished:

Would you go again?: ☐y ☐n Open all year?: ☐y ☐n

- ☐ Archery
- ☐ Biking
- ☐ Birding
- ☐ Boating
- ☐ Camping
- ☐ Caving
- ☐ Geocaching
- ☐ Fishing
- ☐ Hiking
- ☐ Horseback Riding
- ☐ Hunting
- ☐ Off-Roading
- ☐ Paddle Boarding
- ☐ Photography
- ☐ Picnicking
- ☐ Rock Climbing
- ☐ Shooting Range
- ☐ Snowshoeing
- ☐ Stargazing
- ☐ Swimming
- ☐ Tennis
- ☐ Walking
- ☐ Wildlife Watching
- ☐ ______
- ☐ ______
- ☐ ______
- ☐ ______
- ☐ ______

Traveled by:

☐ ☐ ☐ ☐ ☐ ☐ ☐ ☐ ☐ ☐ ☐ ☐

Add your favorite ticket stub, postcard, photo, stamp or drawing here

NOT ALL THOSE WHO WANDER ARE LOST

Fort Cooper State Park

County: Citrus
3100 S. Old Floral City Road, Inverness FL 34450 | 352-726-0315

Website: https://www.floridastateparks.org/parks-and-trails/fort-cooper-state-park
Email: FSP.Feedback@FloridaDEP.gov

Water Body: Lake Holathlikaha

Size: 710 acres
Established: 1977

On the Withlacoochee State Trail

Star Rating ☆☆☆☆☆

What souvenir did you bring home?... Decal Magnet

My favorite thing about this place is...

Why I went ...

Who I went with ...

When I went ...

What I did...

What I saw...

What I learned...

An unforgettable moment...

A laughable moment...

A surprising moment...

An unforeseeable moment...

Snapped a selfie | Location...

Took a park sign selfie? - Y | N

The weather was ...

My List

- ☐
- ☐
- ☐
- ☐
- ☐
- ☐
- ☐
- ☐
- ☐
- ☐
- ☐
- ☐

Plan Your Trip:

☐ Trip Plan Completed

☐ Day Trip ☐ Overnight Stay

Reservations required: ☐y ☐n

Date reservations made: ____________

Refund Policy: ☐y ☐n Site/Room #: ______

Confirmation #: ____________

Miles to travel: ____________

Time traveling: ____________

Dog friendly?: ☐y ☐n

Destination Information:

____

____

Places we discovered along the way

____

____

____

Places to stop and see along the way

____

____

Would you go again?: ☐y ☐n Open all year?: ☐y ☐n

Activities Accomplished:

- ☐ Archery
- ☐ Biking
- ☐ Birding
- ☐ Boating
- ☐ Camping
- ☐ Caving
- ☐ Geocaching
- ☐ Fishing
- ☐ Hiking
- ☐ Horseback Riding
- ☐ Hunting
- ☐ Off-Roading
- ☐ Paddle Boarding
- ☐ Photography
- ☐ Picnicking
- ☐ Rock Climbing
- ☐ Shooting Range
- ☐ Snowshoeing
- ☐ Stargazing
- ☐ Swimming
- ☐ Tennis
- ☐ Walking
- ☐ Wildlife Watching
- ☐ ____________
- ☐ ____________
- ☐ ____________
- ☐ ____________
- ☐ ____________

Traveled by:

☐ ☐ ☐ ☐ ☐ ☐ ☐ ☐ ☐ ☐ ☐ ☐

Add your favorite ticket stub, postcard, photo, stamp or drawing here

Fort Foster State Historic Site

County: Hillsborough
15402 U.S. 301 North, Thonotosassa FL 33592 | 813-987-6771

Website: https://www.floridastateparks.org/parks-and-trails/fort-foster-state-historic-site
Email: FSP.Feedback@FloridaDEP.gov

Water Body: none

Size: 30 acres
Established: 1935

Part of Hillsborough River State Park; replica fort built in 1972

Star Rating ☆☆☆☆☆

What souvenir did you bring home?... Decal Magnet

My favorite thing about this place is...

Why I went ...

Who I went with ...

When I went ...

What I did...

What I saw...

What I learned...

An unforgettable moment...

A laughable moment...

A surprising moment...

An unforeseeable moment...

My List

- ☐
- ☐
- ☐
- ☐
- ☐
- ☐
- ☐
- ☐
- ☐
- ☐
- ☐
- ☐

Snapped a selfie | Location...

Took a park sign selfie? - Y | N

The weather was ...

PLAN YOUR TRIP:

DESTINATION INFORMATION:

☐ Trip Plan Completed

☐ Day Trip ☐ Overnight Stay

Reservations required: ☐y ☐n

Date reservations made: ____

Refund Policy: ☐y ☐n Site/Room #: ____

Confirmation #: ____

Miles to travel: ____

Time traveling: ____

Dog friendly?: ☐y ☐n

PLACES WE DISCOVERED ALONG THE WAY

PLACES TO STOP AND SEE ALONG THE WAY

Would you go again?: ☐y ☐n Open all year?: ☐y ☐n

Activities Accomplished:

☐ Archery
☐ Biking
☐ Birding
☐ Boating
☐ Camping
☐ Caving
☐ Geocaching
☐ Fishing
☐ Hiking
☐ Horseback Riding
☐ Hunting
☐ Off-Roading
☐ Paddle Boarding
☐ Photography
☐ Picnicking
☐ Rock Climbing
☐ Shooting Range
☐ Snowshoeing
☐ Stargazing
☐ Swimming
☐ Tennis
☐ Walking
☐ Wildlife Watching
☐ ____
☐ ____
☐ ____
☐ ____
☐ ____

Traveled by:

☐ ☐ ☐ ☐ ☐ ☐ ☐ ☐ ☐ ☐ ☐ ☐

Add your favorite ticket stub, postcard, photo, stamp or drawing here

N W E S NOT ALL THOSE WHO WANDER ARE LOST

Fort George Island Cultural State Park

County: Duval
11241 Fort George Road, Jacksonville FL 32226 | 904-251-2320

Website: https://www.floridastateparks.org/parks-and-trails/fort-george-island-cultural-state-park
Email: FSP.Feedback@FloridaDEP.gov

Water Body: Atlantic Ocean

Size: 1,600 acres
Established: 1949

Hurricane Dora connected Anastasia Island and Conch Island in 1964

Star Rating ☆☆☆☆☆

What souvenir did you bring home?... Decal Magnet

My favorite thing about this place is...

Why I went ...

Who I went with ...

When I went ...

What I did...

What I saw...

What I learned...

An unforgettable moment...

A laughable moment...

A surprising moment...

An unforeseeable moment...

Snapped a selfie | Location...

Took a park sign selfie? - Y | N

My List

- ☐
- ☐
- ☐
- ☐
- ☐
- ☐
- ☐
- ☐
- ☐
- ☐
- ☐
- ☐

The weather was ... °F

Plan Your Trip:

☐ Trip Plan Completed

☐ Day Trip ☐ Overnight Stay

Reservations required: ☐y ☐n

Date reservations made: ____________

Refund Policy: ☐y ☐n Site/Room #: ______

Confirmation #: ____________

Miles to travel: ____________

Time traveling: ____________

Dog friendly?: ☐y ☐n

Destination Information:

Places we discovered along the way

Places to stop and see along the way

Would you go again?: ☐y ☐n

Open all year?: ☐y ☐n

Activities Accomplished:

- ☐ Archery
- ☐ Biking
- ☐ Birding
- ☐ Boating
- ☐ Camping
- ☐ Caving
- ☐ Geocaching
- ☐ Fishing
- ☐ Hiking
- ☐ Horseback Riding
- ☐ Hunting
- ☐ Off-Roading
- ☐ Paddle Boarding
- ☐ Photography
- ☐ Picnicking
- ☐ Rock Climbing
- ☐ Shooting Range
- ☐ Snowshoeing
- ☐ Stargazing
- ☐ Swimming
- ☐ Tennis
- ☐ Walking
- ☐ Wildlife Watching
- ☐ ____________
- ☐ ____________
- ☐ ____________
- ☐ ____________
- ☐ ____________

Traveled by:

☐ ☐ ☐ ☐ ☐ ☐ ☐ ☐ ☐ ☐ ☐ ☐

Add your favorite ticket stub, postcard, photo, stamp or drawing here

N
E
S
W
NOT ALL THOSE WHO WANDER ARE LOST

Fort Mose Historic State Park

County: St. Johns
15 Fort Mose Trail, St. Augustine FL 32084 | 904-823-2232

Website: https://www.floridastateparks.org/parks-and-trails/fort-mose-historic-state-park
Email: FSP.Feedback@FloridaDEP.gov

Water Body: none

Size: 24 acres
Established: 2005

National Historic Landmark originally known as Gracia Real de Santa Teresa de Mos√©

Star Rating ☆☆☆☆☆

What souvenir did you bring home?... Decal Magnet

My favorite thing about this place is...

Why I went ...

Who I went with ...

When I went ...

What I did...

What I saw...

What I learned...

An unforgettable moment...

A laughable moment...

A surprising moment...

An unforeseeable moment...

Snapped a selfie | Location...

Took a park sign selfie? - Y | N

The weather was ...

My List

- ☐
- ☐
- ☐
- ☐
- ☐
- ☐
- ☐
- ☐
- ☐
- ☐
- ☐
- ☐

Plan Your Trip:

☐ Trip Plan Completed

☐ Day Trip ☐ Overnight Stay

Reservations required: ☐y ☐n

Date reservations made: ____________

Refund Policy: ☐y ☐n Site/Room #: ____

Confirmation #: ____________

Miles to travel: ____________

Time traveling: ____________

Dog friendly?: ☐y ☐n

Destination Information:

____

____

Places we discovered along the way

____

____

____

Places to stop and see along the way

____

____

Activities Accomplished:

Would you go again?: ☐y ☐n Open all year?: ☐y ☐n

- ☐ Archery
- ☐ Biking
- ☐ Birding
- ☐ Boating
- ☐ Camping
- ☐ Caving
- ☐ Geocaching
- ☐ Fishing
- ☐ Hiking
- ☐ Horseback Riding
- ☐ Hunting
- ☐ Off-Roading
- ☐ Paddle Boarding
- ☐ Photography
- ☐ Picnicking
- ☐ Rock Climbing
- ☐ Shooting Range
- ☐ Snowshoeing
- ☐ Stargazing
- ☐ Swimming
- ☐ Tennis
- ☐ Walking
- ☐ Wildlife Watching
- ☐ ____________
- ☐ ____________
- ☐ ____________
- ☐ ____________
- ☐ ____________

Traveled by:

☐ ☐ ☐ ☐ ☐ ☐ ☐ ☐ ☐ ☐ ☐ ☐

Add your favorite ticket stub, postcard, photo, stamp or drawing here

N W E S NOT ALL THOSE WHO WANDER ARE LOST

FORT PIERCE INLET STATE PARK

County: St. Lucie

905 Shorewinds Drive, Fort Pierce FL 34949 | 772-468-3985

Website: https://www.floridastateparks.org/parks-and-trails/fort-pierce-inlet-state-park
Email: FSP.Feedback@FloridaDEP.gov

Water Body: Tucker Cove - Atlantic Ocean

Size: 340 acres
Established: 1973

Used for frogman training during World War II

Star Rating ☆☆☆☆☆

What souvenir did you bring home?... Decal Magnet

My favorite thing about this place is...

Why I went ...

Who I went with ...

When I went ...

What I did...

What I saw...

What I learned...

An unforgettable moment...

A laughable moment...

A surprising moment...

An unforeseeable moment...

MY LIST

- ☐
- ☐
- ☐
- ☐
- ☐
- ☐
- ☐
- ☐
- ☐
- ☐
- ☐
- ☐

Snapped a selfie | Location...

Took a park sign selfie? - Y | N

The weather was ... °F

PLAN YOUR TRIP:

☐ Trip Plan Completed

☐ Day Trip ☐ Overnight Stay

Reservations required: ☐y ☐n

Date reservations made: ____________

Refund Policy: ☐y ☐n Site/Room #: ______

Confirmation #: ____________

Miles to travel: ____________

Time traveling: ____________

Dog friendly?: ☐y ☐n

DESTINATION INFORMATION:

PLACES WE DISCOVERED ALONG THE WAY

PLACES TO STOP AND SEE ALONG THE WAY

Would you go again?: ☐y ☐n

Open all year?: ☐y ☐n

Activities Accomplished:

- ☐ Archery
- ☐ Biking
- ☐ Birding
- ☐ Boating
- ☐ Camping
- ☐ Caving
- ☐ Geocaching
- ☐ Fishing
- ☐ Hiking
- ☐ Horseback Riding
- ☐ Hunting
- ☐ Off-Roading
- ☐ Paddle Boarding
- ☐ Photography
- ☐ Picnicking
- ☐ Rock Climbing
- ☐ Shooting Range
- ☐ Snowshoeing
- ☐ Stargazing
- ☐ Swimming
- ☐ Tennis
- ☐ Walking
- ☐ Wildlife Watching
- ☐ ____________
- ☐ ____________
- ☐ ____________
- ☐ ____________
- ☐ ____________

Traveled by:

☐ ☐ ☐ ☐ ☐ ☐ ☐ ☐ ☐ ☐ ☐ ☐

Add your favorite ticket stub, postcard, photo, stamp or drawing here

N E S W NOT ALL THOSE WHO WANDER ARE LOST

Fort Zachary Taylor Historic State Park

County: Monroe
601 Howard England Way, Key West FL 33040 | 305-292-6713

Website: https://www.floridastateparks.org/parks-and-trails/fort-zachary-taylor-historic-state-park
Email: FSP.Feedback@FloridaDEP.gov

Water Body: Straits of Florida

Size: 87 acres
Established: 1974

Pre-civil war fort abandoned, restoration began in the late 1960s by volunteers

Star Rating ☆☆☆☆☆

What souvenir did you bring home?... Decal Magnet

My favorite thing about this place is...

Why I went ...

Who I went with ...

When I went ...

What I did...

What I saw...

What I learned...

An unforgettable moment...

A laughable moment...

A surprising moment...

An unforeseeable moment...

Snapped a selfie | Location...

Took a park sign selfie? - Y | N

The weather was ...

My List

- ☐
- ☐
- ☐
- ☐
- ☐
- ☐
- ☐
- ☐
- ☐
- ☐
- ☐
- ☐

PLAN YOUR TRIP:

☐ Trip Plan Completed

☐ Day Trip ☐ Overnight Stay

Reservations required: ☐y ☐n

Date reservations made: ____________

Refund Policy: ☐y ☐n Site/Room #: ______

Confirmation #: ____________

Miles to travel: ____________

Time traveling: ____________

Dog friendly?: ☐y ☐n

DESTINATION INFORMATION:

____

____

PLACES WE DISCOVERED ALONG THE WAY

____

____

____

PLACES TO STOP AND SEE ALONG THE WAY

____

____

Would you go again?: ☐y ☐n Open all year?: ☐y ☐n

Activities Accomplished:

☐ Archery
☐ Biking
☐ Birding
☐ Boating
☐ Camping
☐ Caving
☐ Geocaching
☐ Fishing
☐ Hiking
☐ Horseback Riding
☐ Hunting
☐ Off-Roading
☐ Paddle Boarding
☐ Photography
☐ Picnicking
☐ Rock Climbing
☐ Shooting Range
☐ Snowshoeing
☐ Stargazing
☐ Swimming
☐ Tennis
☐ Walking
☐ Wildlife Watching
☐ ____________
☐ ____________
☐ ____________
☐ ____________
☐ ____________

Traveled by:

☐ ☐ ☐ ☐ ☐ ☐ ☐ ☐ ☐ ☐ ☐ ☐

Add your favorite ticket stub, postcard, photo, stamp or drawing here

N W E S NOT ALL THOSE WHO WANDER ARE LOST

Fred Gannon Rocky Bayou State Park

County: Okaloosa
4281 State Road 20, Niceville FL 32578 | 850-833-9144

Website: https://www.floridastateparks.org/parks-and-trails/fred-gannon-rocky-bayou-state-park
Email: FSP.Feedback@FloridaDEP.gov

Water Body: Rocky Bayou

Size: 357 acres
Established: 1966

Named in honor of United States Air Force Colonel who preserved site

Star Rating ☆☆☆☆☆

What souvenir did you bring home?... Decal Magnet

My favorite thing about this place is... ______

Why I went ... ______

Who I went with ... ______

When I went ... ______

What I did... ______

What I saw... ______

What I learned... ______

An unforgettable moment... ______

A laughable moment... ______

A surprising moment... ______

An unforeseeable moment... ______

My List

- ☐ ______
- ☐ ______
- ☐ ______
- ☐ ______
- ☐ ______
- ☐ ______
- ☐ ______
- ☐ ______
- ☐ ______
- ☐ ______
- ☐ ______
- ☐ ______

Snapped a selfie | Location... ______

Took a park sign selfie? - Y | N

The weather was ...

PLAN YOUR TRIP:

DESTINATION INFORMATION:

☐ Trip Plan Completed

☐ Day Trip ☐ Overnight Stay

Reservations required: ☐y ☐n

Date reservations made: ____________

Refund Policy: ☐y ☐n Site/Room #: ______

Confirmation #: ____________

Miles to travel: ____________

Time traveling: ____________

Dog friendly?: ☐y ☐n

PLACES WE DISCOVERED ALONG THE WAY

PLACES TO STOP AND SEE ALONG THE WAY

Activities Accomplished:

Would you go again?: ☐y ☐n

Open all year?: ☐y ☐n

☐ Archery
☐ Biking
☐ Birding
☐ Boating
☐ Camping
☐ Caving
☐ Geocaching
☐ Fishing
☐ Hiking
☐ Horseback Riding
☐ Hunting
☐ Off-Roading
☐ Paddle Boarding
☐ Photography
☐ Picnicking
☐ Rock Climbing
☐ Shooting Range
☐ Snowshoeing
☐ Stargazing
☐ Swimming
☐ Tennis
☐ Walking
☐ Wildlife Watching
☐ ____________
☐ ____________
☐ ____________
☐ ____________
☐ ____________

Traveled by:

☐ ☐ ☐ ☐ ☐ ☐ ☐ ☐ ☐ ☐ ☐ ☐

Add your favorite ticket stub, postcard, photo, stamp or drawing here

N
NOT ALL THOSE WHO WANDER ARE LOST
W E S

Gainesville-Hawthorne State Trail

County: Alachua
3400 S.E. 15th St., Gainesville FL 32641 | 352-466-3397

Website: https://www.floridastateparks.org/parks-and-trails/gainesville-hawthorne-state-trail
Email: FSP.Feedback@FloridaDEP.gov

Water Body: Boulware Springs

Size: 16 miles
Established: 1989

Passes through Paynes Prairie

Star Rating ☆☆☆☆☆

What souvenir did you bring home?... Decal Magnet

My favorite thing about this place is...

Why I went ...

Who I went with ...

When I went ...

What I did...

What I saw...

What I learned...

An unforgettable moment...

A laughable moment...

A surprising moment...

An unforeseeable moment...

Snapped a selfie | Location...

Took a park sign selfie? - Y | N

The weather was ...

My List

- ☐
- ☐
- ☐
- ☐
- ☐
- ☐
- ☐
- ☐
- ☐
- ☐
- ☐
- ☐

Plan Your Trip:

☐ Trip Plan Completed

☐ Day Trip ☐ Overnight Stay

Reservations required: ☐y ☐n

Date reservations made: ____________

Refund Policy: ☐y ☐n Site/Room #: ______

Confirmation #: ____________

Miles to travel: ____________

Time traveling: ____________

Dog friendly?: ☐y ☐n

Destination Information:

____

____

Places we discovered along the way

____

____

____

Places to stop and see along the way

____

____

Would you go again?: ☐y ☐n Open all year?: ☐y ☐n

Activities Accomplished:

☐ Archery	☐ Fishing	☐ Picnicking	☐ Walking
☐ Biking	☐ Hiking	☐ Rock Climbing	☐ Wildlife Watching
☐ Birding	☐ Horseback Riding	☐ Shooting Range	☐ ____________
☐ Boating	☐ Hunting	☐ Snowshoeing	☐ ____________
☐ Camping	☐ Off-Roading	☐ Stargazing	☐ ____________
☐ Caving	☐ Paddle Boarding	☐ Swimming	☐ ____________
☐ Geocaching	☐ Photography	☐ Tennis	☐ ____________

Traveled by:

☐ ☐ ☐ ☐ ☐ ☐ ☐ ☐ ☐ ☐ ☐ ☐

Add your favorite ticket stub, postcard, photo, stamp or drawing here

N W E S NOT ALL THOSE WHO WANDER ARE LOST

Gamble Plantation Historic State Park

County: Manatee
3708 U.S. Highway 301, Ellenton FL 34222 | 941-723-4536

Website: https://www.floridastateparks.org/parks-and-trails/judah-p-benjamin-confederate-memorial-gamble-plantation-historic-state-park
Email: FSP.Feedback@FloridaDEP.gov
Water Body: Manatee River

Size: 87 acres
Established: 1927

Sole surviving antebellum mansion in south Florida, once a 3,500-acre 1,416 ha sugarcane plantation

Star Rating ☆☆☆☆☆

What souvenir did you bring home?... Decal Magnet

My favorite thing about this place is...

Why I went ...

Who I went with ...

When I went ...

What I did...

What I saw...

What I learned...

An unforgettable moment...

A laughable moment...

A surprising moment...

An unforeseeable moment...

My List

- ☐
- ☐
- ☐
- ☐
- ☐
- ☐
- ☐
- ☐
- ☐
- ☐
- ☐
- ☐

Snapped a selfie | Location...

Took a park sign selfie? - Y | N

The weather was ...

PLAN YOUR TRIP:

DESTINATION INFORMATION:

☐ Trip Plan Completed

☐ Day Trip ☐ Overnight Stay

Reservations required: ☐y ☐n

Date reservations made: ____

Refund Policy: ☐y ☐n Site/Room #: ____

Confirmation #: ____

Miles to travel: ____

Time traveling: ____

Dog friendly?: ☐y ☐n

PLACES WE DISCOVERED ALONG THE WAY

PLACES TO STOP AND SEE ALONG THE WAY

Activities Accomplished:

Would you go again?: ☐y ☐n Open all year?: ☐y ☐n

- ☐ Archery
- ☐ Biking
- ☐ Birding
- ☐ Boating
- ☐ Camping
- ☐ Caving
- ☐ Geocaching
- ☐ Fishing
- ☐ Hiking
- ☐ Horseback Riding
- ☐ Hunting
- ☐ Off-Roading
- ☐ Paddle Boarding
- ☐ Photography
- ☐ Picnicking
- ☐ Rock Climbing
- ☐ Shooting Range
- ☐ Snowshoeing
- ☐ Stargazing
- ☐ Swimming
- ☐ Tennis
- ☐ Walking
- ☐ Wildlife Watching
- ☐ ____
- ☐ ____
- ☐ ____
- ☐ ____
- ☐ ____

Traveled by:

☐ ☐ ☐ ☐ ☐ ☐ ☐ ☐ ☐ ☐ ☐ ☐

Add your favorite ticket stub, postcard, photo, stamp or drawing here

N NOT ALL THOSE WHO WANDER ARE LOST E S W

Gamble Rogers Memorial State Recreation Area at Flagler Beach

County: Flagler
3100 S. Oceanshore Blvd., Flagler Beach FL 32136 | 386-517-2086

Website: https://www.floridastateparks.org/parks-and-trails/gamble-rogers-memorial-state-recreation-area-flagler-beach
Email: FSP.Feedback@FloridaDEP.gov

Water Body: Atlantic Ocean

Size: 144 acres
Established: 1961

Renamed from Flagler Beach State Recreation Area in 1992

Star Rating ☆☆☆☆☆

What souvenir did you bring home?... Decal Magnet

My favorite thing about this place is...

Why I went ...

Who I went with ...

When I went ...

What I did...

What I saw...

What I learned...

An unforgettable moment...

A laughable moment...

A surprising moment...

An unforeseeable moment...

Snapped a selfie | Location...

Took a park sign selfie? - Y | N

The weather was ...

My List

- ☐
- ☐
- ☐
- ☐
- ☐
- ☐
- ☐
- ☐
- ☐
- ☐
- ☐
- ☐

PLAN YOUR TRIP:	DESTINATION INFORMATION:

☐ Trip Plan Completed

☐ Day Trip ☐ Overnight Stay

Reservations required: ☐y ☐n

Date reservations made: ____________

Refund Policy: ☐y ☐n Site/Room #: ____

Confirmation #: ____________

Miles to travel: ____________

Time traveling: ____________

Dog friendly?: ☐y ☐n

PLACES WE DISCOVERED ALONG THE WAY

PLACES TO STOP AND SEE ALONG THE WAY

Activities Accomplished:

Would you go again?: ☐y ☐n Open all year?: ☐y ☐n

☐ Archery	☐ Fishing	☐ Picnicking	☐ Walking
☐ Biking	☐ Hiking	☐ Rock Climbing	☐ Wildlife Watching
☐ Birding	☐ Horseback Riding	☐ Shooting Range	☐ ____
☐ Boating	☐ Hunting	☐ Snowshoeing	☐ ____
☐ Camping	☐ Off-Roading	☐ Stargazing	☐ ____
☐ Caving	☐ Paddle Boarding	☐ Swimming	☐ ____
☐ Geocaching	☐ Photography	☐ Tennis	☐ ____

Traveled by:

☐ ☐ ☐ ☐ ☐ ☐ ☐ ☐ ☐ ☐ ☐ ☐

Add your favorite ticket stub, postcard, photo, stamp or drawing here

N W E S NOT ALL THOSE WHO WANDER ARE LOST

Gasparilla Island State Park

County: Charlotte - Lee
880 Belcher Road, Boca Grande FL 33921 | 941-964-0375

Website: https://www.floridastateparks.org/parks-and-trails/gasparilla-island-state-park
Email: FSP.Feedback@FloridaDEP.gov

Water Body: Charlotte Harbor

Size: 128 acres
Established: 1983

Gasparilla Island Lights were lit in 1890

Star Rating ☆☆☆☆☆

What souvenir did you bring home?... Decal Magnet

My favorite thing about this place is...

Why I went ...

Who I went with ...

When I went ...

What I did...

What I saw...

What I learned...

An unforgettable moment...

A laughable moment...

A surprising moment...

An unforeseeable moment...

My List

- ☐
- ☐
- ☐
- ☐
- ☐
- ☐
- ☐
- ☐
- ☐
- ☐
- ☐
- ☐

Snapped a selfie | Location...

Took a park sign selfie? - Y | N

The weather was ...

Plan Your Trip:

☐ Trip Plan Completed

☐ Day Trip ☐ Overnight Stay

Reservations required: ☐y ☐n

Date reservations made: ____________

Refund Policy: ☐y ☐n Site/Room #: ______

Confirmation #: ____________

Miles to travel: ____________

Time traveling: ____________

Dog friendly?: ☐y ☐n

Destination Information:

Places we discovered along the way

Places to stop and see along the way

Would you go again?: ☐y ☐n Open all year?: ☐y ☐n

Activities Accomplished:

☐ Archery
☐ Biking
☐ Birding
☐ Boating
☐ Camping
☐ Caving
☐ Geocaching
☐ Fishing
☐ Hiking
☐ Horseback Riding
☐ Hunting
☐ Off-Roading
☐ Paddle Boarding
☐ Photography
☐ Picnicking
☐ Rock Climbing
☐ Shooting Range
☐ Snowshoeing
☐ Stargazing
☐ Swimming
☐ Tennis
☐ Walking
☐ Wildlife Watching
☐ ____________
☐ ____________
☐ ____________
☐ ____________
☐ ____________

Traveled by:

☐ ☐ ☐ ☐ ☐ ☐ ☐ ☐ ☐ ☐ ☐ ☐

Add your favorite ticket stub, postcard, photo, stamp or drawing here

N E S W NOT ALL THOSE WHO WANDER ARE LOST

George Crady Bridge Fishing Pier

County: Duval

State Road A1A South, Jacksonville FL 32226 | 904-251-2320

Website: https://www.floridastateparks.org/parks-and-trails/george-crady-bridge-fishing-pier-state-park
Email: FSP.Feedback@FloridaDEP.gov

Water Body: Nassau Sound - Atlantic Ocean

Size: 8,000 ft
Established: 1999

Pedestrian-only fishing bridge

Star Rating ☆☆☆☆☆

What souvenir did you bring home?... Decal Magnet

My favorite thing about this place is...

Why I went ...

Who I went with ...

When I went ...

What I did...

What I saw...

What I learned...

An unforgettable moment...

A laughable moment...

A surprising moment...

An unforeseeable moment...

My List

- ☐
- ☐
- ☐
- ☐
- ☐
- ☐
- ☐
- ☐
- ☐
- ☐
- ☐
- ☐

Snapped a selfie | Location...

Took a park sign selfie? - Y | N

The weather was ...

Plan Your Trip:

☐ Trip Plan Completed

☐ Day Trip ☐ Overnight Stay

Reservations required: ☐y ☐n

Date reservations made: ____________

Refund Policy: ☐y ☐n Site/Room #: ______

Confirmation #: ____________

Miles to travel: ____________

Time traveling: ____________

Dog friendly?: ☐y ☐n

Destination Information:

Places we discovered along the way

Places to stop and see along the way

Activities Accomplished:

Would you go again?: ☐y ☐n Open all year?: ☐y ☐n

- ☐ Archery
- ☐ Biking
- ☐ Birding
- ☐ Boating
- ☐ Camping
- ☐ Caving
- ☐ Geocaching
- ☐ Fishing
- ☐ Hiking
- ☐ Horseback Riding
- ☐ Hunting
- ☐ Off-Roading
- ☐ Paddle Boarding
- ☐ Photography
- ☐ Picnicking
- ☐ Rock Climbing
- ☐ Shooting Range
- ☐ Snowshoeing
- ☐ Stargazing
- ☐ Swimming
- ☐ Tennis
- ☐ Walking
- ☐ Wildlife Watching
- ☐ ____________
- ☐ ____________
- ☐ ____________
- ☐ ____________
- ☐ ____________

Traveled by:

☐ ☐ ☐ ☐ ☐ ☐ ☐ ☐ ☐ ☐ ☐ ☐

Add your favorite ticket stub, postcard, photo, stamp or drawing here

N E S W NOT ALL THOSE WHO WANDER ARE LOST

Gilchrist Blue Springs State Park

County: Gilchrist
7450 N.E. 60th St., High Springs FL 32643 | 386-454-1369

Website: https://www.floridastateparks.org/parks-and-trails/ruth-b-kirby-gilchrist-blue-springs-state-park
Email: FSP.Feedback@FloridaDEP.gov

Water Body: Santa Fe River

Size: 407 acres
Established: 2017

Several springs in the park, including a second magnitude spring with 44 million gallons 167 million liters per day.

Star Rating ☆☆☆☆☆

What souvenir did you bring home?... Decal Magnet

My favorite thing about this place is... ______

Why I went ... ______

Who I went with ... ______

When I went ... ______

What I did... ______

What I saw... ______

What I learned... ______

An unforgettable moment... ______

A laughable moment... ______

A surprising moment... ______

An unforeseeable moment... ______

Snapped a selfie | Location... ______

Took a park sign selfie? - Y | N

The weather was ...

My List

- ☐ ______
- ☐ ______
- ☐ ______
- ☐ ______
- ☐ ______
- ☐ ______
- ☐ ______
- ☐ ______
- ☐ ______
- ☐ ______
- ☐ ______
- ☐ ______

Plan Your Trip:	Destination Information:

☐ Trip Plan Completed

☐ Day Trip ☐ Overnight Stay

Reservations required: ☐y ☐n

Date reservations made: ____

Refund Policy: ☐y ☐n Site/Room #: ____

Confirmation #: ____

Miles to travel: ____

Time traveling: ____

Dog friendly?: ☐y ☐n

Places we discovered along the way

Places to stop and see along the way

Would you go again?: ☐y ☐n

Open all year?: ☐y ☐n

Activities Accomplished:

☐ Archery	☐ Fishing	☐ Picnicking	☐ Walking
☐ Biking	☐ Hiking	☐ Rock Climbing	☐ Wildlife Watching
☐ Birding	☐ Horseback Riding	☐ Shooting Range	☐ ____
☐ Boating	☐ Hunting	☐ Snowshoeing	☐ ____
☐ Camping	☐ Off-Roading	☐ Stargazing	☐ ____
☐ Caving	☐ Paddle Boarding	☐ Swimming	☐ ____
☐ Geocaching	☐ Photography	☐ Tennis	☐ ____

Traveled by:

☐ ☐ ☐ ☐ ☐ ☐ ☐ ☐ ☐ ☐ ☐ ☐

Add your favorite ticket stub, postcard, photo, stamp or drawing here

N W E S NOT ALL THOSE WHO WANDER ARE LOST

Grayton Beach State Park

County: Walton
357 Main Park Road, Santa Rosa Beach FL 32459 | 850-267-8300

Website: https://www.floridastateparks.org/graytonbeach
Email: FSP.Feedback@FloridaDEP.gov

Water Body: Western Lake - Gulf of Mexico

Size: 2,200 acres
Established: 1968

Popular pristine beach offers cabins & camping, boating, fishing and trails

Star Rating ☆☆☆☆☆

What souvenir did you bring home?... Decal Magnet ____________

My favorite thing about this place is... ____________

Why I went ... ____________

Who I went with ... ____________

When I went ... ____________

What I did... ____________

What I saw... ____________

What I learned... ____________

An unforgettable moment... ____________

A laughable moment... ____________

A surprising moment... ____________

An unforeseeable moment... ____________

Snapped a selfie | Location... ____________

Took a park sign selfie? - Y | N

The weather was ...

My List

- ☐ ____________
- ☐ ____________
- ☐ ____________
- ☐ ____________
- ☐ ____________
- ☐ ____________
- ☐ ____________
- ☐ ____________
- ☐ ____________
- ☐ ____________
- ☐ ____________
- ☐ ____________

Plan Your Trip:

☐ Trip Plan Completed

☐ Day Trip ☐ Overnight Stay

Reservations required: ☐y ☐n

Date reservations made: ______

Refund Policy: ☐y ☐n Site/Room #: ______

Confirmation #: ______

Miles to travel: ______

Time traveling: ______

Dog friendly?: ☐y ☐n

Destination Information:

______

______

Places we discovered along the way

______

______

______

Places to stop and see along the way

______

______

Would you go again?: ☐y ☐n

Open all year?: ☐y ☐n

Activities Accomplished:

- ☐ Archery
- ☐ Biking
- ☐ Birding
- ☐ Boating
- ☐ Camping
- ☐ Caving
- ☐ Geocaching
- ☐ Fishing
- ☐ Hiking
- ☐ Horseback Riding
- ☐ Hunting
- ☐ Off-Roading
- ☐ Paddle Boarding
- ☐ Photography
- ☐ Picnicking
- ☐ Rock Climbing
- ☐ Shooting Range
- ☐ Snowshoeing
- ☐ Stargazing
- ☐ Swimming
- ☐ Tennis
- ☐ Walking
- ☐ Wildlife Watching
- ☐ ______
- ☐ ______
- ☐ ______
- ☐ ______
- ☐ ______

Traveled by:

☐ ☐ ☐ ☐ ☐ ☐ ☐ ☐ ☐ ☐ ☐ ☐

Add your favorite ticket stub, postcard, photo, stamp or drawing here

N
NOT ALL THOSE WHO WANDER ARE LOST
W E
S

Henderson Beach State Park

County: Okaloosa
17000 Emerald Coast Parkway, Destin FL 32541 | 850-837-7550

Website: https://www.floridastateparks.org/parks-and-trails/henderson-beach-state-park
Email: FSP.Feedback@FloridaDEP.gov

Water Body: Gulf of Mexico

Size: 222 acres
Established: 1983

U.S. Air Force Clausen Tracking site until 1951

Star Rating ☆☆☆☆☆

What souvenir did you bring home?... Decal Magnet

My favorite thing about this place is...

Why I went ...

Who I went with ...

When I went ...

What I did...

What I saw...

What I learned...

An unforgettable moment...

A laughable moment...

A surprising moment...

An unforeseeable moment...

Snapped a selfie | Location...

Took a park sign selfie? - Y | N

The weather was ...

My List

- ☐
- ☐
- ☐
- ☐
- ☐
- ☐
- ☐
- ☐
- ☐
- ☐
- ☐
- ☐

PLAN YOUR TRIP:

- [ ] Trip Plan Completed
- [ ] Day Trip
- [ ] Overnight Stay

Reservations required: ☐y ☐n

Date reservations made: ______

Refund Policy: ☐y ☐n Site/Room #: ______

Confirmation #: ______

Miles to travel: ______

Time traveling: ______

Dog friendly?: ☐y ☐n

DESTINATION INFORMATION:

______

______

PLACES WE DISCOVERED ALONG THE WAY

______

______

______

PLACES TO STOP AND SEE ALONG THE WAY

______

______

Activities Accomplished:

Would you go again?: ☐y ☐n

Open all year?: ☐y ☐n

- [ ] Archery
- [ ] Biking
- [ ] Birding
- [ ] Boating
- [ ] Camping
- [ ] Caving
- [ ] Geocaching
- [ ] Fishing
- [ ] Hiking
- [ ] Horseback Riding
- [ ] Hunting
- [ ] Off-Roading
- [ ] Paddle Boarding
- [ ] Photography
- [ ] Picnicking
- [ ] Rock Climbing
- [ ] Shooting Range
- [ ] Snowshoeing
- [ ] Stargazing
- [ ] Swimming
- [ ] Tennis
- [ ] Walking
- [ ] Wildlife Watching
- [ ] ______
- [ ] ______
- [ ] ______
- [ ] ______
- [ ] ______

Traveled by:

Add your favorite ticket stub, postcard, photo, stamp or drawing here

N E S W
NOT ALL THOSE WHO WANDER ARE LOST

Highlands Hammock State Park

County: Highlands
5931 Hammock Road, Sebring FL 33872 | 863-386-6094

Website: **https://www.floridastateparks.org/parks-and-trails/highlands-hammock-state-park**
Email: **FSP.Feedback@FloridaDEP.gov**

Water Body: none

Size: 9,000 acres
Established: 1931

One of the highest ranking parks in Florida for endemic biodiversity

Star Rating ☆☆☆☆☆

What souvenir did you bring home?... Decal Magnet

My favorite thing about this place is...

Why I went ...

Who I went with ...

When I went ...

What I did...

What I saw...

What I learned...

An unforgettable moment...

A laughable moment...

A surprising moment...

An unforeseeable moment...

Snapped a selfie | Location...

Took a park sign selfie? - Y | N

The weather was ...

My List

- ☐
- ☐
- ☐
- ☐
- ☐
- ☐
- ☐
- ☐
- ☐
- ☐
- ☐
- ☐

Plan Your Trip:

☐ Trip Plan Completed

☐ Day Trip ☐ Overnight Stay

Reservations required: ☐y ☐n

Date reservations made: ____________

Refund Policy: ☐y ☐n Site/Room #: ______

Confirmation #: ____________

Miles to travel: ____________

Time traveling: ____________

Dog friendly?: ☐y ☐n

Destination Information:

____

____

Places we discovered along the way

____

____

____

Places to stop and see along the way

____

____

Would you go again?: ☐y ☐n Open all year?: ☐y ☐n

Activities Accomplished:

☐ Archery
☐ Biking
☐ Birding
☐ Boating
☐ Camping
☐ Caving
☐ Geocaching
☐ Fishing
☐ Hiking
☐ Horseback Riding
☐ Hunting
☐ Off-Roading
☐ Paddle Boarding
☐ Photography
☐ Picnicking
☐ Rock Climbing
☐ Shooting Range
☐ Snowshoeing
☐ Stargazing
☐ Swimming
☐ Tennis
☐ Walking
☐ Wildlife Watching
☐ ____________
☐ ____________
☐ ____________
☐ ____________
☐ ____________

Traveled by:

☐ ☐ ☐ ☐ ☐ ☐ ☐ ☐ ☐ ☐ ☐ ☐

Add your favorite ticket stub, postcard, photo, stamp or drawing here

N
W
E
S
NOT ALL THOSE WHO WANDER ARE LOST

HILLSBOROUGH RIVER STATE PARK

County: Hillsborough

15402 U.S. 301 North, Thonotosassa FL 33592 | 813-987-6771 or 813-326-5867

Website: https://www.floridastateparks.org/parks-and-trails/hillsborough-river-state-park
Email: FSP.Feedback@FloridaDEP.gov

Water Body: Hillsborough River

Size: 3,383 acres
Established: 1935

Fort Foster is inside the park

Star Rating ☆☆☆☆☆

What souvenir did you bring home?... Decal Magnet

My favorite thing about this place is...

Why I went ...

Who I went with ...

When I went ...

What I did...

What I saw...

What I learned...

An unforgettable moment...

A laughable moment...

A surprising moment...

An unforeseeable moment...

MY LIST

- ☐
- ☐
- ☐
- ☐
- ☐
- ☐
- ☐
- ☐
- ☐
- ☐
- ☐
- ☐

 Snapped a selfie | Location...

 Took a park sign selfie? - Y | N

The weather was ... 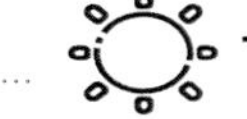      

Plan Your Trip:

☐ Trip Plan Completed

☐ Day Trip ☐ Overnight Stay

Reservations required: ☐y ☐n

Date reservations made: ____________

Refund Policy: ☐y ☐n Site/Room #: ______

Confirmation #: ____________

Miles to travel: ____________

Time traveling: ____________

Dog friendly?: ☐y ☐n

Destination Information:

____

____

Places we discovered along the way

____

____

____

Places to stop and see along the way

____

____

Would you go again?: ☐y ☐n Open all year?: ☐y ☐n

Activities Accomplished:

- ☐ Archery
- ☐ Biking
- ☐ Birding
- ☐ Boating
- ☐ Camping
- ☐ Caving
- ☐ Geocaching
- ☐ Fishing
- ☐ Hiking
- ☐ Horseback Riding
- ☐ Hunting
- ☐ Off-Roading
- ☐ Paddle Boarding
- ☐ Photography
- ☐ Picnicking
- ☐ Rock Climbing
- ☐ Shooting Range
- ☐ Snowshoeing
- ☐ Stargazing
- ☐ Swimming
- ☐ Tennis
- ☐ Walking
- ☐ Wildlife Watching
- ☐ ____________
- ☐ ____________
- ☐ ____________
- ☐ ____________
- ☐ ____________

Traveled by:

☐ ☐ ☐ ☐ ☐ ☐ ☐ ☐ ☐ ☐ ☐ ☐

Add your favorite ticket stub, postcard, photo, stamp or drawing here

N W E S NOT ALL THOSE WHO WANDER ARE LOST

HOMOSASSA SPRINGS WILDLIFE STATE PARK

County: Citrus
4150 S. Suncoast Blvd., Homosassa FL 34446 | 352-628-5343

Website: https://www.floridastateparks.org/parks-and-trails/ellie-schiller-homosassa-springs-wildlife-state-park
Email: FSP.Feedback@FloridaDEP.gov

Water Body: Homosassa River

Size: 210 acres
Established: 1984

Home to numerous manatees

Star Rating
☆☆☆☆☆

What souvenir did you bring home?... Decal Magnet

My favorite thing about this place is...

Why I went ...

Who I went with ...

When I went ...

What I did...

What I saw...

What I learned...

An unforgettable moment...

A laughable moment...

A surprising moment...

An unforeseeable moment...

Snapped a selfie | Location...

Took a park sign selfie? - Y | N

The weather was ...

MY LIST

- ☐
- ☐
- ☐
- ☐
- ☐
- ☐
- ☐
- ☐
- ☐
- ☐
- ☐
- ☐

Plan Your Trip:

☐ Trip Plan Completed

☐ Day Trip ☐ Overnight Stay

Reservations required: ☐y ☐n

Date reservations made: ____

Refund Policy: ☐y ☐n Site/Room #: ____

Confirmation #: ____

Miles to travel: ____

Time traveling: ____

Dog friendly?: ☐y ☐n

Destination Information:

____

____

Places we discovered along the way

____

____

____

Places to stop and see along the way

____

____

Would you go again?: ☐y ☐n Open all year?: ☐y ☐n

Activities Accomplished:

- ☐ Archery
- ☐ Biking
- ☐ Birding
- ☐ Boating
- ☐ Camping
- ☐ Caving
- ☐ Geocaching
- ☐ Fishing
- ☐ Hiking
- ☐ Horseback Riding
- ☐ Hunting
- ☐ Off-Roading
- ☐ Paddle Boarding
- ☐ Photography
- ☐ Picnicking
- ☐ Rock Climbing
- ☐ Shooting Range
- ☐ Snowshoeing
- ☐ Stargazing
- ☐ Swimming
- ☐ Tennis
- ☐ Walking
- ☐ Wildlife Watching
- ☐ ____
- ☐ ____
- ☐ ____
- ☐ ____
- ☐ ____

Traveled by:

☐ ☐ ☐ ☐ ☐ ☐ ☐ ☐ ☐ ☐ ☐ ☐

Add your favorite ticket stub, postcard, photo, stamp or drawing here

N W E S NOT ALL THOSE WHO WANDER ARE LOST

Honeymoon Island State Park

County: Pinellas
#1 Causeway Blvd., Dunedin FL 34698 | 727-241-6106

Website: https://www.floridastateparks.org/honeymoonisland
Email: FSP.Feedback@FloridaDEP.gov

Water Body: Gulf of Mexico

Size: 2,785 acres
Established: 1975

Easily accessible by bridge from Dunedin

Star Rating ☆☆☆☆☆

What souvenir did you bring home?... Decal Magnet

My favorite thing about this place is...

Why I went ...

Who I went with ...

When I went ...

What I did...

What I saw...

What I learned...

An unforgettable moment...

A laughable moment...

A surprising moment...

An unforeseeable moment...

My List

- ☐
- ☐
- ☐
- ☐
- ☐
- ☐
- ☐
- ☐
- ☐
- ☐
- ☐
- ☐

 Snapped a selfie | Location...

 Took a park sign selfie? - Y | N

The weather was ...      

PLAN YOUR TRIP:

☐ Trip Plan Completed

☐ Day Trip ☐ Overnight Stay

Reservations required: ☐y ☐n

Date reservations made: ____________

Refund Policy: ☐y ☐n Site/Room #: ______

Confirmation #: ____________

Miles to travel: ____________

Time traveling: ____________

Dog friendly?: ☐y ☐n

DESTINATION INFORMATION:

PLACES WE DISCOVERED ALONG THE WAY

PLACES TO STOP AND SEE ALONG THE WAY

Activities Accomplished:

Would you go again?: ☐y ☐n

Open all year?: ☐y ☐n

- ☐ Archery
- ☐ Biking
- ☐ Birding
- ☐ Boating
- ☐ Camping
- ☐ Caving
- ☐ Geocaching
- ☐ Fishing
- ☐ Hiking
- ☐ Horseback Riding
- ☐ Hunting
- ☐ Off-Roading
- ☐ Paddle Boarding
- ☐ Photography
- ☐ Picnicking
- ☐ Rock Climbing
- ☐ Shooting Range
- ☐ Snowshoeing
- ☐ Stargazing
- ☐ Swimming
- ☐ Tennis
- ☐ Walking
- ☐ Wildlife Watching
- ☐ ____________
- ☐ ____________
- ☐ ____________
- ☐ ____________
- ☐ ____________

Traveled by:

☐ ☐ ☐ ☐ ☐ ☐ ☐ ☐ ☐ ☐ ☐ ☐

Add your favorite ticket stub, postcard, photo, stamp or drawing here

N W E S NOT ALL THOSE WHO WANDER ARE LOST

Hontoon Island State Park

County: Volusia Lake
2309 River Ridge Road, DeLand FL 32720 | 386-736-5309

Website: https://www.floridastateparks.org/parks-and-trails/hontoon-island-state-park
Email: FSP.Feedback@FloridaDEP.gov

Water Body: St. Johns River - Hontoon Dead River

Size: 1,648 acres
Established: 1960

Accessible only by ferry or boat

Star Rating ☆☆☆☆☆

What souvenir did you bring home?... Decal Magnet

My favorite thing about this place is...

Why I went ...

Who I went with ...

When I went ...

What I did...

What I saw...

What I learned...

An unforgettable moment...

A laughable moment...

A surprising moment...

An unforeseeable moment...

My List

- ☐
- ☐
- ☐
- ☐
- ☐
- ☐
- ☐
- ☐
- ☐
- ☐
- ☐
- ☐

Snapped a selfie | Location...

Took a park sign selfie? - Y | N

The weather was ...

PLAN YOUR TRIP:

DESTINATION INFORMATION:

☐ Trip Plan Completed

☐ Day Trip ☐ Overnight Stay

Reservations required: ☐y ☐n

Date reservations made: ______

Refund Policy: ☐y ☐n Site/Room #: ______

Confirmation #: ______

Miles to travel: ______

Time traveling: ______

Dog friendly?: ☐y ☐n

PLACES WE DISCOVERED ALONG THE WAY

PLACES TO STOP AND SEE ALONG THE WAY

Would you go again?: ☐y ☐n Open all year?: ☐y ☐n

Activities Accomplished:

☐ Archery	☐ Fishing	☐ Picnicking	☐ Walking
☐ Biking	☐ Hiking	☐ Rock Climbing	☐ Wildlife Watching
☐ Birding	☐ Horseback Riding	☐ Shooting Range	☐ ______
☐ Boating	☐ Hunting	☐ Snowshoeing	☐ ______
☐ Camping	☐ Off-Roading	☐ Stargazing	☐ ______
☐ Caving	☐ Paddle Boarding	☐ Swimming	☐ ______
☐ Geocaching	☐ Photography	☐ Tennis	☐ ______

Traveled by:

☐ ☐ ☐ ☐ ☐ ☐ ☐ ☐ ☐ ☐ ☐ ☐

Add your favorite ticket stub, postcard, photo, stamp or drawing here

HUGH TAYLOR BIRCH STATE PARK

County: Broward
3109 E. Sunrise Blvd., Fort Lauderale FL 33304 | 954-564-4521

Website: https://www.floridastateparks.org/HughTaylorBirch
Email: FSP.Feedback@FloridaDEP.gov

Water Body: Atlantic Ocean

Size: 180 acres
Established: 1941

Park is in the middle of urban Fort Lauderdale

Star Rating ☆☆☆☆☆

What souvenir did you bring home?... Decal Magnet

My favorite thing about this place is...

Why I went ...

Who I went with ...

When I went ...

What I did...

What I saw...

What I learned...

An unforgettable moment...

A laughable moment...

A surprising moment...

An unforeseeable moment...

Snapped a selfie | Location...

Took a park sign selfie? - Y | N

The weather was ...

MY LIST

- ☐
- ☐
- ☐
- ☐
- ☐
- ☐
- ☐
- ☐
- ☐
- ☐
- ☐
- ☐

Plan Your Trip:

☐ Trip Plan Completed

☐ Day Trip ☐ Overnight Stay

Reservations required: ☐y ☐n

Date reservations made: ____________

Refund Policy: ☐y ☐n Site/Room #: ______

Confirmation #: ____________

Miles to travel: ____________

Time traveling: ____________

Dog friendly?: ☐y ☐n

Destination Information:

____

____

Places we discovered along the way

____

____

____

Places to stop and see along the way

____

____

Would you go again?: ☐y ☐n

Open all year?: ☐y ☐n

Activities Accomplished:

☐ Archery
☐ Biking
☐ Birding
☐ Boating
☐ Camping
☐ Caving
☐ Geocaching
☐ Fishing
☐ Hiking
☐ Horseback Riding
☐ Hunting
☐ Off-Roading
☐ Paddle Boarding
☐ Photography
☐ Picnicking
☐ Rock Climbing
☐ Shooting Range
☐ Snowshoeing
☐ Stargazing
☐ Swimming
☐ Tennis
☐ Walking
☐ Wildlife Watching
☐ ____________
☐ ____________
☐ ____________
☐ ____________
☐ ____________

Traveled by:

☐ ☐ ☐ ☐ ☐ ☐ ☐ ☐ ☐ ☐ ☐ ☐

Add your favorite ticket stub, postcard, photo, stamp or drawing here

N
NOT ALL THOSE WHO WANDER ARE LOST
W E
S

Ichetucknee Springs State Park

County: Columbia
12087 S.W. U.S. Highway 27, Fort White FL 32038 | 386-497-4690

Website: https://www.floridastateparks.org/parks-and-trails/ichetucknee-springs-state-park
Email: FSP.Feedback@FloridaDEP.gov

Water Body: Ichetucknee River

Size: 2,241 acres
Established: 1972

Drift tubing and certified cave diving

Star Rating ☆☆☆☆☆

What souvenir did you bring home?... Decal Magnet

My favorite thing about this place is...

Why I went ...

Who I went with ...

When I went ...

What I did...

What I saw...

What I learned...

An unforgettable moment...

A laughable moment...

A surprising moment...

An unforeseeable moment...

My List

- ☐
- ☐
- ☐
- ☐
- ☐
- ☐
- ☐
- ☐
- ☐
- ☐
- ☐
- ☐

Snapped a selfie | Location...

Took a park sign selfie? - Y | N

The weather was ...

Plan Your Trip:

☐ Trip Plan Completed

☐ Day Trip ☐ Overnight Stay

Reservations required: ☐y ☐n

Date reservations made: ______

Refund Policy: ☐y ☐n Site/Room #: ______

Confirmation #: ______

Miles to travel: ______

Time traveling: ______

Dog friendly?: ☐y ☐n

Destination Information:

______

______

Places we discovered along the way

______

______

______

Places to stop and see along the way

______

______

Activities Accomplished:

Would you go again?: ☐y ☐n

Open all year?: ☐y ☐n

- ☐ Archery
- ☐ Biking
- ☐ Birding
- ☐ Boating
- ☐ Camping
- ☐ Caving
- ☐ Geocaching
- ☐ Fishing
- ☐ Hiking
- ☐ Horseback Riding
- ☐ Hunting
- ☐ Off-Roading
- ☐ Paddle Boarding
- ☐ Photography
- ☐ Picnicking
- ☐ Rock Climbing
- ☐ Shooting Range
- ☐ Snowshoeing
- ☐ Stargazing
- ☐ Swimming
- ☐ Tennis
- ☐ Walking
- ☐ Wildlife Watching
- ☐ ______
- ☐ ______
- ☐ ______
- ☐ ______
- ☐ ______

Traveled by:

☐ ☐ ☐ ☐ ☐ ☐ ☐ ☐ ☐ ☐ ☐ ☐

Add your favorite ticket stub, postcard, photo, stamp or drawing here

INDIAN KEY HISTORIC STATE PARK

County: Monroe
Offshore Island, Islamorada FL 33036 | 305-664-2540

Website: https://www.floridastateparks.org/IndianKey
Email: FSP.Feedback@FloridaDEP.gov

Water Body: Atlantic Ocean

Size: 10 acres
Established: 1972

First county seat for Dade County; accessible only by boat

Star Rating ☆☆☆☆☆

What souvenir did you bring home?... Decal Magnet

My favorite thing about this place is...

Why I went ...

Who I went with ...

When I went ...

What I did...

What I saw...

What I learned...

An unforgettable moment...

A laughable moment...

A surprising moment...

An unforeseeable moment...

Snapped a selfie | Location...

Took a park sign selfie? - Y | N

The weather was ...

MY LIST

- ☐
- ☐
- ☐
- ☐
- ☐
- ☐
- ☐
- ☐
- ☐
- ☐
- ☐
- ☐

Plan Your Trip:

☐ Trip Plan Completed

☐ Day Trip ☐ Overnight Stay

Reservations required: ☐y ☐n

Date reservations made: ____

Refund Policy: ☐y ☐n Site/Room #: ____

Confirmation #: ____

Miles to travel: ____

Time traveling: ____

Dog friendly?: ☐y ☐n

Destination Information:

____

____

Places we discovered along the way

____

____

____

Places to stop and see along the way

____

____

Would you go again?: ☐y ☐n Open all year?: ☐y ☐n

Activities Accomplished:

- ☐ Archery
- ☐ Biking
- ☐ Birding
- ☐ Boating
- ☐ Camping
- ☐ Caving
- ☐ Geocaching
- ☐ Fishing
- ☐ Hiking
- ☐ Horseback Riding
- ☐ Hunting
- ☐ Off-Roading
- ☐ Paddle Boarding
- ☐ Photography
- ☐ Picnicking
- ☐ Rock Climbing
- ☐ Shooting Range
- ☐ Snowshoeing
- ☐ Stargazing
- ☐ Swimming
- ☐ Tennis
- ☐ Walking
- ☐ Wildlife Watching
- ☐ ____
- ☐ ____
- ☐ ____
- ☐ ____
- ☐ ____

Traveled by:

☐ ☐ ☐ ☐ ☐ ☐ ☐ ☐ ☐ ☐ ☐ ☐

Add your favorite ticket stub, postcard, photo, stamp or drawing here

N W E S NOT ALL THOSE WHO WANDER ARE LOST

John D. MacArthur Beach State Park

County: Palm Beach
10900 Jack Nicklaus Drive, North Palm Beach FL 33408 | 561-624-6950

Website: https://www.floridastateparks.org/parks-and-trails/john-d-macarthur-beach-state-park
Email: FSP.Feedback@FloridaDEP.gov

Water Body: Lake Worth - Atlantic Ocean

Size: 325 acres
Established: 1989

A gift from John D. MacArthur to the people of Florida

Star Rating
☆☆☆☆☆

What souvenir did you bring home?... Decal Magnet

My favorite thing about this place is...

Why I went ...

Who I went with ...

When I went ...

What I did...

What I saw...

What I learned...

An unforgettable moment...

A laughable moment...

A surprising moment...

An unforeseeable moment...

Snapped a selfie | Location...

Took a park sign selfie? - Y | N

The weather was ...

My List

- ☐
- ☐
- ☐
- ☐
- ☐
- ☐
- ☐
- ☐
- ☐
- ☐
- ☐
- ☐

Plan Your Trip:

☐ Trip Plan Completed

☐ Day Trip ☐ Overnight Stay

Reservations required: ☐y ☐n

Date reservations made: ____________

Refund Policy: ☐y ☐n Site/Room #: ______

Confirmation #: ____________

Miles to travel: ____________

Time traveling: ____________

Dog friendly?: ☐y ☐n

Destination Information:

Places we discovered along the way

Places to stop and see along the way

Activities Accomplished:

Would you go again?: ☐y ☐n Open all year?: ☐y ☐n

- ☐ Archery
- ☐ Biking
- ☐ Birding
- ☐ Boating
- ☐ Camping
- ☐ Caving
- ☐ Geocaching
- ☐ Fishing
- ☐ Hiking
- ☐ Horseback Riding
- ☐ Hunting
- ☐ Off-Roading
- ☐ Paddle Boarding
- ☐ Photography
- ☐ Picnicking
- ☐ Rock Climbing
- ☐ Shooting Range
- ☐ Snowshoeing
- ☐ Stargazing
- ☐ Swimming
- ☐ Tennis
- ☐ Walking
- ☐ Wildlife Watching
- ☐ ____________
- ☐ ____________
- ☐ ____________
- ☐ ____________
- ☐ ____________

Traveled by:

☐ ☐ ☐ ☐ ☐ ☐ ☐ ☐ ☐ ☐ ☐ ☐

Add your favorite ticket stub, postcard, photo, stamp or drawing here

N
NOT ALL THOSE WHO
W E
WANDER ARE LOST
S

JOHN GORRIE MUSEUM STATE PARK

County: Franklin
46 Sixth St., Apalachicola FL 32320 | 850-653-9347

Website: https://www.floridastateparks.org/parks-and-trails/john-gorrie-museum-state-park
Email: FSP.Feedback@FloridaDEP.gov

Water Body: none

Size: 1 acres
Established: 1958

Physician John Gorrie patented the first mechanical refrigeration process air conditioning

Star Rating
☆☆☆☆☆

What souvenir did you bring home?... Decal Magnet

My favorite thing about this place is...

Why I went ...

Who I went with ...

When I went ...

What I did...

What I saw...

What I learned...

An unforgettable moment...

A laughable moment...

A surprising moment...

An unforeseeable moment...

MY LIST

- ☐
- ☐
- ☐
- ☐
- ☐
- ☐
- ☐
- ☐
- ☐
- ☐
- ☐
- ☐

Snapped a selfie | Location...

Took a park sign selfie? - Y | N

The weather was ...

Plan Your Trip:

☐ Trip Plan Completed

☐ Day Trip ☐ Overnight Stay

Reservations required: ☐y ☐n

Date reservations made: ____________

Refund Policy: ☐y ☐n Site/Room #: ______

Confirmation #: ____________

Miles to travel: ____________

Time traveling: ____________

Dog friendly?: ☐y ☐n

Destination Information:

Places we discovered along the way

Places to stop and see along the way

Would you go again?: ☐y ☐n Open all year?: ☐y ☐n

Activities Accomplished:

☐ Archery
☐ Biking
☐ Birding
☐ Boating
☐ Camping
☐ Caving
☐ Geocaching
☐ Fishing
☐ Hiking
☐ Horseback Riding
☐ Hunting
☐ Off-Roading
☐ Paddle Boarding
☐ Photography
☐ Picnicking
☐ Rock Climbing
☐ Shooting Range
☐ Snowshoeing
☐ Stargazing
☐ Swimming
☐ Tennis
☐ Walking
☐ Wildlife Watching
☐ ____________
☐ ____________
☐ ____________
☐ ____________
☐ ____________

Traveled by:

☐ ☐ ☐ ☐ ☐ ☐ ☐ ☐ ☐ ☐ ☐ ☐

Add your favorite ticket stub, postcard, photo, stamp or drawing here

N E S W NOT ALL THOSE WHO WANDER ARE LOST

John Pennekamp Coral Reef State Park

County: Monroe
102601 Overseas Highway (MM 102.5), Key Largo, FL 33037 | 305-451-6300

Website: http://pennekamppark.com
Email: info@pennekamppark.com

Water Body: Atlantic Ocean

Size: 53,000 acres
Established: 1963

First underwater park in the United States

Star Rating ☆☆☆☆☆

What souvenir did you bring home?... Decal Magnet

My favorite thing about this place is...

Why I went ...

Who I went with ...

When I went ...

What I did...

What I saw...

What I learned...

An unforgettable moment...

A laughable moment...

A surprising moment...

An unforeseeable moment...

My List

- ☐
- ☐
- ☐
- ☐
- ☐
- ☐
- ☐
- ☐
- ☐
- ☐
- ☐
- ☐

Snapped a selfie | Location...

Took a park sign selfie? - Y | N

The weather was ...

Plan Your Trip:

☐ Trip Plan Completed

☐ Day Trip ☐ Overnight Stay

Reservations required: ☐y ☐n

Date reservations made: ____________

Refund Policy: ☐y ☐n Site/Room #: ______

Confirmation #: ____________

Miles to travel: ____________

Time traveling: ____________

Dog friendly?: ☐y ☐n

Destination Information:

Places we discovered along the way

Places to stop and see along the way

Would you go again?: ☐y ☐n Open all year?: ☐y ☐n

Activities Accomplished:

- ☐ Archery
- ☐ Biking
- ☐ Birding
- ☐ Boating
- ☐ Camping
- ☐ Caving
- ☐ Geocaching
- ☐ Fishing
- ☐ Hiking
- ☐ Horseback Riding
- ☐ Hunting
- ☐ Off-Roading
- ☐ Paddle Boarding
- ☐ Photography
- ☐ Picnicking
- ☐ Rock Climbing
- ☐ Shooting Range
- ☐ Snowshoeing
- ☐ Stargazing
- ☐ Swimming
- ☐ Tennis
- ☐ Walking
- ☐ Wildlife Watching
- ☐ ____________
- ☐ ____________
- ☐ ____________
- ☐ ____________
- ☐ ____________

Traveled by:

☐ ☐ ☐ ☐ ☐ ☐ ☐ ☐ ☐ ☐ ☐ ☐

Add your favorite ticket stub, postcard, photo, stamp or drawing here

Jonathan Dickinson State Park

County: Martin
16450 S.E. Federal Highway, Hobe Sound FL 33455 | 772-546-2771

Website: https://www.floridastateparks.org/parks-and-trails/jonathan-dickinson-state-park
Email: FSP.Feedback@FloridaDEP.gov

Water Body: Loxahatchee River

Size: 11,500 acres
Established: 1950

Formerly a top-secret radar training school during WWII; now hosts the Elsa Kimbell Environmental Education & Research Center

Star Rating
☆☆☆☆☆

What souvenir did you bring home?... Decal Magnet

My favorite thing about this place is...

Why I went ...

Who I went with ...

When I went ...

What I did...

What I saw...

What I learned...

An unforgettable moment...

A laughable moment...

A surprising moment...

An unforeseeable moment...

My List

- ☐
- ☐
- ☐
- ☐
- ☐
- ☐
- ☐
- ☐
- ☐
- ☐
- ☐
- ☐

Snapped a selfie | Location...

Took a park sign selfie? - Y | N

The weather was ...

Plan Your Trip:

☐ Trip Plan Completed

☐ Day Trip ☐ Overnight Stay

Reservations required: ☐y ☐n

Date reservations made: ______

Refund Policy: ☐y ☐n Site/Room #: ______

Confirmation #: ______

Miles to travel: ______

Time traveling: ______

Dog friendly?: ☐y ☐n

Destination Information:

______

______

Places we discovered along the way

______

______

______

Places to stop and see along the way

______

______

Would you go again?: ☐y ☐n

Open all year?: ☐y ☐n

Activities Accomplished:

- ☐ Archery
- ☐ Biking
- ☐ Birding
- ☐ Boating
- ☐ Camping
- ☐ Caving
- ☐ Geocaching
- ☐ Fishing
- ☐ Hiking
- ☐ Horseback Riding
- ☐ Hunting
- ☐ Off-Roading
- ☐ Paddle Boarding
- ☐ Photography
- ☐ Picnicking
- ☐ Rock Climbing
- ☐ Shooting Range
- ☐ Snowshoeing
- ☐ Stargazing
- ☐ Swimming
- ☐ Tennis
- ☐ Walking
- ☐ Wildlife Watching
- ☐ ______
- ☐ ______
- ☐ ______
- ☐ ______
- ☐ ______

Traveled by:

☐ ☐ ☐ ☐ ☐ ☐ ☐ ☐ ☐ ☐ ☐ ☐

Add your favorite ticket stub, postcard, photo, stamp or drawing here

N W E S NOT ALL THOSE WHO WANDER ARE LOST

Kissimmee Prairie Preserve State Park

County: Okeechobee
33104 N.W. 192nd Ave., Okeechobee FL 34972 | 863-462-5360

Website: https://www.floridastateparks.org/parks-and-trails/kissimmee-prairie-preserve-state-park
Email: FSP.Feedback@FloridaDEP.gov

Water Body: none

Size: 54,000 acres
Established: 1997

The U.S. Army used the land to train B-17 bomber crews during World War II

Star Rating ☆☆☆☆☆

What souvenir did you bring home?... Decal Magnet

My favorite thing about this place is...

Why I went ...

Who I went with ...

When I went ...

What I did...

What I saw...

What I learned...

An unforgettable moment...

A laughable moment...

A surprising moment...

An unforeseeable moment...

Snapped a selfie | Location...

Took a park sign selfie? - Y | N

The weather was ...

My List

- ☐
- ☐
- ☐
- ☐
- ☐
- ☐
- ☐
- ☐
- ☐
- ☐
- ☐
- ☐

Plan Your Trip:

☐ Trip Plan Completed

☐ Day Trip ☐ Overnight Stay

Reservations required: ☐y ☐n

Date reservations made: ______

Refund Policy: ☐y ☐n Site/Room #: ______

Confirmation #: ______

Miles to travel: ______

Time traveling: ______

Dog friendly?: ☐y ☐n

Destination Information:

______

______

Places we discovered along the way

______

______

______

Places to stop and see along the way

______

______

Would you go again?: ☐y ☐n Open all year?: ☐y ☐n

Activities Accomplished:

- ☐ Archery
- ☐ Biking
- ☐ Birding
- ☐ Boating
- ☐ Camping
- ☐ Caving
- ☐ Geocaching
- ☐ Fishing
- ☐ Hiking
- ☐ Horseback Riding
- ☐ Hunting
- ☐ Off-Roading
- ☐ Paddle Boarding
- ☐ Photography
- ☐ Picnicking
- ☐ Rock Climbing
- ☐ Shooting Range
- ☐ Snowshoeing
- ☐ Stargazing
- ☐ Swimming
- ☐ Tennis
- ☐ Walking
- ☐ Wildlife Watching
- ☐ ______
- ☐ ______
- ☐ ______
- ☐ ______
- ☐ ______

Traveled by:

☐ ☐ ☐ ☐ ☐ ☐ ☐ ☐ ☐ ☐ ☐ ☐

Add your favorite ticket stub, postcard, photo, stamp or drawing here

NOT ALL THOSE WHO WANDER ARE LOST

KORESHAN STATE HISTORIC SITE

County: Lee
3800 Corkscrew Road, Estero FL 33928 | 239-992-0311

Website: https://www.floridastateparks.org/parks-and-trails/koreshan-state-park
Email: FSP.Feedback@FloridaDEP.gov

Water Body: Estero River

Size: 135 acres
Established: 1983

Home of the Koreshan Unity group

Star Rating ☆☆☆☆☆

What souvenir did you bring home?... Decal Magnet

My favorite thing about this place is...

Why I went ...

Who I went with ...

When I went ...

What I did...

What I saw...

What I learned...

An unforgettable moment...

A laughable moment...

A surprising moment...

An unforeseeable moment...

MY LIST

- ☐
- ☐
- ☐
- ☐
- ☐
- ☐
- ☐
- ☐
- ☐
- ☐
- ☐
- ☐

 Snapped a selfie | Location...

 Took a park sign selfie? - Y | N

The weather was ...  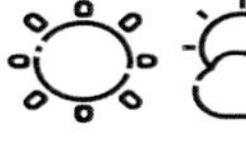     

PLAN YOUR TRIP:

☐ Trip Plan Completed

☐ Day Trip ☐ Overnight Stay

Reservations required: ☐y ☐n

Date reservations made: ______

Refund Policy: ☐y ☐n Site/Room #: ______

Confirmation #: ______

Miles to travel: ______

Time traveling: ______

Dog friendly?: ☐y ☐n

DESTINATION INFORMATION:

PLACES WE DISCOVERED ALONG THE WAY

PLACES TO STOP AND SEE ALONG THE WAY

Would you go again?: ☐y ☐n Open all year?: ☐y ☐n

Activities Accomplished:

- ☐ Archery
- ☐ Biking
- ☐ Birding
- ☐ Boating
- ☐ Camping
- ☐ Caving
- ☐ Geocaching
- ☐ Fishing
- ☐ Hiking
- ☐ Horseback Riding
- ☐ Hunting
- ☐ Off-Roading
- ☐ Paddle Boarding
- ☐ Photography
- ☐ Picnicking
- ☐ Rock Climbing
- ☐ Shooting Range
- ☐ Snowshoeing
- ☐ Stargazing
- ☐ Swimming
- ☐ Tennis
- ☐ Walking
- ☐ Wildlife Watching
- ☐ ______
- ☐ ______
- ☐ ______
- ☐ ______
- ☐ ______

Traveled by:

☐ ☐ ☐ ☐ ☐ ☐ ☐ ☐ ☐ ☐ ☐ ☐

Add your favorite ticket stub, postcard, photo, stamp or drawing here

N W E S NOT ALL THOSE WHO WANDER ARE LOST

Lafayette Blue Springs State Park

County: Lafayette
799 N.W. Blue Spring Road, Mayo FL 32066 | 386-294-3667

Website: https://www.floridastateparks.org/parks-and-trails/lafayette-blue-springs-state-park
Email: FSP.Feedback@FloridaDEP.gov

Water Body: Suwannee River

Size: 702 acres
Established: 2005

First magnitude spring with 168 million gallons 636 million liters per day

Star Rating ☆☆☆☆☆

What souvenir did you bring home?... Decal Magnet

My favorite thing about this place is...

Why I went ...

Who I went with ...

When I went ...

What I did...

What I saw...

What I learned...

An unforgettable moment...

A laughable moment...

A surprising moment...

An unforeseeable moment...

Snapped a selfie | Location...

Took a park sign selfie? - Y | N

The weather was ...

My List

- ☐
- ☐
- ☐
- ☐
- ☐
- ☐
- ☐
- ☐
- ☐
- ☐
- ☐
- ☐

Plan Your Trip:

☐ Trip Plan Completed

☐ Day Trip ☐ Overnight Stay

Reservations required: ☐y ☐n

Date reservations made: ____________

Refund Policy: ☐y ☐n Site/Room #: ______

Confirmation #: ____________

Miles to travel: ____________

Time traveling: ____________

Dog friendly?: ☐y ☐n

Destination Information:

____

____

Places we discovered along the way

____

____

____

Places to stop and see along the way

____

____

Activities Accomplished:

Would you go again?: ☐y ☐n

Open all year?: ☐y ☐n

- ☐ Archery
- ☐ Biking
- ☐ Birding
- ☐ Boating
- ☐ Camping
- ☐ Caving
- ☐ Geocaching
- ☐ Fishing
- ☐ Hiking
- ☐ Horseback Riding
- ☐ Hunting
- ☐ Off-Roading
- ☐ Paddle Boarding
- ☐ Photography
- ☐ Picnicking
- ☐ Rock Climbing
- ☐ Shooting Range
- ☐ Snowshoeing
- ☐ Stargazing
- ☐ Swimming
- ☐ Tennis
- ☐ Walking
- ☐ Wildlife Watching
- ☐ ____________
- ☐ ____________
- ☐ ____________
- ☐ ____________
- ☐ ____________

Traveled by:

☐ ☐ ☐ ☐ ☐ ☐ ☐ ☐ ☐ ☐ ☐ ☐

Add your favorite ticket stub, postcard, photo, stamp or drawing here

N W E S NOT ALL THOSE WHO WANDER ARE LOST

Lake Griffin State Park

County: Lake
3089 U.S. Highway 441-27, Fruitland Park FL 34731 | 352-360-6760

Website: https://www.floridastateparks.org/parks-and-trails/lake-griffin-state-park
Email: FSP.Feedback@FloridaDEP.gov

Water Body: Dead River - Oklawaha River

Size: 578 acres
Established: 1968

Connects Oklawaha to Lake Griffin

Star Rating ☆☆☆☆☆

What souvenir did you bring home?... Decal Magnet

My favorite thing about this place is...

Why I went ...

Who I went with ...

When I went ...

What I did...

What I saw...

What I learned...

An unforgettable moment...

A laughable moment...

A surprising moment...

An unforeseeable moment...

My List

- ☐
- ☐
- ☐
- ☐
- ☐
- ☐
- ☐
- ☐
- ☐
- ☐
- ☐
- ☐

Snapped a selfie | Location...

Took a park sign selfie? - Y | N

The weather was ...

Plan Your Trip:

☐ Trip Plan Completed

☐ Day Trip ☐ Overnight Stay

Reservations required: ☐y ☐n

Date reservations made: ____________

Refund Policy: ☐y ☐n Site/Room #: ______

Confirmation #: ____________

Miles to travel: ____________

Time traveling: ____________

Dog friendly?: ☐y ☐n

Destination Information:

Places we discovered along the way

Places to stop and see along the way

Would you go again?: ☐y ☐n Open all year?: ☐y ☐n

Activities Accomplished:

☐ Archery
☐ Biking
☐ Birding
☐ Boating
☐ Camping
☐ Caving
☐ Geocaching
☐ Fishing
☐ Hiking
☐ Horseback Riding
☐ Hunting
☐ Off-Roading
☐ Paddle Boarding
☐ Photography
☐ Picnicking
☐ Rock Climbing
☐ Shooting Range
☐ Snowshoeing
☐ Stargazing
☐ Swimming
☐ Tennis
☐ Walking
☐ Wildlife Watching
☐ ____________
☐ ____________
☐ ____________
☐ ____________
☐ ____________

Traveled by:

☐ ☐ ☐ ☐ ☐ ☐ ☐ ☐ ☐ ☐ ☐ ☐

Add your favorite ticket stub, postcard, photo, stamp or drawing here

N W E S NOT ALL THOSE WHO WANDER ARE LOST

Lake Jackson Mounds Archaeological State Park

County: Leon
3600 Indian Mounds Road, Tallahassee FL 32303 | 850-487-7989

Website: https://www.floridastateparks.org/parks-and-trails/lake-jackson-mounds-archaeological-state-park
Email: FSP.Feedback@FloridaDEP.gov

Water Body: St. Marks River

Size: 100 acres
Established: 1966

Fort Walton Culture capital from 1050,Äì1500

Star Rating ☆☆☆☆☆

What souvenir did you bring home?... Decal Magnet

My favorite thing about this place is...

Why I went ...

Who I went with ...

When I went ...

What I did...

What I saw...

What I learned...

An unforgettable moment...

A laughable moment...

A surprising moment...

An unforeseeable moment...

Snapped a selfie | Location...

Took a park sign selfie? - Y | N

The weather was ...

My List

- ☐
- ☐
- ☐
- ☐
- ☐
- ☐
- ☐
- ☐
- ☐
- ☐
- ☐
- ☐

PLAN YOUR TRIP:	DESTINATION INFORMATION:

☐ Trip Plan Completed

☐ Day Trip ☐ Overnight Stay

Reservations required: ☐y ☐n

Date reservations made: ______

Refund Policy: ☐y ☐n Site/Room #: ______

Confirmation #: ______

Miles to travel: ______

Time traveling: ______

Dog friendly?: ☐y ☐n

PLACES WE DISCOVERED ALONG THE WAY

PLACES TO STOP AND SEE ALONG THE WAY

Would you go again?: ☐y ☐n Open all year?: ☐y ☐n

Activities Accomplished:

☐ Archery	☐ Fishing	☐ Picnicking	☐ Walking
☐ Biking	☐ Hiking	☐ Rock Climbing	☐ Wildlife Watching
☐ Birding	☐ Horseback Riding	☐ Shooting Range	☐ ______
☐ Boating	☐ Hunting	☐ Snowshoeing	☐ ______
☐ Camping	☐ Off-Roading	☐ Stargazing	☐ ______
☐ Caving	☐ Paddle Boarding	☐ Swimming	☐ ______
☐ Geocaching	☐ Photography	☐ Tennis	☐ ______

Traveled by:

☐ ☐ ☐ ☐ ☐ ☐ ☐ ☐ ☐ ☐ ☐ ☐

Add your favorite ticket stub, postcard, photo, stamp or drawing here

Lake June in Winter Scrub State Park

County: Highlands
Daffodil Road, Lake Placid FL 33852 | 863-386-6094

Website: https://www.floridastateparks.org/parks-and-trails/lake-june-winter-scrub-preserve-state-park
Email: FSP.Feedback@FloridaDEP.gov

Water Body: Lake June in Winter

Size: 845 acres
Established: 1995

Limited facilities; still under development

Star Rating ☆☆☆☆☆

What souvenir did you bring home?... Decal Magnet

My favorite thing about this place is...

Why I went ...

Who I went with ...

When I went ...

What I did...

What I saw...

What I learned...

An unforgettable moment...

A laughable moment...

A surprising moment...

An unforeseeable moment...

Snapped a selfie | Location...

Took a park sign selfie? - Y | N

The weather was ...

My List

- ☐
- ☐
- ☐
- ☐
- ☐
- ☐
- ☐
- ☐
- ☐
- ☐
- ☐
- ☐

Plan Your Trip:

☐ Trip Plan Completed

☐ Day Trip ☐ Overnight Stay

Reservations required: ☐y ☐n

Date reservations made: ____________

Refund Policy: ☐y ☐n Site/Room #: ______

Confirmation #: ____________

Miles to travel: ____________

Time traveling: ____________

Dog friendly?: ☐y ☐n

Destination Information:

____

____

Places we discovered along the way

____

____

____

Places to stop and see along the way

____

____

Activities Accomplished:

Would you go again?: ☐y ☐n Open all year?: ☐y ☐n

- ☐ Archery
- ☐ Biking
- ☐ Birding
- ☐ Boating
- ☐ Camping
- ☐ Caving
- ☐ Geocaching
- ☐ Fishing
- ☐ Hiking
- ☐ Horseback Riding
- ☐ Hunting
- ☐ Off-Roading
- ☐ Paddle Boarding
- ☐ Photography
- ☐ Picnicking
- ☐ Rock Climbing
- ☐ Shooting Range
- ☐ Snowshoeing
- ☐ Stargazing
- ☐ Swimming
- ☐ Tennis
- ☐ Walking
- ☐ Wildlife Watching
- ☐ ____________
- ☐ ____________
- ☐ ____________
- ☐ ____________
- ☐ ____________

Traveled by:

☐ ☐ ☐ ☐ ☐ ☐ ☐ ☐ ☐ ☐ ☐ ☐

Add your favorite ticket stub, postcard, photo, stamp or drawing here

N E S W
NOT ALL THOSE WHO WANDER ARE LOST

Lake Kissimmee State Park

County: Polk

14248 Camp Mack Road, Lake Wales FL 33898 | 863-696-1112

Website: https://www.floridastateparks.org/parks-and-trails/lake-kissimmee-state-park
Email: FSP.Feedback@FloridaDEP.gov

Water Body: Lake Kissimmee

Size: 5,930 acres
Established: 1977

The 1876 Cow Camp is a living history site with Cracker Cowboys

Star Rating ☆☆☆☆☆

What souvenir did you bring home?... Decal Magnet

My favorite thing about this place is...

Why I went ...

Who I went with ...

When I went ...

What I did...

What I saw...

What I learned...

An unforgettable moment...

A laughable moment...

A surprising moment...

An unforeseeable moment...

My List

- ☐
- ☐
- ☐
- ☐
- ☐
- ☐
- ☐
- ☐
- ☐
- ☐
- ☐
- ☐

Snapped a selfie | Location...

Took a park sign selfie? - Y | N

The weather was ... 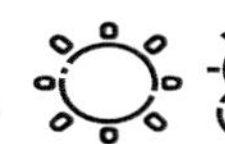     

Plan Your Trip:

Destination Information:

☐ Trip Plan Completed

☐ Day Trip ☐ Overnight Stay

Reservations required: ☐y ☐n

Date reservations made: ____________

Refund Policy: ☐y ☐n Site/Room #: ____

Confirmation #: ____________

Miles to travel: ____________

Time traveling: ____________

Dog friendly?: ☐y ☐n

Places we discovered along the way

Places to stop and see along the way

Would you go again?: ☐y ☐n Open all year?: ☐y ☐n

Activities Accomplished:

☐ Archery
☐ Biking
☐ Birding
☐ Boating
☐ Camping
☐ Caving
☐ Geocaching
☐ Fishing
☐ Hiking
☐ Horseback Riding
☐ Hunting
☐ Off-Roading
☐ Paddle Boarding
☐ Photography
☐ Picnicking
☐ Rock Climbing
☐ Shooting Range
☐ Snowshoeing
☐ Stargazing
☐ Swimming
☐ Tennis
☐ Walking
☐ Wildlife Watching
☐ ____________
☐ ____________
☐ ____________
☐ ____________
☐ ____________

Traveled by:

☐ ☐ ☐ ☐ ☐ ☐ ☐ ☐ ☐ ☐ ☐ ☐

Add your favorite ticket stub, postcard, photo, stamp or drawing here

N W E S NOT ALL THOSE WHO WANDER ARE LOST

LAKE LOUISA STATE PARK

County: Lake
7305 U.S. Highway 27, Clermont FL 34714 | 352-394-3969

Website: https://www.floridastateparks.org/parks-and-trails/lake-louisa-state-park
Email: FSP.Feedback@FloridaDEP.gov

Water Body: Lake Louisa

Size: 4,372 acres
Established: 1974

Park includes the Green Swamp and six lakes

Star Rating ☆☆☆☆☆

What souvenir did you bring home?... Decal Magnet

My favorite thing about this place is...

Why I went ...

Who I went with ...

When I went ...

What I did...

What I saw...

What I learned...

An unforgettable moment...

A laughable moment...

A surprising moment...

An unforeseeable moment...

MY LIST

- ☐
- ☐
- ☐
- ☐
- ☐
- ☐
- ☐
- ☐
- ☐
- ☐
- ☐
- ☐

Snapped a selfie | Location...

Took a park sign selfie? - Y | N

The weather was ...

Plan Your Trip:

☐ Trip Plan Completed

☐ Day Trip ☐ Overnight Stay

Reservations required: ☐y ☐n

Date reservations made: ____________

Refund Policy: ☐y ☐n Site/Room #: ______

Confirmation #: ____________

Miles to travel: ____________

Time traveling: ____________

Dog friendly?: ☐y ☐n

Destination Information:

Places we discovered along the way

Places to stop and see along the way

Would you go again?: ☐y ☐n Open all year?: ☐y ☐n

Activities Accomplished:

☐ Archery
☐ Biking
☐ Birding
☐ Boating
☐ Camping
☐ Caving
☐ Geocaching
☐ Fishing
☐ Hiking
☐ Horseback Riding
☐ Hunting
☐ Off-Roading
☐ Paddle Boarding
☐ Photography
☐ Picnicking
☐ Rock Climbing
☐ Shooting Range
☐ Snowshoeing
☐ Stargazing
☐ Swimming
☐ Tennis
☐ Walking
☐ Wildlife Watching
☐ ____________
☐ ____________
☐ ____________
☐ ____________
☐ ____________

Traveled by:

☐ ☐ ☐ ☐ ☐ ☐ ☐ ☐ ☐ ☐ ☐ ☐

Add your favorite ticket stub, postcard, photo, stamp or drawing here

N W E S NOT ALL THOSE WHO WANDER ARE LOST

Lake Manatee State Park

County: Manatee
20007 State Road 64 East, Bradenton FL 34212 | 941-741-3028

Website: **https://www.floridastateparks.org/parks-and-trails/lake-manatee-state-park**
Email: **FSP.Feedback@FloridaDEP.gov**

Water Body: Lake Manatee

Size: 556 acres
Established: 1970

60-site campground was opened in 1986

Star Rating ☆☆☆☆☆

What souvenir did you bring home?... Decal Magnet

My favorite thing about this place is...

Why I went ...

Who I went with ...

When I went ...

What I did...

What I saw...

What I learned...

An unforgettable moment...

A laughable moment...

A surprising moment...

An unforeseeable moment...

My List

- ☐
- ☐
- ☐
- ☐
- ☐
- ☐
- ☐
- ☐
- ☐
- ☐
- ☐
- ☐

Snapped a selfie | Location...

Took a park sign selfie? - Y | N

The weather was ...

PLAN YOUR TRIP:

DESTINATION INFORMATION:

☐ Trip Plan Completed

☐ Day Trip ☐ Overnight Stay

Reservations required: ☐y ☐n

Date reservations made: ____

Refund Policy: ☐y ☐n Site/Room #: ____

Confirmation #: ____

Miles to travel: ____

Time traveling: ____

Dog friendly?: ☐y ☐n

PLACES WE DISCOVERED ALONG THE WAY

PLACES TO STOP AND SEE ALONG THE WAY

Would you go again?: ☐y ☐n Open all year?: ☐y ☐n

Activities Accomplished:

- ☐ Archery
- ☐ Biking
- ☐ Birding
- ☐ Boating
- ☐ Camping
- ☐ Caving
- ☐ Geocaching
- ☐ Fishing
- ☐ Hiking
- ☐ Horseback Riding
- ☐ Hunting
- ☐ Off-Roading
- ☐ Paddle Boarding
- ☐ Photography
- ☐ Picnicking
- ☐ Rock Climbing
- ☐ Shooting Range
- ☐ Snowshoeing
- ☐ Stargazing
- ☐ Swimming
- ☐ Tennis
- ☐ Walking
- ☐ Wildlife Watching
- ☐ ____
- ☐ ____
- ☐ ____
- ☐ ____
- ☐ ____

Traveled by:

☐ ☐ ☐ ☐ ☐ ☐ ☐ ☐ ☐ ☐ ☐ ☐

Add your favorite ticket stub, postcard, photo, stamp or drawing here

N
NOT ALL THOSE WHO WANDER ARE LOST
W E
S

Lake Talquin State Park

County: Leon Gadsden
14850 Jack Vause Landing Road, Tallahassee FL 32310 | 850-487-7989

Website: https://www.floridastateparks.org/parks-and-trails/lake-talquin-state-park
Email: FSP.Feedback@FloridaDEP.gov

Water Body: Lake Talquin

Size: 526 acres
Established: 1971

Lake Talquin is a 10,000 acre 4,047 ha reservoir created by the Jackson Bluff Dam on the Ochlockonee River

What souvenir did you bring home?... Decal Magnet ____

Star Rating ☆☆☆☆☆

My favorite thing about this place is... ____

Why I went ... ____

Who I went with ... ____

When I went ... ____

What I did... ____

What I saw... ____

What I learned... ____

An unforgettable moment... ____

A laughable moment... ____

A surprising moment... ____

An unforeseeable moment... ____

My List

- ☐ ____
- ☐ ____
- ☐ ____
- ☐ ____
- ☐ ____
- ☐ ____
- ☐ ____
- ☐ ____
- ☐ ____
- ☐ ____
- ☐ ____
- ☐ ____

Snapped a selfie | Location... ____

Took a park sign selfie? - Y | N

The weather was ...

Plan Your Trip:

☐ Trip Plan Completed

☐ Day Trip ☐ Overnight Stay

Reservations required: ☐y ☐n

Date reservations made: ______

Refund Policy: ☐y ☐n Site/Room #: ______

Confirmation #: ______

Miles to travel: ______

Time traveling: ______

Dog friendly?: ☐y ☐n

Destination Information:

______

______

Places we discovered along the way

______

______

______

Places to stop and see along the way

______

______

Would you go again?: ☐y ☐n Open all year?: ☐y ☐n

Activities Accomplished:

☐ Archery
☐ Biking
☐ Birding
☐ Boating
☐ Camping
☐ Caving
☐ Geocaching
☐ Fishing
☐ Hiking
☐ Horseback Riding
☐ Hunting
☐ Off-Roading
☐ Paddle Boarding
☐ Photography
☐ Picnicking
☐ Rock Climbing
☐ Shooting Range
☐ Snowshoeing
☐ Stargazing
☐ Swimming
☐ Tennis
☐ Walking
☐ Wildlife Watching
☐ ______
☐ ______
☐ ______
☐ ______
☐ ______

Traveled by:

☐ ☐ ☐ ☐ ☐ ☐ ☐ ☐ ☐ ☐ ☐ ☐

Add your favorite ticket stub, postcard, photo, stamp or drawing here

N E S W NOT ALL THOSE WHO WANDER ARE LOST

Letchworth-Love Mounds Archaeological State Park

County: Jefferson
4500 Sunray Road South, Tallahassee FL 32309 | 850-487-7989

Website: https://www.floridastateparks.org/parks-and-trails/letchworth-love-mounds-archaeological-state-park
Email: FSP.Feedback@FloridaDEP.gov

Water Body: Lake Miccosukee

Size: 188 acres
Established: 1998

Site of the tallest prehistoric, Native American ceremonial earthwork mound in Florida

Star Rating
☆☆☆☆☆

What souvenir did you bring home?... Decal Magnet

My favorite thing about this place is... ______

Why I went ... ______

Who I went with ... ______

When I went ... ______

What I did... ______

What I saw... ______

What I learned... ______

An unforgettable moment... ______

A laughable moment... ______

A surprising moment... ______

An unforeseeable moment... ______

My List

- ☐ ______
- ☐ ______
- ☐ ______
- ☐ ______
- ☐ ______
- ☐ ______
- ☐ ______
- ☐ ______
- ☐ ______
- ☐ ______
- ☐ ______
- ☐ ______

Snapped a selfie | Location... ______

Took a park sign selfie? - Y | N

The weather was ...

Plan Your Trip:

☐ Trip Plan Completed

☐ Day Trip ☐ Overnight Stay

Reservations required: ☐y ☐n

Date reservations made: ____

Refund Policy: ☐y ☐n Site/Room #: ____

Confirmation #: ____

Miles to travel: ____

Time traveling: ____

Dog friendly?: ☐y ☐n

Destination Information:

____

____

Places we discovered along the way

____

____

____

Places to stop and see along the way

____

____

Would you go again?: ☐y ☐n

Open all year?: ☐y ☐n

Activities Accomplished:

- ☐ Archery
- ☐ Biking
- ☐ Birding
- ☐ Boating
- ☐ Camping
- ☐ Caving
- ☐ Geocaching
- ☐ Fishing
- ☐ Hiking
- ☐ Horseback Riding
- ☐ Hunting
- ☐ Off-Roading
- ☐ Paddle Boarding
- ☐ Photography
- ☐ Picnicking
- ☐ Rock Climbing
- ☐ Shooting Range
- ☐ Snowshoeing
- ☐ Stargazing
- ☐ Swimming
- ☐ Tennis
- ☐ Walking
- ☐ Wildlife Watching
- ☐ ____
- ☐ ____
- ☐ ____
- ☐ ____
- ☐ ____

Traveled by:

☐ ☐ ☐ ☐ ☐ ☐ ☐ ☐ ☐ ☐ ☐ ☐

Add your favorite ticket stub, postcard, photo, stamp or drawing here

N W E S NOT ALL THOSE WHO WANDER ARE LOST

Lignumvitae Key Botanical State Park

County: Monroe
77200 Overseas Highway, Islamorada FL 33036 | 305-664-2540

Website: https://www.floridastateparks.org/LignumvitaeKey
Email: FSP.Feedback@FloridaDEP.gov

Water Body: Florida Bay - Gulf of Mexico

Size: 10,481 acres
Established: 1971

Access via private boat or tour boat; daily visitors are limited

Star Rating ☆☆☆☆☆

What souvenir did you bring home?... Decal Magnet

My favorite thing about this place is...

Why I went ...

Who I went with ...

When I went ...

What I did...

What I saw...

What I learned...

An unforgettable moment...

A laughable moment...

A surprising moment...

An unforeseeable moment...

My List

- ☐
- ☐
- ☐
- ☐
- ☐
- ☐
- ☐
- ☐
- ☐
- ☐
- ☐
- ☐

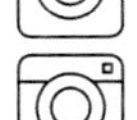 Snapped a selfie | Location...

 Took a park sign selfie? - Y | N

The weather was ...      

Plan Your Trip:

☐ Trip Plan Completed

☐ Day Trip ☐ Overnight Stay

Reservations required: ☐y ☐n

Date reservations made: ______

Refund Policy: ☐y ☐n Site/Room #: ______

Confirmation #: ______

Miles to travel: ______

Time traveling: ______

Dog friendly?: ☐y ☐n

Destination Information:

______

______

Places we discovered along the way

______

______

______

Places to stop and see along the way

______

______

Would you go again?: ☐y ☐n Open all year?: ☐y ☐n

Activities Accomplished:

- ☐ Archery
- ☐ Biking
- ☐ Birding
- ☐ Boating
- ☐ Camping
- ☐ Caving
- ☐ Geocaching
- ☐ Fishing
- ☐ Hiking
- ☐ Horseback Riding
- ☐ Hunting
- ☐ Off-Roading
- ☐ Paddle Boarding
- ☐ Photography
- ☐ Picnicking
- ☐ Rock Climbing
- ☐ Shooting Range
- ☐ Snowshoeing
- ☐ Stargazing
- ☐ Swimming
- ☐ Tennis
- ☐ Walking
- ☐ Wildlife Watching
- ☐ ______
- ☐ ______
- ☐ ______
- ☐ ______
- ☐ ______

Traveled by:

☐ ☐ ☐ ☐ ☐ ☐ ☐ ☐ ☐ ☐ ☐ ☐

Add your favorite ticket stub, postcard, photo, stamp or drawing here

Little Manatee River State Park

County: Hillsborough
215 Lightfoot Road, Wimauma FL 33598 | 813-671-5005

Website: https://www.floridastateparks.org/parks-and-trails/little-manatee-river-state-park
Email: FSP.Feedback@FloridaDEP.gov

Water Body: Little Manatee River

Size: 2,433 acres
Established: 1974

Park includes equestrian trails and campsites

Star Rating
☆☆☆☆☆

What souvenir did you bring home?... Decal Magnet

My favorite thing about this place is...

Why I went ...

Who I went with ...

When I went ...

What I did...

What I saw...

What I learned...

An unforgettable moment...

A laughable moment...

A surprising moment...

An unforeseeable moment...

My List

- ☐
- ☐
- ☐
- ☐
- ☐
- ☐
- ☐
- ☐
- ☐
- ☐
- ☐
- ☐

Snapped a selfie | Location...

Took a park sign selfie? - Y | N

The weather was ...      

Plan Your Trip:

☐ Trip Plan Completed

☐ Day Trip ☐ Overnight Stay

Reservations required: ☐y ☐n

Date reservations made: __________

Refund Policy: ☐y ☐n Site/Room #: _____

Confirmation #: __________

Miles to travel: __________

Time traveling: __________

Dog friendly?: ☐y ☐n

Destination Information:

Places we discovered along the way

Places to stop and see along the way

Would you go again?: ☐y ☐n

Open all year?: ☐y ☐n

Activities Accomplished:

☐ Archery	☐ Fishing	☐ Picnicking	☐ Walking
☐ Biking	☐ Hiking	☐ Rock Climbing	☐ Wildlife Watching
☐ Birding	☐ Horseback Riding	☐ Shooting Range	☐ ________
☐ Boating	☐ Hunting	☐ Snowshoeing	☐ ________
☐ Camping	☐ Off-Roading	☐ Stargazing	☐ ________
☐ Caving	☐ Paddle Boarding	☐ Swimming	☐ ________
☐ Geocaching	☐ Photography	☐ Tennis	☐ ________

Traveled by:

☐ ☐ ☐ ☐ ☐ ☐ ☐ ☐ ☐ ☐ ☐ ☐

Add your favorite ticket stub, postcard, photo, stamp or drawing here

N E S W NOT ALL THOSE WHO WANDER ARE LOST

Little Talbot Island State Park

County: Duval
12157 Heckscher Drive, Jacksonville FL 32226 | 904-251-2320

Website: https://www.floridastateparks.org/parks-and-trails/little-talbot-island-state-park
Email: FSP.Feedback@FloridaDEP.gov

Water Body: Atlantic Ocean

Size: 1,600 acres
Established: 1949

Part of Talbot Islands State Parks

Star Rating ☆☆☆☆☆

What souvenir did you bring home?... Decal Magnet

My favorite thing about this place is...

Why I went ...

Who I went with ...

When I went ...

What I did...

What I saw...

What I learned...

An unforgettable moment...

A laughable moment...

A surprising moment...

An unforeseeable moment...

My List

- ☐
- ☐
- ☐
- ☐
- ☐
- ☐
- ☐
- ☐
- ☐
- ☐
- ☐
- ☐

 Snapped a selfie | Location...

 Took a park sign selfie? - Y | N

The weather was ...  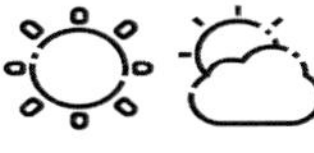     

Plan Your Trip:

☐ Trip Plan Completed

☐ Day Trip ☐ Overnight Stay

Reservations required: ☐y ☐n

Date reservations made: ____________

Refund Policy: ☐y ☐n Site/Room #: ____

Confirmation #: ____________

Miles to travel: ____________

Time traveling: ____________

Dog friendly?: ☐y ☐n

Destination Information:

Places we discovered along the way

Places to stop and see along the way

Would you go again?: ☐y ☐n Open all year?: ☐y ☐n

Activities Accomplished:

☐ Archery	☐ Fishing	☐ Picnicking	☐ Walking
☐ Biking	☐ Hiking	☐ Rock Climbing	☐ Wildlife Watching
☐ Birding	☐ Horseback Riding	☐ Shooting Range	☐ ____
☐ Boating	☐ Hunting	☐ Snowshoeing	☐ ____
☐ Camping	☐ Off-Roading	☐ Stargazing	☐ ____
☐ Caving	☐ Paddle Boarding	☐ Swimming	☐ ____
☐ Geocaching	☐ Photography	☐ Tennis	☐ ____

Traveled by:

☐ ☐ ☐ ☐ ☐ ☐ ☐ ☐ ☐ ☐ ☐ ☐

Add your favorite ticket stub, postcard, photo, stamp or drawing here

Long Key State Park

County: Monroe
67400 Overseas Highway, Long Key FL 33001 | 305-664-4815

Website: https://www.floridastateparks.org/parks-and-trails/long-key-state-park
Email: FSP.Feedback@FloridaDEP.gov

Water Body: Atlantic Ocean

Size: 965 acres
Established: 1969

Grand resort was destroyed by the Labor Day Hurricane of 1935

Star Rating ☆☆☆☆☆

What souvenir did you bring home?... Decal Magnet

My favorite thing about this place is...

Why I went ...

Who I went with ...

When I went ...

What I did...

What I saw...

What I learned...

An unforgettable moment...

A laughable moment...

A surprising moment...

An unforeseeable moment...

My List

- ☐
- ☐
- ☐
- ☐
- ☐
- ☐
- ☐
- ☐
- ☐
- ☐
- ☐
- ☐

Snapped a selfie | Location...

Took a park sign selfie? - Y | N

The weather was ...

Plan Your Trip:

☐ Trip Plan Completed

☐ Day Trip ☐ Overnight Stay

Reservations required: ☐y ☐n

Date reservations made: ____

Refund Policy: ☐y ☐n Site/Room #: ____

Confirmation #: ____

Miles to travel: ____

Time traveling: ____

Dog friendly?: ☐y ☐n

Destination Information:

____

____

Places we discovered along the way

____

____

____

Places to stop and see along the way

____

____

Activities Accomplished:

Would you go again?: ☐y ☐n

Open all year?: ☐y ☐n

☐ Archery
☐ Biking
☐ Birding
☐ Boating
☐ Camping
☐ Caving
☐ Geocaching
☐ Fishing
☐ Hiking
☐ Horseback Riding
☐ Hunting
☐ Off-Roading
☐ Paddle Boarding
☐ Photography
☐ Picnicking
☐ Rock Climbing
☐ Shooting Range
☐ Snowshoeing
☐ Stargazing
☐ Swimming
☐ Tennis
☐ Walking
☐ Wildlife Watching
☐ ____
☐ ____
☐ ____
☐ ____
☐ ____

Traveled by:

☐ ☐ ☐ ☐ ☐ ☐ ☐ ☐ ☐ ☐ ☐ ☐

Add your favorite ticket stub, postcard, photo, stamp or drawing here

N
NOT ALL THOSE WHO WANDER ARE LOST
W E S

Lovers Key State Park

County: Lee
8700 Estero Blvd., Fort Myers Beach FL 33931 | 239-463-4588

Website: https://www.floridastateparks.org/Lovers-Key
Email: FSP.Feedback@FloridaDEP.gov

Water Body: Gulf of Mexico

Size: 712 acres
Established: 1983

Lovers Key State Park merged with Carl Johnson County Park in 1996

Star Rating
☆☆☆☆☆

What souvenir did you bring home?... Decal Magnet

My favorite thing about this place is...

Why I went ...

Who I went with ...

When I went ...

What I did...

What I saw...

What I learned...

An unforgettable moment...

A laughable moment...

A surprising moment...

An unforeseeable moment...

My List

- ☐
- ☐
- ☐
- ☐
- ☐
- ☐
- ☐
- ☐
- ☐
- ☐
- ☐
- ☐

 Snapped a selfie | Location...

 Took a park sign selfie? - Y | N

The weather was ...      

Plan Your Trip:

☐ Trip Plan Completed

☐ Day Trip ☐ Overnight Stay

Reservations required: ☐y ☐n

Date reservations made: ______

Refund Policy: ☐y ☐n Site/Room #: ______

Confirmation #: ______

Miles to travel: ______

Time traveling: ______

Dog friendly?: ☐y ☐n

Destination Information:

______

______

Places we discovered along the way

______

______

______

Places to stop and see along the way

______

______

Would you go again?: ☐y ☐n

Open all year?: ☐y ☐n

Activities Accomplished:

- ☐ Archery
- ☐ Biking
- ☐ Birding
- ☐ Boating
- ☐ Camping
- ☐ Caving
- ☐ Geocaching
- ☐ Fishing
- ☐ Hiking
- ☐ Horseback Riding
- ☐ Hunting
- ☐ Off-Roading
- ☐ Paddle Boarding
- ☐ Photography
- ☐ Picnicking
- ☐ Rock Climbing
- ☐ Shooting Range
- ☐ Snowshoeing
- ☐ Stargazing
- ☐ Swimming
- ☐ Tennis
- ☐ Walking
- ☐ Wildlife Watching
- ☐ ______
- ☐ ______
- ☐ ______
- ☐ ______
- ☐ ______

Traveled by:

☐ ☐ ☐ ☐ ☐ ☐ ☐ ☐ ☐ ☐ ☐ ☐

Add your favorite ticket stub, postcard, photo, stamp or drawing here

N W E S NOT ALL THOSE WHO WANDER ARE LOST

Lower Wekiva River Preserve State Park

County: Lake Seminole
262 Wekiva Park Drive, Sanford FL 32771 | 407-553-4383

Website: https://www.floridastateparks.org/parks-and-trails/lower-wekiva-river-preserve-state-park
Email: FSP.Feedback@FloridaDEP.gov

Water Body: Wekiva River - St. Johns River

Size: 17,405 acres
Established: 1976

Wildlife corridor to the Ocala National Forest

Star Rating ☆☆☆☆☆

What souvenir did you bring home?... Decal Magnet

My favorite thing about this place is...

Why I went ...

Who I went with ...

When I went ...

What I did...

What I saw...

What I learned...

An unforgettable moment...

A laughable moment...

A surprising moment...

An unforeseeable moment...

Snapped a selfie | Location...

Took a park sign selfie? - Y | N

The weather was ...

My List

- ☐
- ☐
- ☐
- ☐
- ☐
- ☐
- ☐
- ☐
- ☐
- ☐
- ☐
- ☐

Plan Your Trip:

☐ Trip Plan Completed

☐ Day Trip ☐ Overnight Stay

Reservations required: ☐y ☐n

Date reservations made: ______

Refund Policy: ☐y ☐n Site/Room #: ______

Confirmation #: ______

Miles to travel: ______

Time traveling: ______

Dog friendly?: ☐y ☐n

Destination Information:

______

______

Places we discovered along the way

______

______

______

Places to stop and see along the way

______

______

Activities Accomplished:

Would you go again?: ☐y ☐n Open all year?: ☐y ☐n

- ☐ Archery
- ☐ Biking
- ☐ Birding
- ☐ Boating
- ☐ Camping
- ☐ Caving
- ☐ Geocaching
- ☐ Fishing
- ☐ Hiking
- ☐ Horseback Riding
- ☐ Hunting
- ☐ Off-Roading
- ☐ Paddle Boarding
- ☐ Photography
- ☐ Picnicking
- ☐ Rock Climbing
- ☐ Shooting Range
- ☐ Snowshoeing
- ☐ Stargazing
- ☐ Swimming
- ☐ Tennis
- ☐ Walking
- ☐ Wildlife Watching
- ☐ ______
- ☐ ______
- ☐ ______
- ☐ ______
- ☐ ______

Traveled by:

☐ ☐ ☐ ☐ ☐ ☐ ☐ ☐ ☐ ☐ ☐ ☐

Add your favorite ticket stub, postcard, photo, stamp or drawing here

Madira Bickel Mound State Archaeological Site

County: Manatee
955 Bayshore Drive, Terra Ceia FL 34250 | 941-723-4536

Website: https://www.floridastateparks.org/parks-and-trails/madira-bickel-mound-state-archaeological-site
Email: FSP.Feedback@FloridaDEP.gov

Water Body: Tampa Bay

Size: 10 acres
Established: 1970

Named for the owners who donated it to the state in 1948

Star Rating
☆☆☆☆☆

What souvenir did you bring home?... Decal Magnet ________

My favorite thing about this place is... ________

Why I went ... ________

Who I went with ... ________

When I went ... ________

What I did... ________

What I saw... ________

What I learned... ________

An unforgettable moment... ________

A laughable moment... ________

A surprising moment... ________

An unforeseeable moment... ________

My List

- ☐ ________
- ☐ ________
- ☐ ________
- ☐ ________
- ☐ ________
- ☐ ________
- ☐ ________
- ☐ ________
- ☐ ________
- ☐ ________
- ☐ ________
- ☐ ________

Snapped a selfie | Location... ________

Took a park sign selfie? - Y | N

The weather was ...

Plan Your Trip:

☐ Trip Plan Completed

☐ Day Trip ☐ Overnight Stay

Reservations required: ☐y ☐n

Date reservations made: ___

Refund Policy: ☐y ☐n Site/Room #: ___

Confirmation #: ___

Miles to travel: ___

Time traveling: ___

Dog friendly?: ☐y ☐n

Destination Information:

___

___

Places we discovered along the way

___

___

___

Places to stop and see along the way

___

___

Would you go again?: ☐y ☐n

Open all year?: ☐y ☐n

Activities Accomplished:

- ☐ Archery
- ☐ Biking
- ☐ Birding
- ☐ Boating
- ☐ Camping
- ☐ Caving
- ☐ Geocaching
- ☐ Fishing
- ☐ Hiking
- ☐ Horseback Riding
- ☐ Hunting
- ☐ Off-Roading
- ☐ Paddle Boarding
- ☐ Photography
- ☐ Picnicking
- ☐ Rock Climbing
- ☐ Shooting Range
- ☐ Snowshoeing
- ☐ Stargazing
- ☐ Swimming
- ☐ Tennis
- ☐ Walking
- ☐ Wildlife Watching
- ☐ ___
- ☐ ___
- ☐ ___
- ☐ ___
- ☐ ___

Traveled by:

☐ ☐ ☐ ☐ ☐ ☐ ☐ ☐ ☐ ☐ ☐ ☐

Add your favorite ticket stub, postcard, photo, stamp or drawing here

N E S W NOT ALL THOSE WHO WANDER ARE LOST

Madison Blue Spring State Park

County: Madison
8300 N.E. State Road 6, Lee FL 32059 | 850-971-5003

Website: https://www.floridastateparks.org/parks-and-trails/madison-blue-spring-state-park
Email: FSP.Feedback@FloridaDEP.gov

Water Body: Withlacoochee River

Size: 1 acres
Established: 2000

First magnitude spring

Star Rating ☆☆☆☆☆

What souvenir did you bring home?... Decal Magnet

My favorite thing about this place is...

Why I went ...

Who I went with ...

When I went ...

What I did...

What I saw...

What I learned...

An unforgettable moment...

A laughable moment...

A surprising moment...

An unforeseeable moment...

Snapped a selfie | Location...

Took a park sign selfie? - Y | N

The weather was ...

My List

- ☐
- ☐
- ☐
- ☐
- ☐
- ☐
- ☐
- ☐
- ☐
- ☐
- ☐
- ☐

PLAN YOUR TRIP:

☐ Trip Plan Completed

☐ Day Trip ☐ Overnight Stay

Reservations required: ☐y ☐n

Date reservations made: ____

Refund Policy: ☐y ☐n Site/Room #: ____

Confirmation #: ____

Miles to travel: ____

Time traveling: ____

Dog friendly?: ☐y ☐n

DESTINATION INFORMATION:

PLACES WE DISCOVERED ALONG THE WAY

PLACES TO STOP AND SEE ALONG THE WAY

Would you go again?: ☐y ☐n Open all year?: ☐y ☐n

Activities Accomplished:

- ☐ Archery
- ☐ Biking
- ☐ Birding
- ☐ Boating
- ☐ Camping
- ☐ Caving
- ☐ Geocaching
- ☐ Fishing
- ☐ Hiking
- ☐ Horseback Riding
- ☐ Hunting
- ☐ Off-Roading
- ☐ Paddle Boarding
- ☐ Photography
- ☐ Picnicking
- ☐ Rock Climbing
- ☐ Shooting Range
- ☐ Snowshoeing
- ☐ Stargazing
- ☐ Swimming
- ☐ Tennis
- ☐ Walking
- ☐ Wildlife Watching
- ☐ ____
- ☐ ____
- ☐ ____
- ☐ ____
- ☐ ____

Traveled by:

☐ ☐ ☐ ☐ ☐ ☐ ☐ ☐ ☐ ☐ ☐ ☐

Add your favorite ticket stub, postcard, photo, stamp or drawing here

MANATEE SPRINGS STATE PARK

County: Levy
11650 N.W. 115 St., Chiefland FL 32626 | 352-493-6072

Website: https://www.floridastateparks.org/parks-and-trails/manatee-springs-state-park
Email: FSP.Feedback@FloridaDEP.gov

Water Body: Manatee Springs

Size: 2,443 acres
Established: 1949

First magnitude spring

Star Rating ☆☆☆☆☆

What souvenir did you bring home?... Decal Magnet

My favorite thing about this place is...

Why I went ...

Who I went with ...

When I went ...

What I did...

What I saw...

What I learned...

An unforgettable moment...

A laughable moment...

A surprising moment...

An unforeseeable moment...

MY LIST

- ☐
- ☐
- ☐
- ☐
- ☐
- ☐
- ☐
- ☐
- ☐
- ☐
- ☐
- ☐

Snapped a selfie | Location...

Took a park sign selfie? - Y | N

The weather was ...

PLAN YOUR TRIP:

☐ Trip Plan Completed

☐ Day Trip ☐ Overnight Stay

Reservations required: ☐y ☐n

Date reservations made: ____________

Refund Policy: ☐y ☐n Site/Room #: ____

Confirmation #: ____________

Miles to travel: ____________

Time traveling: ____________

Dog friendly?: ☐y ☐n

DESTINATION INFORMATION:

____

____

PLACES WE DISCOVERED ALONG THE WAY

____

____

____

PLACES TO STOP AND SEE ALONG THE WAY

____

____

Would you go again?: ☐y ☐n

Open all year?: ☐y ☐n

Activities Accomplished:

- ☐ Archery
- ☐ Biking
- ☐ Birding
- ☐ Boating
- ☐ Camping
- ☐ Caving
- ☐ Geocaching
- ☐ Fishing
- ☐ Hiking
- ☐ Horseback Riding
- ☐ Hunting
- ☐ Off-Roading
- ☐ Paddle Boarding
- ☐ Photography
- ☐ Picnicking
- ☐ Rock Climbing
- ☐ Shooting Range
- ☐ Snowshoeing
- ☐ Stargazing
- ☐ Swimming
- ☐ Tennis
- ☐ Walking
- ☐ Wildlife Watching
- ☐ ____________
- ☐ ____________
- ☐ ____________
- ☐ ____________
- ☐ ____________

Traveled by:

☐ ☐ ☐ ☐ ☐ ☐ ☐ ☐ ☐ ☐ ☐ ☐

Add your favorite ticket stub, postcard, photo, stamp or drawing here

N
NOT ALL THOSE WHO WANDER ARE LOST
W E
S

Marjorie Kinnan Rawlings Historic State Park

County: Alachua
18700 S. County Road 325, Cross Creek FL 32640 | 352-466-3672

Website: https://www.floridastateparks.org/parks-and-trails/marjorie-kinnan-rawlings-historic-state-park
Email: FSP.Feedback@FloridaDEP.gov

Water Body: none

Size: 99 acres
Established: 1970

1930s farm and citrus orchard

Star Rating ☆☆☆☆☆

What souvenir did you bring home?... Decal Magnet

My favorite thing about this place is...

Why I went ...

Who I went with ...

When I went ...

What I did...

What I saw...

What I learned...

An unforgettable moment...

A laughable moment...

A surprising moment...

An unforeseeable moment...

My List

- ☐
- ☐
- ☐
- ☐
- ☐
- ☐
- ☐
- ☐
- ☐
- ☐
- ☐
- ☐

Snapped a selfie | Location...

Took a park sign selfie? - Y | N

The weather was ...

Plan Your Trip:

☐ Trip Plan Completed

☐ Day Trip ☐ Overnight Stay

Reservations required: ☐y ☐n

Date reservations made: ____________

Refund Policy: ☐y ☐n Site/Room #: ____

Confirmation #: ____________

Miles to travel: ____________

Time traveling: ____________

Dog friendly?: ☐y ☐n

Destination Information:

____

____

Places we discovered along the way

____

____

____

Places to stop and see along the way

____

____

Activities Accomplished:

Would you go again?: ☐y ☐n

Open all year?: ☐y ☐n

- ☐ Archery
- ☐ Biking
- ☐ Birding
- ☐ Boating
- ☐ Camping
- ☐ Caving
- ☐ Geocaching
- ☐ Fishing
- ☐ Hiking
- ☐ Horseback Riding
- ☐ Hunting
- ☐ Off-Roading
- ☐ Paddle Boarding
- ☐ Photography
- ☐ Picnicking
- ☐ Rock Climbing
- ☐ Shooting Range
- ☐ Snowshoeing
- ☐ Stargazing
- ☐ Swimming
- ☐ Tennis
- ☐ Walking
- ☐ Wildlife Watching
- ☐ ____________
- ☐ ____________
- ☐ ____________
- ☐ ____________
- ☐ ____________

Traveled by:

☐ ☐ ☐ ☐ ☐ ☐ ☐ ☐ ☐ ☐ ☐ ☐

Add your favorite ticket stub, postcard, photo, stamp or drawing here

N NOT ALL THOSE WHO WANDER ARE LOST E S W

Mike Roess Gold Head Branch State Park

County: Clay

6239 State Road 21, Keystone Heights FL 32656 | 352-473-4701

Website: https://www.floridastateparks.org/parks-and-trails/mike-roess-gold-head-branch-state-park
Email: FSP.Feedback@FloridaDEP.gov

Water Body: Little Lake Johnson

Size: 2,000 acres
Established: 1935

Hiking and Equestrian trails

Star Rating ☆☆☆☆☆

What souvenir did you bring home?... Decal Magnet

My favorite thing about this place is...

Why I went ...

Who I went with ...

When I went ...

What I did...

What I saw...

What I learned...

An unforgettable moment...

A laughable moment...

A surprising moment...

An unforeseeable moment...

My List

- ☐
- ☐
- ☐
- ☐
- ☐
- ☐
- ☐
- ☐
- ☐
- ☐
- ☐
- ☐

Snapped a selfie | Location...

Took a park sign selfie? - Y | N

The weather was ...

Plan Your Trip:

☐ Trip Plan Completed

☐ Day Trip ☐ Overnight Stay

Reservations required: ☐y ☐n

Date reservations made: ____________

Refund Policy: ☐y ☐n Site/Room #: ______

Confirmation #: ____________

Miles to travel: ____________

Time traveling: ____________

Dog friendly?: ☐y ☐n

Destination Information:

Places we discovered along the way

Places to stop and see along the way

Would you go again?: ☐y ☐n Open all year?: ☐y ☐n

Activities Accomplished:

☐ Archery
☐ Biking
☐ Birding
☐ Boating
☐ Camping
☐ Caving
☐ Geocaching
☐ Fishing
☐ Hiking
☐ Horseback Riding
☐ Hunting
☐ Off-Roading
☐ Paddle Boarding
☐ Photography
☐ Picnicking
☐ Rock Climbing
☐ Shooting Range
☐ Snowshoeing
☐ Stargazing
☐ Swimming
☐ Tennis
☐ Walking
☐ Wildlife Watching
☐ ____________
☐ ____________
☐ ____________
☐ ____________
☐ ____________

Traveled by:

☐ ☐ ☐ ☐ ☐ ☐ ☐ ☐ ☐ ☐ ☐ ☐

Add your favorite ticket stub, postcard, photo, stamp or drawing here

N W E S NOT ALL THOSE WHO WANDER ARE LOST

MOUND KEY ARCHAEOLOGICAL STATE PARK

County: Lee

Located in Estero Bay, visitors typically launch from Koreshan State Park or Lovers Key State Park to access the park. | 239-992-0311

Website: https://www.floridastateparks.org/parks-and-trails/mound-key-archaeological-state-park
Email: FSP.Feedback@FloridaDEP.gov

Water Body: Estero Bay

Size: 113 acres
Established: 1970

Accessible only by boat - no facilities

Star Rating ☆☆☆☆☆

What souvenir did you bring home?... Decal Magnet

My favorite thing about this place is...

Why I went ...

Who I went with ...

When I went ...

What I did...

What I saw...

What I learned...

An unforgettable moment...

A laughable moment...

A surprising moment...

An unforeseeable moment...

MY LIST

- ☐
- ☐
- ☐
- ☐
- ☐
- ☐
- ☐
- ☐
- ☐
- ☐
- ☐
- ☐

Snapped a selfie | Location...

Took a park sign selfie? - Y | N

The weather was ...

Plan Your Trip:

☐ Trip Plan Completed

☐ Day Trip ☐ Overnight Stay

Reservations required: ☐y ☐n

Date reservations made: ______

Refund Policy: ☐y ☐n Site/Room #: ______

Confirmation #: ______

Miles to travel: ______

Time traveling: ______

Dog friendly?: ☐y ☐n

Destination Information:

______

______

Places we discovered along the way

______

______

______

Places to stop and see along the way

______

______

Activities Accomplished:

Would you go again?: ☐y ☐n

Open all year?: ☐y ☐n

☐ Archery
☐ Biking
☐ Birding
☐ Boating
☐ Camping
☐ Caving
☐ Geocaching
☐ Fishing
☐ Hiking
☐ Horseback Riding
☐ Hunting
☐ Off-Roading
☐ Paddle Boarding
☐ Photography
☐ Picnicking
☐ Rock Climbing
☐ Shooting Range
☐ Snowshoeing
☐ Stargazing
☐ Swimming
☐ Tennis
☐ Walking
☐ Wildlife Watching
☐ ______
☐ ______
☐ ______
☐ ______
☐ ______

Traveled by:

☐ ☐ ☐ ☐ ☐ ☐ ☐ ☐ ☐ ☐ ☐ ☐

Add your favorite ticket stub, postcard, photo, stamp or drawing here

N W E S NOT ALL THOSE WHO WANDER ARE LOST

Myakka River State Park

County: Sarasota Manatee
13208 State Road 72, Sarasota FL 34241 | 941-361-6511

Website: https://www.floridastateparks.org/parks-and-trails/myakka-river-state-park
Email: FSP.Feedback@FloridaDEP.gov

Water Body: Myakka River - Upper Myakka Lake

Size: 37,000 acres
Established: 1941

Land partly donated by Bertha Palmer, pioneer farmer, rancher & developer

Star Rating ☆☆☆☆☆

What souvenir did you bring home?... Decal Magnet

My favorite thing about this place is...

Why I went ...

Who I went with ...

When I went ...

What I did...

What I saw...

What I learned...

An unforgettable moment...

A laughable moment...

A surprising moment...

An unforeseeable moment...

Snapped a selfie | Location...

Took a park sign selfie? - Y | N

My List

- ☐
- ☐
- ☐
- ☐
- ☐
- ☐
- ☐
- ☐
- ☐
- ☐
- ☐
- ☐

The weather was ... F

Plan Your Trip:

☐ Trip Plan Completed

☐ Day Trip ☐ Overnight Stay

Reservations required: ☐y ☐n

Date reservations made: ____________

Refund Policy: ☐y ☐n Site/Room #: ______

Confirmation #: ____________

Miles to travel: ____________

Time traveling: ____________

Dog friendly?: ☐y ☐n

Destination Information:

____

____

Places we discovered along the way

____

____

____

Places to stop and see along the way

____

____

Activities Accomplished:

Would you go again?: ☐y ☐n

Open all year?: ☐y ☐n

☐ Archery
☐ Biking
☐ Birding
☐ Boating
☐ Camping
☐ Caving
☐ Geocaching
☐ Fishing
☐ Hiking
☐ Horseback Riding
☐ Hunting
☐ Off-Roading
☐ Paddle Boarding
☐ Photography
☐ Picnicking
☐ Rock Climbing
☐ Shooting Range
☐ Snowshoeing
☐ Stargazing
☐ Swimming
☐ Tennis
☐ Walking
☐ Wildlife Watching
☐ ____________
☐ ____________
☐ ____________
☐ ____________
☐ ____________

Traveled by:

☐ ☐ ☐ ☐ ☐ ☐ ☐ ☐ ☐ ☐ ☐ ☐

Add your favorite ticket stub, postcard, photo, stamp or drawing here

N E S W NOT ALL THOSE WHO WANDER ARE LOST

Natural Bridge Battlefield Historic State Park

County: Leon
7502 Natural Bridge Road, Tallahassee FL 32305 | 850-487-7989

Website: https://www.floridastateparks.org/parks-and-trails/natural-bridge-battlefield-historic-state-park
Email: FSP.Feedback@FloridaDEP.gov

Water Body: St. Marks River

Size: 113 acres
Established: 1949

Site of the second largest Civil War battle in Florida

Star Rating ☆☆☆☆☆

What souvenir did you bring home?... Decal Magnet

My favorite thing about this place is... ______

Why I went ... ______

Who I went with ... ______

When I went ... ______

What I did... ______

What I saw... ______

What I learned... ______

An unforgettable moment... ______

A laughable moment... ______

A surprising moment... ______

An unforeseeable moment... ______

Snapped a selfie | Location... ______

Took a park sign selfie? - Y | N

The weather was ...

My List

- ☐ ______
- ☐ ______
- ☐ ______
- ☐ ______
- ☐ ______
- ☐ ______
- ☐ ______
- ☐ ______
- ☐ ______
- ☐ ______
- ☐ ______
- ☐ ______

PLAN YOUR TRIP:

☐ Trip Plan Completed

☐ Day Trip ☐ Overnight Stay

Reservations required: ☐y ☐n

Date reservations made: ______

Refund Policy: ☐y ☐n Site/Room #: ______

Confirmation #: ______

Miles to travel: ______

Time traveling: ______

Dog friendly?: ☐y ☐n

DESTINATION INFORMATION:

______

______

PLACES WE DISCOVERED ALONG THE WAY

______

______

______

PLACES TO STOP AND SEE ALONG THE WAY

______

______

Activities Accomplished:

Would you go again?: ☐y ☐n Open all year?: ☐y ☐n

☐ Archery
☐ Biking
☐ Birding
☐ Boating
☐ Camping
☐ Caving
☐ Geocaching
☐ Fishing
☐ Hiking
☐ Horseback Riding
☐ Hunting
☐ Off-Roading
☐ Paddle Boarding
☐ Photography
☐ Picnicking
☐ Rock Climbing
☐ Shooting Range
☐ Snowshoeing
☐ Stargazing
☐ Swimming
☐ Tennis
☐ Walking
☐ Wildlife Watching
☐ ______
☐ ______
☐ ______
☐ ______
☐ ______

Traveled by:

☐ ☐ ☐ ☐ ☐ ☐ ☐ ☐ ☐ ☐ ☐ ☐

Add your favorite ticket stub, postcard, photo, stamp or drawing here

North Peninsula State Park

County: Volusia
40 Highbridge Road, Ormond by the Sea FL 32176 | 386-517-2086

Website: https://www.floridastateparks.org/parks-and-trails/north-peninsula-state-park
Email: FSP.Feedback@FloridaDEP.gov

Water Body: Atlantic Ocean

Size: 534 acres
Established: 1984

Metal pieces from the wreck of the North Western, which sank prior to World War II, have emerged on the beach

Star Rating
☆☆☆☆☆

What souvenir did you bring home?... Decal Magnet
My favorite thing about this place is...

Why I went ...
Who I went with ...
When I went ...

What I did...
What I saw...

What I learned...

An unforgettable moment...

A laughable moment...

A surprising moment...

An unforeseeable moment...

Snapped a selfie | Location...
Took a park sign selfie? - Y | N

The weather was ...

My List

- ☐
- ☐
- ☐
- ☐
- ☐
- ☐
- ☐
- ☐
- ☐
- ☐
- ☐
- ☐

Plan Your Trip:

☐ Trip Plan Completed

☐ Day Trip ☐ Overnight Stay

Reservations required: ☐y ☐n

Date reservations made: ____________

Refund Policy: ☐y ☐n Site/Room #: ______

Confirmation #: ____________

Miles to travel: ____________

Time traveling: ____________

Dog friendly?: ☐y ☐n

Destination Information:

____

____

Places we discovered along the way

____

____

____

Places to stop and see along the way

____

____

Activities Accomplished:

Would you go again?: ☐y ☐n

Open all year?: ☐y ☐n

☐ Archery
☐ Biking
☐ Birding
☐ Boating
☐ Camping
☐ Caving
☐ Geocaching
☐ Fishing
☐ Hiking
☐ Horseback Riding
☐ Hunting
☐ Off-Roading
☐ Paddle Boarding
☐ Photography
☐ Picnicking
☐ Rock Climbing
☐ Shooting Range
☐ Snowshoeing
☐ Stargazing
☐ Swimming
☐ Tennis
☐ Walking
☐ Wildlife Watching
☐ ____________
☐ ____________
☐ ____________
☐ ____________
☐ ____________

Traveled by:

☐ ☐ ☐ ☐ ☐ ☐ ☐ ☐ ☐ ☐ ☐ ☐

Add your favorite ticket stub, postcard, photo, stamp or drawing here

N W E S NOT ALL THOSE WHO WANDER ARE LOST

Okeechobee Battlefield State Park

County: Okeechobee
3500 S.E. 38th Ave., Okeechobee FL 34974 | 863-462-5360

Website: https://www.floridastateparks.org/parks-and-trails/okeechobee-battlefield-historic-state-park
Email: FSP.Feedback@FloridaDEP.gov

Water Body: Lake Okeechobee

Size: 211 acres
Established: 2007

Battle site during the Second Seminole War

Star Rating ☆☆☆☆☆

What souvenir did you bring home?... Decal Magnet ____________

My favorite thing about this place is... ____________

____

Why I went ... ____________

Who I went with ... ____________

When I went ... ____________

____

What I did... ____________

What I saw... ____________

____

____

What I learned... ____________

____

____

An unforgettable moment... ____________

____

____

____

A laughable moment... ____________

____

____

A surprising moment... ____________

____

____

____

An unforeseeable moment... ____________

____

____

My List

- ☐ ____________
- ☐ ____________
- ☐ ____________
- ☐ ____________
- ☐ ____________
- ☐ ____________
- ☐ ____________
- ☐ ____________
- ☐ ____________
- ☐ ____________
- ☐ ____________
- ☐ ____________

Snapped a selfie | Location... ____________

Took a park sign selfie? - Y | N

The weather was ...

Plan Your Trip:

☐ Trip Plan Completed

☐ Day Trip ☐ Overnight Stay

Reservations required: ☐y ☐n

Date reservations made: ______

Refund Policy: ☐y ☐n Site/Room #: ______

Confirmation #: ______

Miles to travel: ______

Time traveling: ______

Dog friendly?: ☐y ☐n

Destination Information:

Places we discovered along the way

Places to stop and see along the way

Activities Accomplished:

Would you go again?: ☐y ☐n

Open all year?: ☐y ☐n

- ☐ Archery
- ☐ Biking
- ☐ Birding
- ☐ Boating
- ☐ Camping
- ☐ Caving
- ☐ Geocaching
- ☐ Fishing
- ☐ Hiking
- ☐ Horseback Riding
- ☐ Hunting
- ☐ Off-Roading
- ☐ Paddle Boarding
- ☐ Photography
- ☐ Picnicking
- ☐ Rock Climbing
- ☐ Shooting Range
- ☐ Snowshoeing
- ☐ Stargazing
- ☐ Swimming
- ☐ Tennis
- ☐ Walking
- ☐ Wildlife Watching
- ☐ ______
- ☐ ______
- ☐ ______
- ☐ ______
- ☐ ______

Traveled by:

☐ ☐ ☐ ☐ ☐ ☐ ☐ ☐ ☐ ☐ ☐ ☐

Add your favorite ticket stub, postcard, photo, stamp or drawing here

N
NOT ALL THOSE WHO WANDER ARE LOST
W E
S

O'Leno State Park

County: Columbia

410 S.E. O'Leno Park Road, High Springs FL 32643 | 386-454-1853

Website: https://www.floridastateparks.org/parks-and-trails/oleno-state-park
Email: FSP.Feedback@FloridaDEP.gov

Water Body: Santa Fe River

Size: 6,000 acres
Established: 1940

Many facilities built by the Civilian Conservation Corps in the 1930s

Star Rating ☆☆☆☆☆

What souvenir did you bring home?... Decal Magnet

My favorite thing about this place is...

Why I went ...

Who I went with ...

When I went ...

What I did...

What I saw...

What I learned...

An unforgettable moment...

A laughable moment...

A surprising moment...

An unforeseeable moment...

My List

- ☐
- ☐
- ☐
- ☐
- ☐
- ☐
- ☐
- ☐
- ☐
- ☐
- ☐
- ☐

Snapped a selfie | Location...

Took a park sign selfie? - Y | N

The weather was ...

Plan Your Trip:

☐ Trip Plan Completed

☐ Day Trip ☐ Overnight Stay

Reservations required: ☐y ☐n

Date reservations made: ____________

Refund Policy: ☐y ☐n Site/Room #: ______

Confirmation #: ____________

Miles to travel: ____________

Time traveling: ____________

Dog friendly?: ☐y ☐n

Destination Information:

Places we discovered along the way

Places to stop and see along the way

Activities Accomplished:

Would you go again?: ☐y ☐n Open all year?: ☐y ☐n

- ☐ Archery
- ☐ Biking
- ☐ Birding
- ☐ Boating
- ☐ Camping
- ☐ Caving
- ☐ Geocaching
- ☐ Fishing
- ☐ Hiking
- ☐ Horseback Riding
- ☐ Hunting
- ☐ Off-Roading
- ☐ Paddle Boarding
- ☐ Photography
- ☐ Picnicking
- ☐ Rock Climbing
- ☐ Shooting Range
- ☐ Snowshoeing
- ☐ Stargazing
- ☐ Swimming
- ☐ Tennis
- ☐ Walking
- ☐ Wildlife Watching
- ☐ ____________
- ☐ ____________
- ☐ ____________
- ☐ ____________
- ☐ ____________

Traveled by:

☐ ☐ ☐ ☐ ☐ ☐ ☐ ☐ ☐ ☐ ☐ ☐

Add your favorite ticket stub, postcard, photo, stamp or drawing here

N E S W NOT ALL THOSE WHO WANDER ARE LOST

OCHLOCKONEE RIVER STATE PARK

County: Wakulla
429 State Park Road, Sopchoppy FL 32358 | 850-962-2771

Website: https://www.floridastateparks.org/parks-and-trails/ochlockonee-river-state-park
Email: FSP.Feedback@FloridaDEP.gov

Water Body: Ochlockonee River - Dead River

Size: 392 acres
Established: 1970

Many older trees show scars from turpentine industry

Star Rating ☆☆☆☆☆

What souvenir did you bring home?... Decal Magnet

My favorite thing about this place is...

Why I went ...

Who I went with ...

When I went ...

What I did...

What I saw...

What I learned...

An unforgettable moment...

A laughable moment...

A surprising moment...

An unforeseeable moment...

MY LIST

- ☐
- ☐
- ☐
- ☐
- ☐
- ☐
- ☐
- ☐
- ☐
- ☐
- ☐
- ☐

 Snapped a selfie | Location...

 Took a park sign selfie? - Y | N

The weather was ... 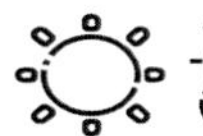     

Plan Your Trip:

☐ Trip Plan Completed

☐ Day Trip ☐ Overnight Stay

Reservations required: ☐y ☐n

Date reservations made: ______

Refund Policy: ☐y ☐n Site/Room #: ______

Confirmation #: ______

Miles to travel: ______

Time traveling: ______

Dog friendly?: ☐y ☐n

Destination Information:

______

______

Places we discovered along the way

______

______

______

Places to stop and see along the way

______

______

Would you go again?: ☐y ☐n Open all year?: ☐y ☐n

Activities Accomplished:

- ☐ Archery
- ☐ Biking
- ☐ Birding
- ☐ Boating
- ☐ Camping
- ☐ Caving
- ☐ Geocaching
- ☐ Fishing
- ☐ Hiking
- ☐ Horseback Riding
- ☐ Hunting
- ☐ Off-Roading
- ☐ Paddle Boarding
- ☐ Photography
- ☐ Picnicking
- ☐ Rock Climbing
- ☐ Shooting Range
- ☐ Snowshoeing
- ☐ Stargazing
- ☐ Swimming
- ☐ Tennis
- ☐ Walking
- ☐ Wildlife Watching
- ☐ ______
- ☐ ______
- ☐ ______
- ☐ ______
- ☐ ______

Traveled by:

☐ ☐ ☐ ☐ ☐ ☐ ☐ ☐ ☐ ☐ ☐ ☐

Add your favorite ticket stub, postcard, photo, stamp or drawing here

N W E S NOT ALL THOSE WHO WANDER ARE LOST

Oleta River State Park

County: Miami-Dade
3400 N.E. 163rd St., North Miami Beach FL 33160 | 305-919-1846

Website: https://www.floridastateparks.org/OletaRiver
Email: FSP.Feedback@FloridaDEP.gov

Water Body: Oleta River - Biscayne Bay

Size: 1,043 acres
Established: 1986

Park has high numbers of the invasive species Casuarina Australian pine

Star Rating ☆☆☆☆☆

What souvenir did you bring home?... Decal Magnet

My favorite thing about this place is... ______

Why I went ... ______

Who I went with ... ______

When I went ... ______

What I did... ______

What I saw... ______

What I learned... ______

An unforgettable moment... ______

A laughable moment... ______

A surprising moment... ______

An unforeseeable moment... ______

My List

- ☐
- ☐
- ☐
- ☐
- ☐
- ☐
- ☐
- ☐
- ☐
- ☐
- ☐
- ☐

Snapped a selfie | Location... ______

Took a park sign selfie? - Y | N

The weather was ...

Plan Your Trip:

☐ Trip Plan Completed

☐ Day Trip ☐ Overnight Stay

Reservations required: ☐y ☐n

Date reservations made: ______

Refund Policy: ☐y ☐n Site/Room #: ______

Confirmation #: ______

Miles to travel: ______

Time traveling: ______

Dog friendly?: ☐y ☐n

Destination Information:

______

______

Places we discovered along the way

______

______

______

Places to stop and see along the way

______

______

Activities Accomplished:

Would you go again?: ☐y ☐n

Open all year?: ☐y ☐n

- ☐ Archery
- ☐ Biking
- ☐ Birding
- ☐ Boating
- ☐ Camping
- ☐ Caving
- ☐ Geocaching
- ☐ Fishing
- ☐ Hiking
- ☐ Horseback Riding
- ☐ Hunting
- ☐ Off-Roading
- ☐ Paddle Boarding
- ☐ Photography
- ☐ Picnicking
- ☐ Rock Climbing
- ☐ Shooting Range
- ☐ Snowshoeing
- ☐ Stargazing
- ☐ Swimming
- ☐ Tennis
- ☐ Walking
- ☐ Wildlife Watching
- ☐ ______
- ☐ ______
- ☐ ______
- ☐ ______
- ☐ ______

Traveled by:

☐ ☐ ☐ ☐ ☐ ☐ ☐ ☐ ☐ ☐ ☐ ☐

Add your favorite ticket stub, postcard, photo, stamp or drawing here

N W E S NOT ALL THOSE WHO WANDER ARE LOST

Olustee Battlefield Historic State Park

County: Baker
5815 Battlefield Trail Road, Olustee FL 32087 | 386-758-0400

Website: https://www.floridastateparks.org/parks-and-trails/olustee-battlefield-historic-state-park
Email: FSP.Feedback@FloridaDEP.gov

Water Body: none

Size: 43 acres
Established: 1949

First State Historic Monument in 1909

Star Rating ☆☆☆☆☆

What souvenir did you bring home?... Decal Magnet

My favorite thing about this place is...

Why I went ...

Who I went with ...

When I went ...

What I did...

What I saw...

What I learned...

An unforgettable moment...

A laughable moment...

A surprising moment...

An unforeseeable moment...

Snapped a selfie | Location...

Took a park sign selfie? - Y | N

The weather was ...

My List

- ☐
- ☐
- ☐
- ☐
- ☐
- ☐
- ☐
- ☐
- ☐
- ☐
- ☐
- ☐

Plan Your Trip:

☐ Trip Plan Completed

☐ Day Trip ☐ Overnight Stay

Reservations required: ☐y ☐n

Date reservations made: ____________

Refund Policy: ☐y ☐n Site/Room #: ____

Confirmation #: ____________

Miles to travel: ____________

Time traveling: ____________

Dog friendly?: ☐y ☐n

Destination Information:

____

____

Places we discovered along the way

____

____

____

Places to stop and see along the way

____

____

Would you go again?: ☐y ☐n

Open all year?: ☐y ☐n

Activities Accomplished:

- ☐ Archery
- ☐ Biking
- ☐ Birding
- ☐ Boating
- ☐ Camping
- ☐ Caving
- ☐ Geocaching
- ☐ Fishing
- ☐ Hiking
- ☐ Horseback Riding
- ☐ Hunting
- ☐ Off-Roading
- ☐ Paddle Boarding
- ☐ Photography
- ☐ Picnicking
- ☐ Rock Climbing
- ☐ Shooting Range
- ☐ Snowshoeing
- ☐ Stargazing
- ☐ Swimming
- ☐ Tennis
- ☐ Walking
- ☐ Wildlife Watching
- ☐ ____________
- ☐ ____________
- ☐ ____________
- ☐ ____________
- ☐ ____________

Traveled by:

☐ ☐ ☐ ☐ ☐ ☐ ☐ ☐ ☐ ☐ ☐ ☐

Add your favorite ticket stub, postcard, photo, stamp or drawing here

N W E S NOT ALL THOSE WHO WANDER ARE LOST

Orman House Historic State Park

County: Franklin
177 Fifth St., Apalachicola FL 32320 | 850-653-1209

Website: **https://www.floridastateparks.org/parks-and-trails/orman-house-historic-state-park**
Email: **FSP.Feedback@FloridaDEP.gov**

Water Body: Apalachicola River

Size: 1 acres
Established: 2001

House built in 1838

Star Rating ☆☆☆☆☆

What souvenir did you bring home?... Decal Magnet ________

My favorite thing about this place is... ________

Why I went ... ________

Who I went with ... ________

When I went ... ________

What I did... ________

What I saw... ________

What I learned... ________

An unforgettable moment... ________

A laughable moment... ________

A surprising moment... ________

An unforeseeable moment... ________

My List

- ☐ ________
- ☐ ________
- ☐ ________
- ☐ ________
- ☐ ________
- ☐ ________
- ☐ ________
- ☐ ________
- ☐ ________
- ☐ ________
- ☐ ________
- ☐ ________

Snapped a selfie | Location... ________

Took a park sign selfie? - Y | N

The weather was ...

PLAN YOUR TRIP:

☐ Trip Plan Completed

☐ Day Trip ☐ Overnight Stay

Reservations required: ☐y ☐n

Date reservations made: ____________

Refund Policy: ☐y ☐n Site/Room #: ____

Confirmation #: ____________

Miles to travel: ____________

Time traveling: ____________

Dog friendly?: ☐y ☐n

DESTINATION INFORMATION:

PLACES WE DISCOVERED ALONG THE WAY

PLACES TO STOP AND SEE ALONG THE WAY

Activities Accomplished:

Would you go again?: ☐y ☐n Open all year?: ☐y ☐n

☐ Archery
☐ Biking
☐ Birding
☐ Boating
☐ Camping
☐ Caving
☐ Geocaching
☐ Fishing
☐ Hiking
☐ Horseback Riding
☐ Hunting
☐ Off-Roading
☐ Paddle Boarding
☐ Photography
☐ Picnicking
☐ Rock Climbing
☐ Shooting Range
☐ Snowshoeing
☐ Stargazing
☐ Swimming
☐ Tennis
☐ Walking
☐ Wildlife Watching
☐ ____________
☐ ____________
☐ ____________
☐ ____________
☐ ____________

Traveled by:

☐ ☐ ☐ ☐ ☐ ☐ ☐ ☐ ☐ ☐ ☐ ☐

Add your favorite ticket stub, postcard, photo, stamp or drawing here

N NOT ALL THOSE WHO WANDER ARE LOST S W E

Oscar Scherer State Park

County: Sarasota
1843 S. Tamiami Trail, Osprey FL 34229 | 941-483-5956

Website: https://www.floridastateparks.org/parks-and-trails/oscar-scherer-state-park
Email: FSP.Feedback@FloridaDEP.gov

Water Body: South Creek - Lake Osprey

Size: 1,400 acres
Established: 1956

Major habitat of the Florida Scrub Jay

Star Rating ☆☆☆☆☆

What souvenir did you bring home?... Decal Magnet

My favorite thing about this place is...

Why I went ...

Who I went with ...

When I went ...

What I did...

What I saw...

What I learned...

An unforgettable moment...

A laughable moment...

A surprising moment...

An unforeseeable moment...

Snapped a selfie | Location...

Took a park sign selfie? - Y | N

The weather was ...

My List

- ☐
- ☐
- ☐
- ☐
- ☐
- ☐
- ☐
- ☐
- ☐
- ☐
- ☐
- ☐

Plan Your Trip:

☐ Trip Plan Completed

☐ Day Trip ☐ Overnight Stay

Reservations required: ☐y ☐n

Date reservations made: ____________

Refund Policy: ☐y ☐n Site/Room #: ______

Confirmation #: ____________

Miles to travel: ____________

Time traveling: ____________

Dog friendly?: ☐y ☐n

Destination Information:

____

____

Places we discovered along the way

____

____

____

Places to stop and see along the way

____

____

Would you go again?: ☐y ☐n Open all year?: ☐y ☐n

Activities Accomplished:

- ☐ Archery
- ☐ Biking
- ☐ Birding
- ☐ Boating
- ☐ Camping
- ☐ Caving
- ☐ Geocaching
- ☐ Fishing
- ☐ Hiking
- ☐ Horseback Riding
- ☐ Hunting
- ☐ Off-Roading
- ☐ Paddle Boarding
- ☐ Photography
- ☐ Picnicking
- ☐ Rock Climbing
- ☐ Shooting Range
- ☐ Snowshoeing
- ☐ Stargazing
- ☐ Swimming
- ☐ Tennis
- ☐ Walking
- ☐ Wildlife Watching
- ☐ ____________
- ☐ ____________
- ☐ ____________
- ☐ ____________
- ☐ ____________

Traveled by:

☐ ☐ ☐ ☐ ☐ ☐ ☐ ☐ ☐ ☐ ☐ ☐

Add your favorite ticket stub, postcard, photo, stamp or drawing here

N W E S NOT ALL THOSE WHO WANDER ARE LOST

PAYNES CREEK HISTORIC STATE PARK

County: Hardee
888 Lake Branch Road, Bowling Green FL 33834 | 863-375-4717

Website: https://www.floridastateparks.org/parks-and-trails/paynes-creek-historic-state-park
Email: FSP.Feedback@FloridaDEP.gov

Water Body: Paynes Creek

Size: 410 acres
Established: 1981

Site of Fort Chokonikla and the Kennedy-Darling trading post during the Seminole Wars

Star Rating ☆☆☆☆☆

What souvenir did you bring home?... Decal Magnet

My favorite thing about this place is...

Why I went ...

Who I went with ...

When I went ...

What I did...

What I saw...

What I learned...

An unforgettable moment...

A laughable moment...

A surprising moment...

An unforeseeable moment...

Snapped a selfie | Location...

Took a park sign selfie? - Y | N

The weather was ...

MY LIST

- ☐
- ☐
- ☐
- ☐
- ☐
- ☐
- ☐
- ☐
- ☐
- ☐
- ☐
- ☐

PLAN YOUR TRIP:

☐ Trip Plan Completed

☐ Day Trip ☐ Overnight Stay

Reservations required: ☐y ☐n

Date reservations made: ______

Refund Policy: ☐y ☐n Site/Room #: ______

Confirmation #: ______

Miles to travel: ______

Time traveling: ______

Dog friendly?: ☐y ☐n

DESTINATION INFORMATION:

______

______

PLACES WE DISCOVERED ALONG THE WAY

______

______

______

PLACES TO STOP AND SEE ALONG THE WAY

______

______

Activities Accomplished:

Would you go again?: ☐y ☐n

Open all year?: ☐y ☐n

- ☐ Archery
- ☐ Biking
- ☐ Birding
- ☐ Boating
- ☐ Camping
- ☐ Caving
- ☐ Geocaching
- ☐ Fishing
- ☐ Hiking
- ☐ Horseback Riding
- ☐ Hunting
- ☐ Off-Roading
- ☐ Paddle Boarding
- ☐ Photography
- ☐ Picnicking
- ☐ Rock Climbing
- ☐ Shooting Range
- ☐ Snowshoeing
- ☐ Stargazing
- ☐ Swimming
- ☐ Tennis
- ☐ Walking
- ☐ Wildlife Watching
- ☐ ______
- ☐ ______
- ☐ ______
- ☐ ______
- ☐ ______

Traveled by:

☐ ☐ ☐ ☐ ☐ ☐ ☐ ☐ ☐ ☐ ☐ ☐

Add your favorite ticket stub, postcard, photo, stamp or drawing here

N W E S NOT ALL THOSE WHO WANDER ARE LOST

Paynes Prairie Preserve State Park

County: Alachua
100 Savannah Blvd., Micanopy FL 32667 | 352-466-3397

Website: https://www.floridastateparks.org/parks-and-trails/paynes-prairie-preserve-state-park
Email: FSP.Feedback@FloridaDEP.gov

Water Body: Lake Wauburg

Size: 21,000 acres
Established: 1971

Savanna formerly occupied by Seminole Indians

Star Rating ☆☆☆☆☆

What souvenir did you bring home?... Decal Magnet

My favorite thing about this place is...

Why I went ...

Who I went with ...

When I went ...

What I did...

What I saw...

What I learned...

An unforgettable moment...

A laughable moment...

A surprising moment...

An unforeseeable moment...

My List

- ☐
- ☐
- ☐
- ☐
- ☐
- ☐
- ☐
- ☐
- ☐
- ☐
- ☐
- ☐

Snapped a selfie | Location...

Took a park sign selfie? - Y | N

The weather was ...

Plan Your Trip:

☐ Trip Plan Completed

☐ Day Trip ☐ Overnight Stay

Reservations required: ☐y ☐n

Date reservations made: ____________

Refund Policy: ☐y ☐n Site/Room #: ______

Confirmation #: ____________

Miles to travel: ____________

Time traveling: ____________

Dog friendly?: ☐y ☐n

Destination Information:

Places we discovered along the way

Places to stop and see along the way

Activities Accomplished:

Would you go again?: ☐y ☐n Open all year?: ☐y ☐n

☐ Archery	☐ Fishing	☐ Picnicking	☐ Walking
☐ Biking	☐ Hiking	☐ Rock Climbing	☐ Wildlife Watching
☐ Birding	☐ Horseback Riding	☐ Shooting Range	☐ ______
☐ Boating	☐ Hunting	☐ Snowshoeing	☐ ______
☐ Camping	☐ Off-Roading	☐ Stargazing	☐ ______
☐ Caving	☐ Paddle Boarding	☐ Swimming	☐ ______
☐ Geocaching	☐ Photography	☐ Tennis	☐ ______

Traveled by:

☐ ☐ ☐ ☐ ☐ ☐ ☐ ☐ ☐ ☐ ☐ ☐

Add your favorite ticket stub, postcard, photo, stamp or drawing here

N E S W NOT ALL THOSE WHO WANDER ARE LOST

PERDIDO KEY STATE PARK

County: Escambia

15301 Perdido Key Drive, Pensacola FL 32507 | 850-492-1595

Website: https://www.floridastateparks.org/parks-and-trails/perdido-key-state-park
Email: FSP.Feedback@FloridaDEP.gov

Water Body: Gulf of Mexico

Size: 290 acres
Established: 1978

A barrier island

Star Rating ☆☆☆☆☆

What souvenir did you bring home?... Decal Magnet

My favorite thing about this place is...

Why I went ...

Who I went with ...

When I went ...

What I did...

What I saw...

What I learned...

An unforgettable moment...

A laughable moment...

A surprising moment...

An unforeseeable moment...

MY LIST

- ☐
- ☐
- ☐
- ☐
- ☐
- ☐
- ☐
- ☐
- ☐
- ☐
- ☐
- ☐

Snapped a selfie | Location...

Took a park sign selfie? - Y | N

The weather was ...

Plan Your Trip:

☐ Trip Plan Completed

☐ Day Trip ☐ Overnight Stay

Reservations required: ☐y ☐n

Date reservations made: ____________

Refund Policy: ☐y ☐n Site/Room #: ____

Confirmation #: ____________

Miles to travel: ____________

Time traveling: ____________

Dog friendly?: ☐y ☐n

Destination Information:

____

____

Places we discovered along the way

____

____

____

Places to stop and see along the way

____

____

Would you go again?: ☐y ☐n

Open all year?: ☐y ☐n

Activities Accomplished:

☐ Archery	☐ Fishing	☐ Picnicking	☐ Walking
☐ Biking	☐ Hiking	☐ Rock Climbing	☐ Wildlife Watching
☐ Birding	☐ Horseback Riding	☐ Shooting Range	☐ ________
☐ Boating	☐ Hunting	☐ Snowshoeing	☐ ________
☐ Camping	☐ Off-Roading	☐ Stargazing	☐ ________
☐ Caving	☐ Paddle Boarding	☐ Swimming	☐ ________
☐ Geocaching	☐ Photography	☐ Tennis	☐ ________

Traveled by:

☐ ☐ ☐ ☐ ☐ ☐ ☐ ☐ ☐ ☐ ☐ ☐

Add your favorite ticket stub, postcard, photo, stamp or drawing here

N E S W NOT ALL THOSE WHO WANDER ARE LOST

PRICE'S SCRUB STATE PARK

County: Marion
9555 N.W. Highway 320, Micanopy FL 32667 | 352-466-3397

Website: https://www.floridastateparks.org/parks-and-trails/prices-scrub-state-park
Email: FSP.Feedback@FloridaDEP.gov

Water Body: Sinkhole lakes

Size: 962.28 acres
Established: 2002

Contains woodland, marsh, scrub, scrubby flatwoods, and sinkhole lakes

Star Rating
☆☆☆☆☆

What souvenir did you bring home?... Decal Magnet

My favorite thing about this place is... ______

Why I went ... ______

Who I went with ... ______

When I went ... ______

What I did... ______

What I saw... ______

What I learned... ______

An unforgettable moment... ______

A laughable moment... ______

A surprising moment... ______

An unforeseeable moment... ______

MY LIST

- ☐ ______
- ☐ ______
- ☐ ______
- ☐ ______
- ☐ ______
- ☐ ______
- ☐ ______
- ☐ ______
- ☐ ______
- ☐ ______
- ☐ ______
- ☐ ______

 Snapped a selfie | Location... ______

 Took a park sign selfie? - Y | N

The weather was ... 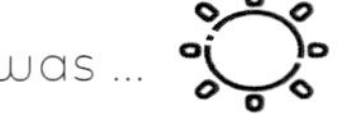      

Plan Your Trip:

☐ Trip Plan Completed

☐ Day Trip ☐ Overnight Stay

Reservations required: ☐y ☐n

Date reservations made: ____________

Refund Policy: ☐y ☐n Site/Room #: ______

Confirmation #: ____________

Miles to travel: ____________

Time traveling: ____________

Dog friendly?: ☐y ☐n

Destination Information:

____

____

Places we discovered along the way

____

____

____

Places to stop and see along the way

____

____

Would you go again?: ☐y ☐n Open all year?: ☐y ☐n

Activities Accomplished:

- ☐ Archery
- ☐ Biking
- ☐ Birding
- ☐ Boating
- ☐ Camping
- ☐ Caving
- ☐ Geocaching
- ☐ Fishing
- ☐ Hiking
- ☐ Horseback Riding
- ☐ Hunting
- ☐ Off-Roading
- ☐ Paddle Boarding
- ☐ Photography
- ☐ Picnicking
- ☐ Rock Climbing
- ☐ Shooting Range
- ☐ Snowshoeing
- ☐ Stargazing
- ☐ Swimming
- ☐ Tennis
- ☐ Walking
- ☐ Wildlife Watching
- ☐ ____________
- ☐ ____________
- ☐ ____________
- ☐ ____________
- ☐ ____________

Traveled by:

☐ ☐ ☐ ☐ ☐ ☐ ☐ ☐ ☐ ☐ ☐ ☐

Add your favorite ticket stub, postcard, photo, stamp or drawing here

N W E S NOT ALL THOSE WHO WANDER ARE LOST

Ponce de Leon Springs State Park

County: Holmes

2860 Ponce de Leon Springs Road, Ponce de Leon FL 32455 | 850-836-4281

Website: https://www.floridastateparks.org/parks-and-trails/ponce-de-leon-springs-state-park
Email: FSP.Feedback@FloridaDEP.gov

Water Body: Mill Creek - Sandy Creek

Size: 420 acres
Established: 1970

14 million gallons 53 million liters of 68 ¬∞F 20 ¬∞C water outflow daily

Star Rating ☆☆☆☆☆

What souvenir did you bring home?... Decal Magnet

My favorite thing about this place is...

Why I went ...

Who I went with ...

When I went ...

What I did...

What I saw...

What I learned...

An unforgettable moment...

A laughable moment...

A surprising moment...

An unforeseeable moment...

My List

- ☐
- ☐
- ☐
- ☐
- ☐
- ☐
- ☐
- ☐
- ☐
- ☐
- ☐
- ☐

Snapped a selfie | Location...

Took a park sign selfie? - Y | N

The weather was ...

Plan Your Trip:

☐ Trip Plan Completed

☐ Day Trip ☐ Overnight Stay

Reservations required: ☐y ☐n

Date reservations made: ____________

Refund Policy: ☐y ☐n Site/Room #: ______

Confirmation #: ____________

Miles to travel: ____________

Time traveling: ____________

Dog friendly?: ☐y ☐n

Destination Information:

Places we discovered along the way

Places to stop and see along the way

Would you go again?: ☐y ☐n Open all year?: ☐y ☐n

Activities Accomplished:

☐ Archery	☐ Fishing	☐ Picnicking	☐ Walking
☐ Biking	☐ Hiking	☐ Rock Climbing	☐ Wildlife Watching
☐ Birding	☐ Horseback Riding	☐ Shooting Range	☐ ____________
☐ Boating	☐ Hunting	☐ Snowshoeing	☐ ____________
☐ Camping	☐ Off-Roading	☐ Stargazing	☐ ____________
☐ Caving	☐ Paddle Boarding	☐ Swimming	☐ ____________
☐ Geocaching	☐ Photography	☐ Tennis	☐ ____________

Traveled by:

Add your favorite ticket stub, postcard, photo, stamp or drawing here

PUMPKIN HILL CREEK PRESERVE STATE PARK

County: Duval
13802 Pumpkin Hill Road, Jacksonville FL 32226 | 904-696-5980

Website: https://www.floridastateparks.org/parks-and-trails/pumpkin-hill-creek-preserve-state-park
Email: FSP.Feedback@FloridaDEP.gov

Water Body: Atlantic Ocean

Size: 3,896 acres
Established: 2003

Part of Talbot Islands State Parks

Star Rating ☆☆☆☆☆

What souvenir did you bring home?... Decal Magnet

My favorite thing about this place is...

Why I went ...

Who I went with ...

When I went ...

What I did...

What I saw...

What I learned...

An unforgettable moment...

A laughable moment...

A surprising moment...

An unforeseeable moment...

MY LIST

- ☐
- ☐
- ☐
- ☐
- ☐
- ☐
- ☐
- ☐
- ☐
- ☐
- ☐
- ☐

Snapped a selfie | Location...

Took a park sign selfie? - Y | N

The weather was ...

Plan Your Trip:

☐ Trip Plan Completed

☐ Day Trip ☐ Overnight Stay

Reservations required: ☐y ☐n

Date reservations made: ____________

Refund Policy: ☐y ☐n Site/Room #: ______

Confirmation #: ____________

Miles to travel: ____________

Time traveling: ____________

Dog friendly?: ☐y ☐n

Destination Information:

____

____

Places we discovered along the way

____

____

____

Places to stop and see along the way

____

____

Activities Accomplished:

Would you go again?: ☐y ☐n Open all year?: ☐y ☐n

☐ Archery
☐ Biking
☐ Birding
☐ Boating
☐ Camping
☐ Caving
☐ Geocaching
☐ Fishing
☐ Hiking
☐ Horseback Riding
☐ Hunting
☐ Off-Roading
☐ Paddle Boarding
☐ Photography
☐ Picnicking
☐ Rock Climbing
☐ Shooting Range
☐ Snowshoeing
☐ Stargazing
☐ Swimming
☐ Tennis
☐ Walking
☐ Wildlife Watching
☐ ____________
☐ ____________
☐ ____________
☐ ____________
☐ ____________

Traveled by:

☐ ☐ ☐ ☐ ☐ ☐ ☐ ☐ ☐ ☐ ☐ ☐

Add your favorite ticket stub, postcard, photo, stamp or drawing here

Rainbow Springs State Park

County: Marion
19158 S.W. 81st Place Road, Dunnellon FL 34432 | 352-465-8555

Website: https://www.floridastateparks.org/parks-and-trails/rainbow-springs-state-park
Email: FSP.Feedback@FloridaDEP.gov

Water Body: Rainbow River

Size: 1,472 acres
Established: 1990

600 million gallons 2.3 billion liters of 68 ¬∞F 20 ¬∞C water outflow daily

Star Rating
☆☆☆☆☆

What souvenir did you bring home?... Decal Magnet

My favorite thing about this place is...

Why I went ...

Who I went with ...

When I went ...

What I did...

What I saw...

What I learned...

An unforgettable moment...

A laughable moment...

A surprising moment...

An unforeseeable moment...

My List

- ☐
- ☐
- ☐
- ☐
- ☐
- ☐
- ☐
- ☐
- ☐
- ☐
- ☐
- ☐

 Snapped a selfie | Location...

 Took a park sign selfie? - y | n

The weather was ...       

Plan Your Trip:

☐ Trip Plan Completed

☐ Day Trip ☐ Overnight Stay

Reservations required: ☐y ☐n

Date reservations made: ______

Refund Policy: ☐y ☐n Site/Room #: ______

Confirmation #: ______

Miles to travel: ______

Time traveling: ______

Dog friendly?: ☐y ☐n

Destination Information:

______

______

Places we discovered along the way

______

______

______

Places to stop and see along the way

______

______

Activities Accomplished:

Would you go again?: ☐y ☐n

Open all year?: ☐y ☐n

- ☐ Archery
- ☐ Biking
- ☐ Birding
- ☐ Boating
- ☐ Camping
- ☐ Caving
- ☐ Geocaching
- ☐ Fishing
- ☐ Hiking
- ☐ Horseback Riding
- ☐ Hunting
- ☐ Off-Roading
- ☐ Paddle Boarding
- ☐ Photography
- ☐ Picnicking
- ☐ Rock Climbing
- ☐ Shooting Range
- ☐ Snowshoeing
- ☐ Stargazing
- ☐ Swimming
- ☐ Tennis
- ☐ Walking
- ☐ Wildlife Watching
- ☐ ______
- ☐ ______
- ☐ ______
- ☐ ______
- ☐ ______

Traveled by:

☐ ☐ ☐ ☐ ☐ ☐ ☐ ☐ ☐ ☐ ☐ ☐

Add your favorite ticket stub, postcard, photo, stamp or drawing here

N NOT ALL THOSE WHO WANDER ARE LOST E S W

Ravine Gardens State Park

County: Putnam
1600 Twigg St., Palatka FL 32177 | 386-329-3721

Website: https://www.floridastateparks.org/parks-and-trails/ravine-gardens-state-park
Email: FSP.Feedback@FloridaDEP.gov

Water Body: St. Johns River

Size: 59 acres
Established: 1934

Gardens built by Works Progress Administration in 1933

Star Rating ☆☆☆☆☆

What souvenir did you bring home?... Decal Magnet

My favorite thing about this place is...

Why I went ...

Who I went with ...

When I went ...

What I did...

What I saw...

What I learned...

An unforgettable moment...

A laughable moment...

A surprising moment...

An unforeseeable moment...

My List

- ☐
- ☐
- ☐
- ☐
- ☐
- ☐
- ☐
- ☐
- ☐
- ☐
- ☐
- ☐

Snapped a selfie | Location...

Took a park sign selfie? - Y | N

The weather was ...

Plan Your Trip:

☐ Trip Plan Completed

☐ Day Trip ☐ Overnight Stay

Reservations required: ☐y ☐n

Date reservations made: ______

Refund Policy: ☐y ☐n Site/Room #: ______

Confirmation #: ______

Miles to travel: ______

Time traveling: ______

Dog friendly?: ☐y ☐n

Destination Information:

______

______

Places we discovered along the way

______

______

______

Places to stop and see along the way

______

______

Would you go again?: ☐y ☐n

Open all year?: ☐y ☐n

Activities Accomplished:

- ☐ Archery
- ☐ Biking
- ☐ Birding
- ☐ Boating
- ☐ Camping
- ☐ Caving
- ☐ Geocaching
- ☐ Fishing
- ☐ Hiking
- ☐ Horseback Riding
- ☐ Hunting
- ☐ Off-Roading
- ☐ Paddle Boarding
- ☐ Photography
- ☐ Picnicking
- ☐ Rock Climbing
- ☐ Shooting Range
- ☐ Snowshoeing
- ☐ Stargazing
- ☐ Swimming
- ☐ Tennis
- ☐ Walking
- ☐ Wildlife Watching
- ☐ ______
- ☐ ______
- ☐ ______
- ☐ ______
- ☐ ______

Traveled by:

☐ ☐ ☐ ☐ ☐ ☐ ☐ ☐ ☐ ☐ ☐ ☐

Add your favorite ticket stub, postcard, photo, stamp or drawing here

N
NOT ALL THOSE WHO WANDER ARE LOST
W E
S

River Rise Preserve State Park

County: Columbia
373 S.W. U.S. Highway 27, Fort White FL 32643 | 386-454-1853

Website: https://www.floridastateparks.org/riverrise
Email: FSP.Feedback@FloridaDEP.gov

Water Body: Santa Fe River

Size: 4,500 acres
Established: 1974

Location where Santa Fe River reemerges after 3 miles 4.8 km underground

Star Rating ☆☆☆☆☆

What souvenir did you bring home?... Decal Magnet

My favorite thing about this place is...

Why I went ...

Who I went with ...

When I went ...

What I did...

What I saw...

What I learned...

An unforgettable moment...

A laughable moment...

A surprising moment...

An unforeseeable moment...

My List

- ☐
- ☐
- ☐
- ☐
- ☐
- ☐
- ☐
- ☐
- ☐
- ☐
- ☐
- ☐

 Snapped a selfie | Location...

 Took a park sign selfie? - Y | N

The weather was ...      

Plan Your Trip:

☐ Trip Plan Completed

☐ Day Trip ☐ Overnight Stay

Reservations required: ☐y ☐n

Date reservations made: ______

Refund Policy: ☐y ☐n Site/Room #: ______

Confirmation #: ______

Miles to travel: ______

Time traveling: ______

Dog friendly?: ☐y ☐n

Destination Information:

Places we discovered along the way

Places to stop and see along the way

Would you go again?: ☐y ☐n Open all year?: ☐y ☐n

Activities Accomplished:

☐ Archery
☐ Biking
☐ Birding
☐ Boating
☐ Camping
☐ Caving
☐ Geocaching
☐ Fishing
☐ Hiking
☐ Horseback Riding
☐ Hunting
☐ Off-Roading
☐ Paddle Boarding
☐ Photography
☐ Picnicking
☐ Rock Climbing
☐ Shooting Range
☐ Snowshoeing
☐ Stargazing
☐ Swimming
☐ Tennis
☐ Walking
☐ Wildlife Watching
☐ ______
☐ ______
☐ ______
☐ ______
☐ ______

Traveled by:

☐ ☐ ☐ ☐ ☐ ☐ ☐ ☐ ☐ ☐ ☐ ☐

Add your favorite ticket stub, postcard, photo, stamp or drawing here

N E S W
NOT ALL THOSE WHO WANDER ARE LOST

Rock Springs Run State Reserve

County: Lake

30601 County Road 433, Sorrento FL 32776 | 407-553-4383

Website: **https://www.floridastateparks.org/parks-and-trails/rock-springs-run-state-reserve**
Email: FSP.Feedback@FloridaDEP.gov

Water Body: Wekiva River

Size: 14,150 acres
Established: 1983

Joins Wekiwa Spring run to create the Wekiva River

Star Rating ☆☆☆☆☆

What souvenir did you bring home?... Decal Magnet

My favorite thing about this place is...

Why I went ...

Who I went with ...

When I went ...

What I did...

What I saw...

What I learned...

An unforgettable moment...

A laughable moment...

A surprising moment...

An unforeseeable moment...

My List

- ☐
- ☐
- ☐
- ☐
- ☐
- ☐
- ☐
- ☐
- ☐
- ☐
- ☐
- ☐

Snapped a selfie | Location...

Took a park sign selfie? - Y | N

The weather was ...

Plan Your Trip:

☐ Trip Plan Completed

☐ Day Trip ☐ Overnight Stay

Reservations required: ☐y ☐n

Date reservations made: ____________

Refund Policy: ☐y ☐n Site/Room #: ____

Confirmation #: ____________

Miles to travel: ____________

Time traveling: ____________

Dog friendly?: ☐y ☐n

Destination Information:

Places we discovered along the way

Places to stop and see along the way

Would you go again?: ☐y ☐n Open all year?: ☐y ☐n

Activities Accomplished:

- ☐ Archery
- ☐ Biking
- ☐ Birding
- ☐ Boating
- ☐ Camping
- ☐ Caving
- ☐ Geocaching
- ☐ Fishing
- ☐ Hiking
- ☐ Horseback Riding
- ☐ Hunting
- ☐ Off-Roading
- ☐ Paddle Boarding
- ☐ Photography
- ☐ Picnicking
- ☐ Rock Climbing
- ☐ Shooting Range
- ☐ Snowshoeing
- ☐ Stargazing
- ☐ Swimming
- ☐ Tennis
- ☐ Walking
- ☐ Wildlife Watching
- ☐ ____________
- ☐ ____________
- ☐ ____________
- ☐ ____________
- ☐ ____________

Traveled by:

☐ ☐ ☐ ☐ ☐ ☐ ☐ ☐ ☐ ☐ ☐ ☐

Add your favorite ticket stub, postcard, photo, stamp or drawing here

N W E S NOT ALL THOSE WHO WANDER ARE LOST

San Felasco Hammock Preserve State Park

County: Alachua
13201 San Felasco Parkway, Alachua FL 32615 | 386-462-7905

Website: https://www.floridastateparks.org/parks-and-trails/san-felasco-hammock-preserve-state-park
Email: FSP.Feedback@FloridaDEP.gov

Water Body: small water bodies

Size: 7,360 acres
Established: 1974

A mature Florida forest and wildlife habitat with hiking, biking, and horse trails

Star Rating ☆☆☆☆☆

What souvenir did you bring home?... Decal Magnet

My favorite thing about this place is...

Why I went ...

Who I went with ...

When I went ...

What I did...

What I saw...

What I learned...

An unforgettable moment...

A laughable moment...

A surprising moment...

An unforeseeable moment...

My List

- ☐
- ☐
- ☐
- ☐
- ☐
- ☐
- ☐
- ☐
- ☐
- ☐
- ☐
- ☐

Snapped a selfie | Location...

Took a park sign selfie? - Y | N

The weather was ...

Plan Your Trip:

☐ Trip Plan Completed

☐ Day Trip ☐ Overnight Stay

Reservations required: ☐y ☐n

Date reservations made: ____________

Refund Policy: ☐y ☐n Site/Room #: ____

Confirmation #: ____________

Miles to travel: ____________

Time traveling: ____________

Dog friendly?: ☐y ☐n

Destination Information:

____

____

Places we discovered along the way

____

____

____

Places to stop and see along the way

____

____

Activities Accomplished:

Would you go again?: ☐y ☐n Open all year?: ☐y ☐n

☐ Archery
☐ Biking
☐ Birding
☐ Boating
☐ Camping
☐ Caving
☐ Geocaching
☐ Fishing
☐ Hiking
☐ Horseback Riding
☐ Hunting
☐ Off-Roading
☐ Paddle Boarding
☐ Photography
☐ Picnicking
☐ Rock Climbing
☐ Shooting Range
☐ Snowshoeing
☐ Stargazing
☐ Swimming
☐ Tennis
☐ Walking
☐ Wildlife Watching
☐ ____________
☐ ____________
☐ ____________
☐ ____________
☐ ____________

Traveled by:

☐ ☐ ☐ ☐ ☐ ☐ ☐ ☐ ☐ ☐ ☐ ☐

Add your favorite ticket stub, postcard, photo, stamp or drawing here

N E S W NOT ALL THOSE WHO WANDER ARE LOST

San Marcos de Apalache Historic State Park

County: Wakulla
148 Old Fort Road, St. Marks FL 32355 | 850-925-6216

Website: https://www.floridastateparks.org/parks-and-trails/san-marcos-de-apalache-historic-state-park
Email: FSP.Feedback@FloridaDEP.gov

Water Body: Wakulla River - St. Marks River

Size: 17 acres
Established: 1964

History of this national landmark dates to 1528

Star Rating ☆☆☆☆☆

What souvenir did you bring home?... Decal Magnet

My favorite thing about this place is... ______

Why I went ... ______

Who I went with ... ______

When I went ... ______

What I did... ______

What I saw... ______

What I learned... ______

An unforgettable moment... ______

A laughable moment... ______

A surprising moment... ______

An unforeseeable moment... ______

Snapped a selfie | Location... ______

Took a park sign selfie? - Y | N

The weather was ...

My List

- ☐ ______
- ☐ ______
- ☐ ______
- ☐ ______
- ☐ ______
- ☐ ______
- ☐ ______
- ☐ ______
- ☐ ______
- ☐ ______
- ☐ ______
- ☐ ______

Plan Your Trip:

☐ Trip Plan Completed

☐ Day Trip ☐ Overnight Stay

Reservations required: ☐y ☐n

Date reservations made: ____________

Refund Policy: ☐y ☐n Site/Room #: ____

Confirmation #: ____________

Miles to travel: ____________

Time traveling: ____________

Dog friendly?: ☐y ☐n

Destination Information:

Places we discovered along the way

Places to stop and see along the way

Would you go again?: ☐y ☐n Open all year?: ☐y ☐n

Activities Accomplished:

- ☐ Archery
- ☐ Biking
- ☐ Birding
- ☐ Boating
- ☐ Camping
- ☐ Caving
- ☐ Geocaching
- ☐ Fishing
- ☐ Hiking
- ☐ Horseback Riding
- ☐ Hunting
- ☐ Off-Roading
- ☐ Paddle Boarding
- ☐ Photography
- ☐ Picnicking
- ☐ Rock Climbing
- ☐ Shooting Range
- ☐ Snowshoeing
- ☐ Stargazing
- ☐ Swimming
- ☐ Tennis
- ☐ Walking
- ☐ Wildlife Watching
- ☐ ____________
- ☐ ____________
- ☐ ____________
- ☐ ____________
- ☐ ____________

Traveled by:

☐ ☐ ☐ ☐ ☐ ☐ ☐ ☐ ☐ ☐ ☐ ☐

Add your favorite ticket stub, postcard, photo, stamp or drawing here

N
NOT ALL THOSE WHO WANDER ARE LOST
W E
S

San Pedro Underwater Archaeological Preserve State Park

County: Monroe
77200 Overseas Highway, Islamorada FL 33036 | 305-664-2540

Website: https://www.floridastateparks.org/SanPedro
Email: FSP.Feedback@FloridaDEP.gov

Water Body: Atlantic Ocean

Size: 644 acres
Established: 1989

Dutch-built ship sank in a hurricane on July 13, 1733

Star Rating ☆☆☆☆☆

What souvenir did you bring home?... Decal Magnet ____

My favorite thing about this place is... ____

Why I went ... ____

Who I went with ... ____

When I went ... ____

What I did... ____

What I saw... ____

What I learned... ____

An unforgettable moment... ____

A laughable moment... ____

A surprising moment... ____

An unforeseeable moment... ____

My List

- ☐ ____
- ☐ ____
- ☐ ____
- ☐ ____
- ☐ ____
- ☐ ____
- ☐ ____
- ☐ ____
- ☐ ____
- ☐ ____
- ☐ ____
- ☐ ____

 Snapped a selfie | Location... ____

 Took a park sign selfie? - Y | N

The weather was ... 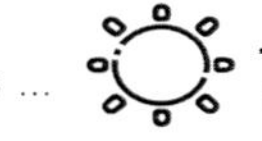     

Plan Your Trip:

☐ Trip Plan Completed

☐ Day Trip ☐ Overnight Stay

Reservations required: ☐y ☐n

Date reservations made: ____________

Refund Policy: ☐y ☐n Site/Room #: ______

Confirmation #: ____________

Miles to travel: ____________

Time traveling: ____________

Dog friendly?: ☐y ☐n

Destination Information:

____

____

Places we discovered along the way

____

____

____

Places to stop and see along the way

____

____

Would you go again?: ☐y ☐n Open all year?: ☐y ☐n

Activities Accomplished:

☐ Archery	☐ Fishing	☐ Picnicking	☐ Walking
☐ Biking	☐ Hiking	☐ Rock Climbing	☐ Wildlife Watching
☐ Birding	☐ Horseback Riding	☐ Shooting Range	☐ ____________
☐ Boating	☐ Hunting	☐ Snowshoeing	☐ ____________
☐ Camping	☐ Off-Roading	☐ Stargazing	☐ ____________
☐ Caving	☐ Paddle Boarding	☐ Swimming	☐ ____________
☐ Geocaching	☐ Photography	☐ Tennis	☐ ____________

Traveled by:

☐ ☐ ☐ ☐ ☐ ☐ ☐ ☐ ☐ ☐ ☐ ☐

Add your favorite ticket stub, postcard, photo, stamp or drawing here

N W E S NOT ALL THOSE WHO WANDER ARE LOST

Savannas Preserve State Park

County: St. Lucie Martin
2541 S.E .Walton Road, Port St. Lucie FL 34952 | 772-398-2779

Website: https://www.floridastateparks.org/parks-and-trails/savannas-preserve-state-park
Email: FSP.Feedback@FloridaDEP.gov

Water Body: Indian River

Size: 6,000 acres
Established: 1977

Area around Jensen Beach was known as the "Pineapple Capital of the World" from 1895 to 1920

Star Rating ☆☆☆☆☆

What souvenir did you bring home?... Decal Magnet

My favorite thing about this place is...

Why I went ...

Who I went with ...

When I went ...

What I did...

What I saw...

What I learned...

An unforgettable moment...

A laughable moment...

A surprising moment...

An unforeseeable moment...

Snapped a selfie | Location...

Took a park sign selfie? - Y | N

The weather was ...

My List

- [ ]
- [ ]
- [ ]
- [ ]
- [ ]
- [ ]
- [ ]
- [ ]
- [ ]
- [ ]
- [ ]
- [ ]

Plan Your Trip:

☐ Trip Plan Completed

☐ Day Trip ☐ Overnight Stay

Reservations required: ☐y ☐n

Date reservations made: ______

Refund Policy: ☐y ☐n Site/Room #: ______

Confirmation #: ______

Miles to travel: ______

Time traveling: ______

Dog friendly?: ☐y ☐n

Destination Information:

______

______

Places we discovered along the way

______

______

______

Places to stop and see along the way

______

______

Would you go again?: ☐y ☐n Open all year?: ☐y ☐n

Activities Accomplished:

- ☐ Archery
- ☐ Biking
- ☐ Birding
- ☐ Boating
- ☐ Camping
- ☐ Caving
- ☐ Geocaching
- ☐ Fishing
- ☐ Hiking
- ☐ Horseback Riding
- ☐ Hunting
- ☐ Off-Roading
- ☐ Paddle Boarding
- ☐ Photography
- ☐ Picnicking
- ☐ Rock Climbing
- ☐ Shooting Range
- ☐ Snowshoeing
- ☐ Stargazing
- ☐ Swimming
- ☐ Tennis
- ☐ Walking
- ☐ Wildlife Watching
- ☐ ______
- ☐ ______
- ☐ ______
- ☐ ______
- ☐ ______

Traveled by:

☐ ☐ ☐ ☐ ☐ ☐ ☐ ☐ ☐ ☐ ☐ ☐

Add your favorite ticket stub, postcard, photo, stamp or drawing here

N W E S NOT ALL THOSE WHO WANDER ARE LOST

Seabranch Preserve State Park

County: Martin

Trailhead - 6093 S.E. Dixie Highway, Stuart FL 34997 | 772-219-1880

Website: https://www.floridastateparks.org/parks-and-trails/seabranch-preserve-state-park
Email: FSP.Feedback@FloridaDEP.gov

Water Body: Indian River lagoon

Size: 7,360 acres
Established: 1992

Four different natural habitats within short distance

Star Rating ☆☆☆☆☆

What souvenir did you bring home?... Decal Magnet

My favorite thing about this place is...

Why I went ...

Who I went with ...

When I went ...

What I did...

What I saw...

What I learned...

An unforgettable moment...

A laughable moment...

A surprising moment...

An unforeseeable moment...

My List

- ☐
- ☐
- ☐
- ☐
- ☐
- ☐
- ☐
- ☐
- ☐
- ☐
- ☐
- ☐

 Snapped a selfie | Location...

 Took a park sign selfie? - Y | N

The weather was ...      

Plan Your Trip:

☐ Trip Plan Completed

☐ Day Trip ☐ Overnight Stay

Reservations required: ☐y ☐n

Date reservations made: ______

Refund Policy: ☐y ☐n Site/Room #: ______

Confirmation #: ______

Miles to travel: ______

Time traveling: ______

Dog friendly?: ☐y ☐n

Destination Information:

______

______

Places we discovered along the way

______

______

______

Places to stop and see along the way

______

______

Activities Accomplished:

Would you go again?: ☐y ☐n

Open all year?: ☐y ☐n

- ☐ Archery
- ☐ Biking
- ☐ Birding
- ☐ Boating
- ☐ Camping
- ☐ Caving
- ☐ Geocaching
- ☐ Fishing
- ☐ Hiking
- ☐ Horseback Riding
- ☐ Hunting
- ☐ Off-Roading
- ☐ Paddle Boarding
- ☐ Photography
- ☐ Picnicking
- ☐ Rock Climbing
- ☐ Shooting Range
- ☐ Snowshoeing
- ☐ Stargazing
- ☐ Swimming
- ☐ Tennis
- ☐ Walking
- ☐ Wildlife Watching
- ☐ ______
- ☐ ______
- ☐ ______
- ☐ ______
- ☐ ______

Traveled by:

☐ ☐ ☐ ☐ ☐ ☐ ☐ ☐ ☐ ☐ ☐ ☐

Add your favorite ticket stub, postcard, photo, stamp or drawing here

N E S W NOT ALL THOSE WHO WANDER ARE LOST

SEBASTIAN INLET STATE PARK

County: Brevard Indian River
9700 South Highway A1A, Melbourne Beach FL 32951 | 321-984-4852

Website: https://www.floridastateparks.org/Sebastian-Inlet
Email: FSP.Feedback@FloridaDEP.gov

Water Body: Sebastian Inlet

Size: 755 acres
Established: 1970

Park never closes; second most visited Florida park

Star Rating ☆☆☆☆☆

What souvenir did you bring home?... Decal Magnet

My favorite thing about this place is...

Why I went ...

Who I went with ...

When I went ...

What I did...

What I saw...

What I learned...

An unforgettable moment...

A laughable moment...

A surprising moment...

An unforeseeable moment...

MY LIST

- ☐
- ☐
- ☐
- ☐
- ☐
- ☐
- ☐
- ☐
- ☐
- ☐
- ☐
- ☐

Snapped a selfie | Location...

Took a park sign selfie? - Y | N

The weather was ...

Plan Your Trip:

☐ Trip Plan Completed

☐ Day Trip ☐ Overnight Stay

Reservations required: ☐y ☐n

Date reservations made: ______

Refund Policy: ☐y ☐n Site/Room #: ______

Confirmation #: ______

Miles to travel: ______

Time traveling: ______

Dog friendly?: ☐y ☐n

Destination Information:

______

______

Places we discovered along the way

______

______

______

Places to stop and see along the way

______

______

Activities Accomplished:

Would you go again?: ☐y ☐n

Open all year?: ☐y ☐n

☐ Archery
☐ Biking
☐ Birding
☐ Boating
☐ Camping
☐ Caving
☐ Geocaching
☐ Fishing
☐ Hiking
☐ Horseback Riding
☐ Hunting
☐ Off-Roading
☐ Paddle Boarding
☐ Photography
☐ Picnicking
☐ Rock Climbing
☐ Shooting Range
☐ Snowshoeing
☐ Stargazing
☐ Swimming
☐ Tennis
☐ Walking
☐ Wildlife Watching
☐ ______
☐ ______
☐ ______
☐ ______
☐ ______

Traveled by:

☐ ☐ ☐ ☐ ☐ ☐ ☐ ☐ ☐ ☐ ☐ ☐

Add your favorite ticket stub, postcard, photo, stamp or drawing here

N E S W NOT ALL THOSE WHO WANDER ARE LOST

Silver Springs State Park

County: Marion

5656 E Silver Springs Blvd, Silver Springs, FL 34488 | 352-261-5840

Website: https://silversprings.com
Email: Info@silversprings.com

Water Body: Silver River

Size: 5,000 acres
Established: 1987

The headspring area was the focal point of Silver Springs Nature Theme Park, a now-defunct commercial attraction

Star Rating ☆☆☆☆☆

What souvenir did you bring home?... Decal Magnet

My favorite thing about this place is...

Why I went ...

Who I went with ...

When I went ...

What I did...

What I saw...

What I learned...

An unforgettable moment...

A laughable moment...

A surprising moment...

An unforeseeable moment...

Snapped a selfie | Location...

Took a park sign selfie? - Y | N

The weather was ...

My List

- ☐
- ☐
- ☐
- ☐
- ☐
- ☐
- ☐
- ☐
- ☐
- ☐
- ☐
- ☐

Plan Your Trip:

☐ Trip Plan Completed

☐ Day Trip ☐ Overnight Stay

Reservations required: ☐y ☐n

Date reservations made: ____________

Refund Policy: ☐y ☐n Site/Room #: ______

Confirmation #: ____________

Miles to travel: ____________

Time traveling: ____________

Dog friendly?: ☐y ☐n

Destination Information:

Places we discovered along the way

Places to stop and see along the way

Would you go again?: ☐y ☐n

Open all year?: ☐y ☐n

Activities Accomplished:

☐ Archery	☐ Fishing	☐ Picnicking	☐ Walking
☐ Biking	☐ Hiking	☐ Rock Climbing	☐ Wildlife Watching
☐ Birding	☐ Horseback Riding	☐ Shooting Range	☐ ______
☐ Boating	☐ Hunting	☐ Snowshoeing	☐ ______
☐ Camping	☐ Off-Roading	☐ Stargazing	☐ ______
☐ Caving	☐ Paddle Boarding	☐ Swimming	☐ ______
☐ Geocaching	☐ Photography	☐ Tennis	☐ ______

Traveled by:

☐ ☐ ☐ ☐ ☐ ☐ ☐ ☐ ☐ ☐ ☐ ☐

Add your favorite ticket stub, postcard, photo, stamp or drawing here

N
NOT ALL THOSE WHO WANDER ARE LOST
W E S

Skyway Fishing Pier State Park

County: Hillsborough Manatee
4905 34th St. South #5000, St. Petersburg FL 33711 | 727-865-0668

Website: https://www.floridastateparks.org/parks-and-trails/skyway-fishing-pier-state-park
Email: FSP.Feedback@FloridaDEP.gov

Water Body: Tampa Bay

Size: 26,000 ft
Established: 1994

Utilizes approaches to old Sunshine Skyway Bridge, following the 1980 collision by MV Summit Venture and construction of a new bridge

Star Rating ☆☆☆☆☆

What souvenir did you bring home?... Decal Magnet

My favorite thing about this place is...

Why I went ...

Who I went with ...

When I went ...

What I did...

What I saw...

What I learned...

An unforgettable moment...

A laughable moment...

A surprising moment...

An unforeseeable moment...

My List

- ☐
- ☐
- ☐
- ☐
- ☐
- ☐
- ☐
- ☐
- ☐
- ☐
- ☐
- ☐

Snapped a selfie | Location...

Took a park sign selfie? - Y | N

The weather was ...

Plan Your Trip:

☐ Trip Plan Completed

☐ Day Trip ☐ Overnight Stay

Reservations required: ☐y ☐n

Date reservations made: ____

Refund Policy: ☐y ☐n Site/Room #: ____

Confirmation #: ____

Miles to travel: ____

Time traveling: ____

Dog friendly?: ☐y ☐n

Destination Information:

____

____

Places we discovered along the way

____

____

____

Places to stop and see along the way

____

____

Activities Accomplished:

Would you go again?: ☐y ☐n

Open all year?: ☐y ☐n

☐ Archery
☐ Biking
☐ Birding
☐ Boating
☐ Camping
☐ Caving
☐ Geocaching
☐ Fishing
☐ Hiking
☐ Horseback Riding
☐ Hunting
☐ Off-Roading
☐ Paddle Boarding
☐ Photography
☐ Picnicking
☐ Rock Climbing
☐ Shooting Range
☐ Snowshoeing
☐ Stargazing
☐ Swimming
☐ Tennis
☐ Walking
☐ Wildlife Watching
☐ ____
☐ ____
☐ ____
☐ ____
☐ ____

Traveled by:

☐ ☐ ☐ ☐ ☐ ☐ ☐ ☐ ☐ ☐ ☐ ☐

Add your favorite ticket stub, postcard, photo, stamp or drawing here

N E S W NOT ALL THOSE WHO WANDER ARE LOST

St. Andrews State Park

County: Bay

4607 State Park Lane, Panama City Beach FL 32408 | 850-708-6100

Website: https://www.floridastateparks.org/parks-and-trails/st-andrews-state-park
Email: FSP.Feedback@FloridaDEP.gov

Water Body: Gulf of Mexico - Grand Lagoon

Size: 1,200 acres
Established: 1950

Named "America's Best Beach" in 1995

Star Rating ☆☆☆☆☆

What souvenir did you bring home?... Decal Magnet

My favorite thing about this place is...

Why I went ...

Who I went with ...

When I went ...

What I did...

What I saw...

What I learned...

An unforgettable moment...

A laughable moment...

A surprising moment...

An unforeseeable moment...

My List

- ☐
- ☐
- ☐
- ☐
- ☐
- ☐
- ☐
- ☐
- ☐
- ☐
- ☐
- ☐

Snapped a selfie | Location...

Took a park sign selfie? - Y | N

The weather was ...

Plan Your Trip:

☐ Trip Plan Completed

☐ Day Trip ☐ Overnight Stay

Reservations required: ☐y ☐n

Date reservations made: ____

Refund Policy: ☐y ☐n Site/Room #: ____

Confirmation #: ____

Miles to travel: ____

Time traveling: ____

Dog friendly?: ☐y ☐n

Destination Information:

____

____

Places we discovered along the way

____

____

____

Places to stop and see along the way

____

____

Would you go again?: ☐y ☐n

Open all year?: ☐y ☐n

Activities Accomplished:

- ☐ Archery
- ☐ Biking
- ☐ Birding
- ☐ Boating
- ☐ Camping
- ☐ Caving
- ☐ Geocaching
- ☐ Fishing
- ☐ Hiking
- ☐ Horseback Riding
- ☐ Hunting
- ☐ Off-Roading
- ☐ Paddle Boarding
- ☐ Photography
- ☐ Picnicking
- ☐ Rock Climbing
- ☐ Shooting Range
- ☐ Snowshoeing
- ☐ Stargazing
- ☐ Swimming
- ☐ Tennis
- ☐ Walking
- ☐ Wildlife Watching
- ☐ ____
- ☐ ____
- ☐ ____
- ☐ ____
- ☐ ____

Traveled by:

☐ ☐ ☐ ☐ ☐ ☐ ☐ ☐ ☐ ☐ ☐ ☐

Add your favorite ticket stub, postcard, photo, stamp or drawing here

N E S W

NOT ALL THOSE WHO WANDER ARE LOST

St. George Island State Park

County: Franklin
1900 E. Gulf Beach Drive, St. George Island FL 32328 | 850-927-2111

Website: https://www.floridastateparks.org/parks-and-trails/dr-julian-g-bruce-st-george-island-state-park
Email: FSP.Feedback@FloridaDEP.gov

Water Body: Gulf of Mexico

Size: 1,962 acres
Established: 1963

Named "6th Best Beach in America" for 2011 after Hurricane Dennis destroyed the facilities in 2005

Star Rating ☆☆☆☆☆

What souvenir did you bring home?... Decal Magnet

My favorite thing about this place is...

Why I went ...

Who I went with ...

When I went ...

What I did...

What I saw...

What I learned...

An unforgettable moment...

A laughable moment...

A surprising moment...

An unforeseeable moment...

My List

- ☐
- ☐
- ☐
- ☐
- ☐
- ☐
- ☐
- ☐
- ☐
- ☐
- ☐
- ☐

Snapped a selfie | Location...

Took a park sign selfie? - Y | N

The weather was ...

Plan Your Trip:

☐ Trip Plan Completed

☐ Day Trip ☐ Overnight Stay

Reservations required: ☐y ☐n

Date reservations made: ____________

Refund Policy: ☐y ☐n Site/Room #: ______

Confirmation #: ____________

Miles to travel: ____________

Time traveling: ____________

Dog friendly?: ☐y ☐n

Destination Information:

Places we discovered along the way

Places to stop and see along the way

Would you go again?: ☐y ☐n Open all year?: ☐y ☐n

Activities Accomplished:

☐ Archery	☐ Fishing	☐ Picnicking	☐ Walking
☐ Biking	☐ Hiking	☐ Rock Climbing	☐ Wildlife Watching
☐ Birding	☐ Horseback Riding	☐ Shooting Range	☐ ____________
☐ Boating	☐ Hunting	☐ Snowshoeing	☐ ____________
☐ Camping	☐ Off-Roading	☐ Stargazing	☐ ____________
☐ Caving	☐ Paddle Boarding	☐ Swimming	☐ ____________
☐ Geocaching	☐ Photography	☐ Tennis	☐ ____________

Traveled by:

☐ ☐ ☐ ☐ ☐ ☐ ☐ ☐ ☐ ☐ ☐ ☐

Add your favorite ticket stub, postcard, photo, stamp or drawing here

N W E S NOT ALL THOSE WHO WANDER ARE LOST

St. Lucie Inlet Preserve State Park

County: Martin
Offshore Island, Port Salerno FL 34997 | 772-219-1880

Website: https://www.floridastateparks.org/parks-and-trails/st-lucie-inlet-preserve-state-park
Email: FSP.Feedback@FloridaDEP.gov

Water Body: Atlantic Ocean

Size: 928 acres
Established: 1965

Barrier island accessible only by boat

Star Rating ☆☆☆☆☆

What souvenir did you bring home?... Decal Magnet ________

My favorite thing about this place is... ________

Why I went ... ________

Who I went with ... ________

When I went ... ________

What I did... ________

What I saw... ________

What I learned... ________

An unforgettable moment... ________

A laughable moment... ________

A surprising moment... ________

An unforeseeable moment... ________

Snapped a selfie | Location... ________

Took a park sign selfie? - Y | N

The weather was ...

My List

- ☐ ________
- ☐ ________
- ☐ ________
- ☐ ________
- ☐ ________
- ☐ ________
- ☐ ________
- ☐ ________
- ☐ ________
- ☐ ________
- ☐ ________
- ☐ ________

Plan Your Trip:

☐ Trip Plan Completed

☐ Day Trip ☐ Overnight Stay

Reservations required: ☐y ☐n

Date reservations made: ______

Refund Policy: ☐y ☐n Site/Room #: ______

Confirmation #: ______

Miles to travel: ______

Time traveling: ______

Dog friendly?: ☐y ☐n

Destination Information:

______

______

Places we discovered along the way

______

______

______

Places to stop and see along the way

______

______

Would you go again?: ☐y ☐n

Open all year?: ☐y ☐n

Activities Accomplished:

- ☐ Archery
- ☐ Biking
- ☐ Birding
- ☐ Boating
- ☐ Camping
- ☐ Caving
- ☐ Geocaching
- ☐ Fishing
- ☐ Hiking
- ☐ Horseback Riding
- ☐ Hunting
- ☐ Off-Roading
- ☐ Paddle Boarding
- ☐ Photography
- ☐ Picnicking
- ☐ Rock Climbing
- ☐ Shooting Range
- ☐ Snowshoeing
- ☐ Stargazing
- ☐ Swimming
- ☐ Tennis
- ☐ Walking
- ☐ Wildlife Watching
- ☐ ______
- ☐ ______
- ☐ ______
- ☐ ______
- ☐ ______

Traveled by:

☐ ☐ ☐ ☐ ☐ ☐ ☐ ☐ ☐ ☐ ☐ ☐

Add your favorite ticket stub, postcard, photo, stamp or drawing here

N W E S NOT ALL THOSE WHO WANDER ARE LOST

St. Marks River Preserve State Park

County: Leon
11950 Tram Road, Tallahassee FL 32311 | 850-487-7989

Website: https://www.floridastateparks.org/parks-and-trails/st-marks-river-preserve-state-park
Email: FSP.Feedback@FloridaDEP.gov

Water Body: St. Marks River

Size: 2,589 acres
Established: 2007

The St. Marks River flows from the wetlands east of Tallahassee to the Gulf of Mexico

Star Rating ☆☆☆☆☆

What souvenir did you bring home?... Decal Magnet

My favorite thing about this place is...

Why I went ...

Who I went with ...

When I went ...

What I did...

What I saw...

What I learned...

An unforgettable moment...

A laughable moment...

A surprising moment...

An unforeseeable moment...

Snapped a selfie | Location...

Took a park sign selfie? - Y | N

The weather was ...

My List

- ☐
- ☐
- ☐
- ☐
- ☐
- ☐
- ☐
- ☐
- ☐
- ☐
- ☐
- ☐

PLAN YOUR TRIP:

☐ Trip Plan Completed

☐ Day Trip ☐ Overnight Stay

Reservations required: ☐y ☐n

Date reservations made: ______

Refund Policy: ☐y ☐n Site/Room #: ______

Confirmation #: ______

Miles to travel: ______

Time traveling: ______

Dog friendly?: ☐y ☐n

DESTINATION INFORMATION:

______

______

PLACES WE DISCOVERED ALONG THE WAY

______

______

______

PLACES TO STOP AND SEE ALONG THE WAY

______

______

Would you go again?: ☐y ☐n

Open all year?: ☐y ☐n

Activities Accomplished:

- ☐ Archery
- ☐ Biking
- ☐ Birding
- ☐ Boating
- ☐ Camping
- ☐ Caving
- ☐ Geocaching
- ☐ Fishing
- ☐ Hiking
- ☐ Horseback Riding
- ☐ Hunting
- ☐ Off-Roading
- ☐ Paddle Boarding
- ☐ Photography
- ☐ Picnicking
- ☐ Rock Climbing
- ☐ Shooting Range
- ☐ Snowshoeing
- ☐ Stargazing
- ☐ Swimming
- ☐ Tennis
- ☐ Walking
- ☐ Wildlife Watching
- ☐ ______
- ☐ ______
- ☐ ______
- ☐ ______
- ☐ ______

Traveled by:

☐ ☐ ☐ ☐ ☐ ☐ ☐ ☐ ☐ ☐ ☐ ☐

Add your favorite ticket stub, postcard, photo, stamp or drawing here

St. Sebastian River Preserve State Park

County: Brevard - Indian River
1000 Buffer Preserve Drive, Fellsmere FL 32948 | 321-953-5005

Website: https://www.floridastateparks.org/St-Sebastian
Email: FSP.Feedback@FloridaDEP.gov

Water Body: St. Sebastian River

Size: 22,000 acres
Established: 1995

The Hern√°ndez,ÄìCapron Trail was built to link St. Augustine with Fort Pierce during the Second Seminole War

Star Rating
☆☆☆☆☆

What souvenir did you bring home?... Decal Magnet

My favorite thing about this place is... ______

Why I went ... ______

Who I went with ... ______

When I went ... ______

What I did... ______

What I saw... ______

What I learned... ______

An unforgettable moment... ______

A laughable moment... ______

A surprising moment... ______

An unforeseeable moment... ______

My List

- ☐ ______
- ☐ ______
- ☐ ______
- ☐ ______
- ☐ ______
- ☐ ______
- ☐ ______
- ☐ ______
- ☐ ______
- ☐ ______
- ☐ ______
- ☐ ______

Snapped a selfie | Location... ______

Took a park sign selfie? - Y | N

The weather was ...

Plan Your Trip:

☐ Trip Plan Completed

☐ Day Trip ☐ Overnight Stay

Reservations required: ☐y ☐n

Date reservations made: ______

Refund Policy: ☐y ☐n Site/Room #: ______

Confirmation #: ______

Miles to travel: ______

Time traveling: ______

Dog friendly?: ☐y ☐n

Destination Information:

______

______

Places we discovered along the way

______

______

______

Places to stop and see along the way

______

______

Would you go again?: ☐y ☐n Open all year?: ☐y ☐n

Activities Accomplished:

☐ Archery
☐ Biking
☐ Birding
☐ Boating
☐ Camping
☐ Caving
☐ Geocaching
☐ Fishing
☐ Hiking
☐ Horseback Riding
☐ Hunting
☐ Off-Roading
☐ Paddle Boarding
☐ Photography
☐ Picnicking
☐ Rock Climbing
☐ Shooting Range
☐ Snowshoeing
☐ Stargazing
☐ Swimming
☐ Tennis
☐ Walking
☐ Wildlife Watching
☐ ______
☐ ______
☐ ______
☐ ______
☐ ______

Traveled by:

☐ ☐ ☐ ☐ ☐ ☐ ☐ ☐ ☐ ☐ ☐ ☐

Add your favorite ticket stub, postcard, photo, stamp or drawing here

N W E S NOT ALL THOSE WHO WANDER ARE LOST

Stephen Foster Folk Culture Center State Park

County: Hamilton
11016 Lillian Saunders Drive/U.S. Highway 41, White Springs FL 32096 | 386-397-4331

Website: https://www.floridastateparks.org/parks-and-trails/stephen-foster-folk-culture-center-state-park
Email: FSP.Feedback@FloridaDEP.gov

Water Body: Suwannee River

Size: 800 acres
Established: 1950

Carillon tower with 97 tubular bells plays Foster's songs every day

Star Rating ☆☆☆☆☆

What souvenir did you bring home?... Decal Magnet ______

My favorite thing about this place is... ______

Why I went ... ______

Who I went with ... ______

When I went ... ______

What I did... ______

What I saw... ______

What I learned... ______

An unforgettable moment... ______

A laughable moment... ______

A surprising moment... ______

An unforeseeable moment... ______

My List

- ☐ ______
- ☐ ______
- ☐ ______
- ☐ ______
- ☐ ______
- ☐ ______
- ☐ ______
- ☐ ______
- ☐ ______
- ☐ ______
- ☐ ______
- ☐ ______

Snapped a selfie | Location... ______

Took a park sign selfie? - Y | N

The weather was ... °F

PLAN YOUR TRIP:

☐ Trip Plan Completed

☐ Day Trip ☐ Overnight Stay

Reservations required: ☐y ☐n

Date reservations made: ____________

Refund Policy: ☐y ☐n Site/Room #: ______

Confirmation #: ____________

Miles to travel: ____________

Time traveling: ____________

Dog friendly?: ☐y ☐n

DESTINATION INFORMATION:

PLACES WE DISCOVERED ALONG THE WAY

PLACES TO STOP AND SEE ALONG THE WAY

Activities Accomplished:

Would you go again?: ☐y ☐n

Open all year?: ☐y ☐n

☐ Archery	☐ Fishing	☐ Picnicking	☐ Walking
☐ Biking	☐ Hiking	☐ Rock Climbing	☐ Wildlife Watching
☐ Birding	☐ Horseback Riding	☐ Shooting Range	☐ ______
☐ Boating	☐ Hunting	☐ Snowshoeing	☐ ______
☐ Camping	☐ Off-Roading	☐ Stargazing	☐ ______
☐ Caving	☐ Paddle Boarding	☐ Swimming	☐ ______
☐ Geocaching	☐ Photography	☐ Tennis	☐ ______

Traveled by:

☐ ☐ ☐ ☐ ☐ ☐ ☐ ☐ ☐ ☐ ☐ ☐

Add your favorite ticket stub, postcard, photo, stamp or drawing here

Stump Pass Beach State Park

County: Charlotte

900 Gulf Blvd., South end of Manasota Key, Englewood FL 34233 | 941-964-0375

Website: https://www.floridastateparks.org/parks-and-trails/stump-pass-beach-state-park
Email: FSP.Feedback@FloridaDEP.gov

Water Body: Gulf of Mexico

Size: 245 acres
Established: 1971

Day park consisting of three islands offer swimming and boating, shelling and hiking, fishing and diving

Star Rating ☆☆☆☆☆

What souvenir did you bring home?... Decal Magnet

My favorite thing about this place is...

Why I went ...

Who I went with ...

When I went ...

What I did...

What I saw...

What I learned...

An unforgettable moment...

A laughable moment...

A surprising moment...

An unforeseeable moment...

Snapped a selfie | Location...

Took a park sign selfie? - Y | N

The weather was ...

My List

- ☐
- ☐
- ☐
- ☐
- ☐
- ☐
- ☐
- ☐
- ☐
- ☐
- ☐
- ☐

PLAN YOUR TRIP:

☐ Trip Plan Completed

☐ Day Trip ☐ Overnight Stay

Reservations required: ☐y ☐n

Date reservations made: ____________

Refund Policy: ☐y ☐n Site/Room #: ______

Confirmation #: ____________

Miles to travel: ____________

Time traveling: ____________

Dog friendly?: ☐y ☐n

DESTINATION INFORMATION:

PLACES WE DISCOVERED ALONG THE WAY

PLACES TO STOP AND SEE ALONG THE WAY

Would you go again?: ☐y ☐n Open all year?: ☐y ☐n

Activities Accomplished:

☐ Archery
☐ Biking
☐ Birding
☐ Boating
☐ Camping
☐ Caving
☐ Geocaching
☐ Fishing
☐ Hiking
☐ Horseback Riding
☐ Hunting
☐ Off-Roading
☐ Paddle Boarding
☐ Photography
☐ Picnicking
☐ Rock Climbing
☐ Shooting Range
☐ Snowshoeing
☐ Stargazing
☐ Swimming
☐ Tennis
☐ Walking
☐ Wildlife Watching
☐ ____________
☐ ____________
☐ ____________
☐ ____________
☐ ____________

Traveled by:

☐ ☐ ☐ ☐ ☐ ☐ ☐ ☐ ☐ ☐ ☐ ☐

Add your favorite ticket stub, postcard, photo, stamp or drawing here

N W E S NOT ALL THOSE WHO WANDER ARE LOST

Suwannee River State Park

County: Suwannee
3631 201st Path, Live Oak FL 32060 | 386-362-2746

Website: **https://www.floridastateparks.org/parks-and-trails/suwannee-river-state-park**
Email: **FSP.Feedback@FloridaDEP.gov**

Water Body: Suwannee River - Withlacoochee River

Size: 1,800 acres
Established: 1951

The 1860 Columbus Cemetery, pieces from an 1800s sawmill, and Civil War earthworks are points of interest

What souvenir did you bring home?... Decal Magnet

Star Rating ☆☆☆☆☆

My favorite thing about this place is...

Why I went ...

Who I went with ...

When I went ...

What I did...

What I saw...

What I learned...

An unforgettable moment...

A laughable moment...

A surprising moment...

An unforeseeable moment...

My List

- ☐
- ☐
- ☐
- ☐
- ☐
- ☐
- ☐
- ☐
- ☐
- ☐
- ☐
- ☐

Snapped a selfie | Location...

Took a park sign selfie? - Y | N

The weather was ...

Plan Your Trip:

☐ Trip Plan Completed

☐ Day Trip ☐ Overnight Stay

Reservations required: ☐y ☐n

Date reservations made: ____________

Refund Policy: ☐y ☐n Site/Room #: ______

Confirmation #: ____________

Miles to travel: ____________

Time traveling: ____________

Dog friendly?: ☐y ☐n

Destination Information:

Places we discovered along the way

Places to stop and see along the way

Would you go again?: ☐y ☐n Open all year?: ☐y ☐n

Activities Accomplished:

☐ Archery	☐ Fishing	☐ Picnicking	☐ Walking
☐ Biking	☐ Hiking	☐ Rock Climbing	☐ Wildlife Watching
☐ Birding	☐ Horseback Riding	☐ Shooting Range	☐ ____________
☐ Boating	☐ Hunting	☐ Snowshoeing	☐ ____________
☐ Camping	☐ Off-Roading	☐ Stargazing	☐ ____________
☐ Caving	☐ Paddle Boarding	☐ Swimming	☐ ____________
☐ Geocaching	☐ Photography	☐ Tennis	☐ ____________

Traveled by:

☐ ☐ ☐ ☐ ☐ ☐ ☐ ☐ ☐ ☐ ☐ ☐

Add your favorite ticket stub, postcard, photo, stamp or drawing here

N E S W NOT ALL THOSE WHO WANDER ARE LOST

T.H. STONE MEMORIAL ST. JOSEPH PENINSULA STATE PARK

County: Gulf
8899 Cape San Blas Road, Port St. Joe FL 32456 | 850-227-1327

Website: https://www.floridastateparks.org/parks-and-trails/th-stone-memorial-st-joseph-peninsula-state-park
Email: FSP.Feedback@FloridaDEP.gov

Water Body: Gulf of Mexico

Size: 1,900 acres
Established: 1967

Dedicated to the former owner, who sold it to the U.S. Army in World War II

Star Rating ☆☆☆☆☆

What souvenir did you bring home?... Decal Magnet

My favorite thing about this place is...

Why I went ...

Who I went with ...

When I went ...

What I did...

What I saw...

What I learned...

An unforgettable moment...

A laughable moment...

A surprising moment...

An unforeseeable moment...

MY LIST

- ☐
- ☐
- ☐
- ☐
- ☐
- ☐
- ☐
- ☐
- ☐
- ☐
- ☐
- ☐

Snapped a selfie | Location...

Took a park sign selfie? - Y | N

The weather was ...

Plan Your Trip:

☐ Trip Plan Completed

☐ Day Trip ☐ Overnight Stay

Reservations required: ☐y ☐n

Date reservations made: ____________

Refund Policy: ☐y ☐n Site/Room #: ______

Confirmation #: ____________

Miles to travel: ____________

Time traveling: ____________

Dog friendly?: ☐y ☐n

Destination Information:

____

____

Places we discovered along the way

____

____

____

Places to stop and see along the way

____

____

Activities Accomplished:

Would you go again?: ☐y ☐n

Open all year?: ☐y ☐n

- ☐ Archery
- ☐ Biking
- ☐ Birding
- ☐ Boating
- ☐ Camping
- ☐ Caving
- ☐ Geocaching
- ☐ Fishing
- ☐ Hiking
- ☐ Horseback Riding
- ☐ Hunting
- ☐ Off-Roading
- ☐ Paddle Boarding
- ☐ Photography
- ☐ Picnicking
- ☐ Rock Climbing
- ☐ Shooting Range
- ☐ Snowshoeing
- ☐ Stargazing
- ☐ Swimming
- ☐ Tennis
- ☐ Walking
- ☐ Wildlife Watching
- ☐ ____________
- ☐ ____________
- ☐ ____________
- ☐ ____________
- ☐ ____________

Traveled by:

☐ ☐ ☐ ☐ ☐ ☐ ☐ ☐ ☐ ☐ ☐ ☐

Add your favorite ticket stub, postcard, photo, stamp or drawing here

N E S W NOT ALL THOSE WHO WANDER ARE LOST

TARKILN BAYOU PRESERVE STATE PARK

County: Escambia
2401 Bauer Road, Pensacola FL 32507 | 850-492-1595

Website: **https://www.floridastateparks.org/parks-and-trails/tarkiln-bayou-preserve-state-park**
Email: **FSP.Feedback@FloridaDEP.gov**

Water Body: Perdido Bay

Size: 4,290 acres
Established: 1998

Limited facilities; nature trails, picnic tables and a bathroom

Star Rating ☆☆☆☆☆

What souvenir did you bring home?... Decal Magnet

My favorite thing about this place is...

Why I went ...

Who I went with ...

When I went ...

What I did...

What I saw...

What I learned...

An unforgettable moment...

A laughable moment...

A surprising moment...

An unforeseeable moment...

Snapped a selfie | Location...

Took a park sign selfie? - Y | N

The weather was ...

MY LIST

- ☐
- ☐
- ☐
- ☐
- ☐
- ☐
- ☐
- ☐
- ☐
- ☐
- ☐
- ☐

PLAN YOUR TRIP:

DESTINATION INFORMATION:

☐ Trip Plan Completed

☐ Day Trip ☐ Overnight Stay

Reservations required: ☐y ☐n

Date reservations made: ____________

Refund Policy: ☐y ☐n Site/Room #: ______

Confirmation #: ____________

Miles to travel: ____________

Time traveling: ____________

Dog friendly?: ☐y ☐n

PLACES WE DISCOVERED ALONG THE WAY

PLACES TO STOP AND SEE ALONG THE WAY

Activities Accomplished:

Would you go again?: ☐y ☐n Open all year?: ☐y ☐n

- ☐ Archery
- ☐ Biking
- ☐ Birding
- ☐ Boating
- ☐ Camping
- ☐ Caving
- ☐ Geocaching
- ☐ Fishing
- ☐ Hiking
- ☐ Horseback Riding
- ☐ Hunting
- ☐ Off-Roading
- ☐ Paddle Boarding
- ☐ Photography
- ☐ Picnicking
- ☐ Rock Climbing
- ☐ Shooting Range
- ☐ Snowshoeing
- ☐ Stargazing
- ☐ Swimming
- ☐ Tennis
- ☐ Walking
- ☐ Wildlife Watching
- ☐ ____________
- ☐ ____________
- ☐ ____________
- ☐ ____________
- ☐ ____________

Traveled by:

☐ ☐ ☐ ☐ ☐ ☐ ☐ ☐ ☐ ☐ ☐ ☐

Add your favorite ticket stub, postcard, photo, stamp or drawing here

N
NOT ALL THOSE WHO WANDER ARE LOST
W E
S

Terra Ceia Preserve State Park

County: Manatee
130 Terra Ceia Rd. Terra Ceia, Fl 34606 | 941-723-4536

Website: https://www.floridastateparks.org/parks-and-trails/terra-ceia-preserve-state-park
Email: FSP.Feedback@FloridaDEP.gov

Water Body: Tampa Bay

Size: 1,932 acres
Established: 2000?

Land acquired by the state and Southwest Florida Water Management District

Star Rating ☆☆☆☆☆

What souvenir did you bring home?... Decal Magnet

My favorite thing about this place is...

Why I went ...

Who I went with ...

When I went ...

What I did...

What I saw...

What I learned...

An unforgettable moment...

A laughable moment...

A surprising moment...

An unforeseeable moment...

Snapped a selfie | Location...

Took a park sign selfie? - Y | N

The weather was ...

My List

- ☐
- ☐
- ☐
- ☐
- ☐
- ☐
- ☐
- ☐
- ☐
- ☐
- ☐
- ☐

Plan Your Trip:

☐ Trip Plan Completed

☐ Day Trip ☐ Overnight Stay

Reservations required: ☐y ☐n

Date reservations made: ____________

Refund Policy: ☐y ☐n Site/Room #: ______

Confirmation #: ____________

Miles to travel: ____________

Time traveling: ____________

Dog friendly?: ☐y ☐n

Destination Information:

Places we discovered along the way

Places to stop and see along the way

Would you go again?: ☐y ☐n Open all year?: ☐y ☐n

Activities Accomplished:

- ☐ Archery
- ☐ Biking
- ☐ Birding
- ☐ Boating
- ☐ Camping
- ☐ Caving
- ☐ Geocaching
- ☐ Fishing
- ☐ Hiking
- ☐ Horseback Riding
- ☐ Hunting
- ☐ Off-Roading
- ☐ Paddle Boarding
- ☐ Photography
- ☐ Picnicking
- ☐ Rock Climbing
- ☐ Shooting Range
- ☐ Snowshoeing
- ☐ Stargazing
- ☐ Swimming
- ☐ Tennis
- ☐ Walking
- ☐ Wildlife Watching
- ☐ ____________
- ☐ ____________
- ☐ ____________
- ☐ ____________
- ☐ ____________

Traveled by:

☐ ☐ ☐ ☐ ☐ ☐ ☐ ☐ ☐ ☐ ☐ ☐

Add your favorite ticket stub, postcard, photo, stamp or drawing here

N W E S NOT ALL THOSE WHO WANDER ARE LOST

THREE RIVERS STATE PARK

County: Jackson

7908 Three Rivers Park Road, Sneads FL 32460 | 850-482-9006

Website: https://www.floridastateparks.org/parks-and-trails/three-rivers-state-park
Email: FSP.Feedback@FloridaDEP.gov

Water Body: Chattahoochee River; Flint River, Lake Seminole

Size: 686 acres
Established: 1955

The 1947 Jim Woodruff Dam created Lake Seminole; the outflow is the Apalachicola River

Star Rating ☆☆☆☆☆

What souvenir did you bring home?... Decal Magnet

My favorite thing about this place is...

Why I went ...

Who I went with ...

When I went ...

What I did...

What I saw...

What I learned...

An unforgettable moment...

A laughable moment...

A surprising moment...

An unforeseeable moment...

MY LIST

- ☐
- ☐
- ☐
- ☐
- ☐
- ☐
- ☐
- ☐
- ☐
- ☐
- ☐
- ☐

Snapped a selfie | Location...

Took a park sign selfie? - Y | N

The weather was ...

Notes

Notes

Plan Your Trip:

☐ Trip Plan Completed

☐ Day Trip ☐ Overnight Stay

Reservations required: ☐y ☐n

Date reservations made: ______

Refund Policy: ☐y ☐n Site/Room #: ______

Confirmation #: ______

Miles to travel: ______

Time traveling: ______

Dog friendly?: ☐y ☐n

Destination Information:

______

______

Places we discovered along the way

______

______

______

Places to stop and see along the way

______

______

Would you go again?: ☐y ☐n

Open all year?: ☐y ☐n

Activities Accomplished:

- ☐ Archery
- ☐ Biking
- ☐ Birding
- ☐ Boating
- ☐ Camping
- ☐ Caving
- ☐ Geocaching
- ☐ Fishing
- ☐ Hiking
- ☐ Horseback Riding
- ☐ Hunting
- ☐ Off-Roading
- ☐ Paddle Boarding
- ☐ Photography
- ☐ Picnicking
- ☐ Rock Climbing
- ☐ Shooting Range
- ☐ Snowshoeing
- ☐ Stargazing
- ☐ Swimming
- ☐ Tennis
- ☐ Walking
- ☐ Wildlife Watching
- ☐ ______
- ☐ ______
- ☐ ______
- ☐ ______
- ☐ ______

Traveled by:

☐ ☐ ☐ ☐ ☐ ☐ ☐ ☐ ☐ ☐ ☐ ☐

Add your favorite ticket stub, postcard, photo, stamp or drawing here

N E S W NOT ALL THOSE WHO WANDER ARE LOST

Tomoka State Park

County: Volusia
2099 N. Beach St., Ormond Beach FL 32174 | 386-676-4050

Website: https://www.floridastateparks.org/Tomoka
Email: FSP.Feedback@FloridaDEP.gov

Water Body: Tomoka River

Size: 1,800 acres
Established: 1945

Urban park completely surrounded by development

Star Rating ☆☆☆☆☆

What souvenir did you bring home?... Decal Magnet

My favorite thing about this place is...

Why I went ...

Who I went with ...

When I went ...

What I did...

What I saw...

What I learned...

An unforgettable moment...

A laughable moment...

A surprising moment...

An unforeseeable moment...

My List

- ☐
- ☐
- ☐
- ☐
- ☐
- ☐
- ☐
- ☐
- ☐
- ☐
- ☐
- ☐

 Snapped a selfie | Location...

 Took a park sign selfie? - Y | N

The weather was ...      

PLAN YOUR TRIP:

☐ Trip Plan Completed

☐ Day Trip ☐ Overnight Stay

Reservations required: ☐y ☐n

Date reservations made: __________

Refund Policy: ☐y ☐n Site/Room #: _____

Confirmation #: __________

Miles to travel: __________

Time traveling: __________

Dog friendly?: ☐y ☐n

DESTINATION INFORMATION:

PLACES WE DISCOVERED ALONG THE WAY

PLACES TO STOP AND SEE ALONG THE WAY

Would you go again?: ☐y ☐n

Open all year?: ☐y ☐n

Activities Accomplished:

☐ Archery
☐ Biking
☐ Birding
☐ Boating
☐ Camping
☐ Caving
☐ Geocaching
☐ Fishing
☐ Hiking
☐ Horseback Riding
☐ Hunting
☐ Off-Roading
☐ Paddle Boarding
☐ Photography
☐ Picnicking
☐ Rock Climbing
☐ Shooting Range
☐ Snowshoeing
☐ Stargazing
☐ Swimming
☐ Tennis
☐ Walking
☐ Wildlife Watching
☐ __________
☐ __________
☐ __________
☐ __________
☐ __________

Traveled by:

☐ ☐ ☐ ☐ ☐ ☐ ☐ ☐ ☐ ☐ ☐ ☐

Add your favorite ticket stub, postcard, photo, stamp or drawing here

N E S W
NOT ALL THOSE WHO WANDER ARE LOST

Topsail Hill Preserve State Park

County: Walton
7525 W. County Highway 30A, Santa Rosa Beach FL 32459 | 850-267-8330

Website: https://www.floridastateparks.org/parks-and-trails/topsail-hill-preserve-state-park
Email: FSP.Feedback@FloridaDEP.gov

Water Body: Gulf of Mexico

Size: 1,643 acres
Established: 1992

Site of munitions testing range during World War II

Star Rating ☆☆☆☆☆

What souvenir did you bring home?... Decal Magnet

My favorite thing about this place is...

Why I went ...

Who I went with ...

When I went ...

What I did...

What I saw...

What I learned...

An unforgettable moment...

A laughable moment...

A surprising moment...

An unforeseeable moment...

Snapped a selfie | Location...

Took a park sign selfie? - Y | N

The weather was ...

My List

- ☐
- ☐
- ☐
- ☐
- ☐
- ☐
- ☐
- ☐
- ☐
- ☐
- ☐
- ☐

Plan Your Trip:

☐ Trip Plan Completed

☐ Day Trip ☐ Overnight Stay

Reservations required: ☐y ☐n

Date reservations made: ____________

Refund Policy: ☐y ☐n Site/Room #: ______

Confirmation #: ____________

Miles to travel: ____________

Time traveling: ____________

Dog friendly?: ☐y ☐n

Destination Information:

____

____

Places we discovered along the way

____

____

____

Places to stop and see along the way

____

____

Activities Accomplished:

Would you go again?: ☐y ☐n Open all year?: ☐y ☐n

- ☐ Archery
- ☐ Biking
- ☐ Birding
- ☐ Boating
- ☐ Camping
- ☐ Caving
- ☐ Geocaching
- ☐ Fishing
- ☐ Hiking
- ☐ Horseback Riding
- ☐ Hunting
- ☐ Off-Roading
- ☐ Paddle Boarding
- ☐ Photography
- ☐ Picnicking
- ☐ Rock Climbing
- ☐ Shooting Range
- ☐ Snowshoeing
- ☐ Stargazing
- ☐ Swimming
- ☐ Tennis
- ☐ Walking
- ☐ Wildlife Watching
- ☐ ____________
- ☐ ____________
- ☐ ____________
- ☐ ____________
- ☐ ____________

Traveled by:

☐ ☐ ☐ ☐ ☐ ☐ ☐ ☐ ☐ ☐ ☐ ☐

Add your favorite ticket stub, postcard, photo, stamp or drawing here

N S E W NOT ALL THOSE WHO WANDER ARE LOST

Torreya State Park

County: Liberty
2576 N.W. Torreya Park Road, Bristol FL 32321 | 850-643-2674

Website: https://www.floridastateparks.org/parks-and-trails/torreya-state-park
Email: FSP.Feedback@FloridaDEP.gov

Water Body: Apalachicola River

Size: 13,737 acres
Established: 1935

Park named after the endangered Torreya tree

Star Rating ☆☆☆☆☆

What souvenir did you bring home?... Decal Magnet

My favorite thing about this place is...

Why I went ...

Who I went with ...

When I went ...

What I did...

What I saw...

What I learned...

An unforgettable moment...

A laughable moment...

A surprising moment...

An unforeseeable moment...

My List

- ☐
- ☐
- ☐
- ☐
- ☐
- ☐
- ☐
- ☐
- ☐
- ☐
- ☐
- ☐

Snapped a selfie | Location...

Took a park sign selfie? - Y | N

The weather was ... °F

Plan Your Trip:

☐ Trip Plan Completed

☐ Day Trip ☐ Overnight Stay

Reservations required: ☐y ☐n

Date reservations made: ____________

Refund Policy: ☐y ☐n Site/Room #: ____

Confirmation #: ____________

Miles to travel: ____________

Time traveling: ____________

Dog friendly?: ☐y ☐n

Destination Information:

____

____

Places we discovered along the way

____

____

____

Places to stop and see along the way

____

____

Would you go again?: ☐y ☐n

Open all year?: ☐y ☐n

Activities Accomplished:

- ☐ Archery
- ☐ Biking
- ☐ Birding
- ☐ Boating
- ☐ Camping
- ☐ Caving
- ☐ Geocaching
- ☐ Fishing
- ☐ Hiking
- ☐ Horseback Riding
- ☐ Hunting
- ☐ Off-Roading
- ☐ Paddle Boarding
- ☐ Photography
- ☐ Picnicking
- ☐ Rock Climbing
- ☐ Shooting Range
- ☐ Snowshoeing
- ☐ Stargazing
- ☐ Swimming
- ☐ Tennis
- ☐ Walking
- ☐ Wildlife Watching
- ☐ ____________
- ☐ ____________
- ☐ ____________
- ☐ ____________
- ☐ ____________

Traveled by:

☐ ☐ ☐ ☐ ☐ ☐ ☐ ☐ ☐ ☐ ☐ ☐

Add your favorite ticket stub, postcard, photo, stamp or drawing here

N W E S NOT ALL THOSE WHO WANDER ARE LOST

TROY SPRING STATE PARK

County: Suwannee - Lafayette
674 N.E. Troy Springs Road, Branford FL 32008 | 386-935-4835

Website: https://www.floridastateparks.org/parks-and-trails/troy-spring-state-park
Email: FSP.Feedback@FloridaDEP.gov

Water Body: Suwannee River

Size: 84 acres
Established: 1995

First magnitude spring; the Civil War steamboat "Madison" was scuttled there in 1863

Star Rating ☆☆☆☆☆

What souvenir did you bring home?... Decal Magnet

My favorite thing about this place is...

Why I went ...

Who I went with ...

When I went ...

What I did...

What I saw...

What I learned...

An unforgettable moment...

A laughable moment...

A surprising moment...

An unforeseeable moment...

MY LIST

- ☐
- ☐
- ☐
- ☐
- ☐
- ☐
- ☐
- ☐
- ☐
- ☐
- ☐
- ☐

Snapped a selfie | Location...

Took a park sign selfie? - Y | N

The weather was ...

Plan Your Trip:

☐ Trip Plan Completed

☐ Day Trip ☐ Overnight Stay

Reservations required: ☐y ☐n

Date reservations made: ____________

Refund Policy: ☐y ☐n Site/Room #: ______

Confirmation #: ____________

Miles to travel: ____________

Time traveling: ____________

Dog friendly?: ☐y ☐n

Destination Information:

Places we discovered along the way

Places to stop and see along the way

Activities Accomplished:

Would you go again?: ☐y ☐n Open all year?: ☐y ☐n

☐ Archery
☐ Biking
☐ Birding
☐ Boating
☐ Camping
☐ Caving
☐ Geocaching
☐ Fishing
☐ Hiking
☐ Horseback Riding
☐ Hunting
☐ Off-Roading
☐ Paddle Boarding
☐ Photography
☐ Picnicking
☐ Rock Climbing
☐ Shooting Range
☐ Snowshoeing
☐ Stargazing
☐ Swimming
☐ Tennis
☐ Walking
☐ Wildlife Watching
☐ ____________
☐ ____________
☐ ____________
☐ ____________
☐ ____________

Traveled by:

☐ ☐ ☐ ☐ ☐ ☐ ☐ ☐ ☐ ☐ ☐ ☐

Add your favorite ticket stub, postcard, photo, stamp or drawing here

N E S W NOT ALL THOSE WHO WANDER ARE LOST

Waccasassa Bay Preserve State Park

County: Levy

Waccasassa River Boat Ramp, 29.214050, -82.763564, Gulf Hammock FL 34449 | 352-543-5567

Website: https://www.floridastateparks.org/parks-and-trails/waccasassa-bay-preserve-state-park
Email: FSP.Feedback@FloridaDEP.gov

Water Body: Gulf of Mexico

Size: 30,784 acres
Established: 2005

Accessible only by boat; no recreational facilities

Star Rating ☆☆☆☆☆

What souvenir did you bring home?... Decal Magnet

My favorite thing about this place is...

Why I went ...

Who I went with ...

When I went ...

What I did...

What I saw...

What I learned...

An unforgettable moment...

A laughable moment...

A surprising moment...

An unforeseeable moment...

Snapped a selfie | Location...

Took a park sign selfie? - Y | N

The weather was ...

My List

- ☐
- ☐
- ☐
- ☐
- ☐
- ☐
- ☐
- ☐
- ☐
- ☐
- ☐
- ☐

Plan Your Trip:

☐ Trip Plan Completed

☐ Day Trip ☐ Overnight Stay

Reservations required: ☐y ☐n

Date reservations made: ____

Refund Policy: ☐y ☐n Site/Room #: ____

Confirmation #: ____

Miles to travel: ____

Time traveling: ____

Dog friendly?: ☐y ☐n

Destination Information:

Places we discovered along the way

Places to stop and see along the way

Activities Accomplished:

Would you go again?: ☐y ☐n

Open all year?: ☐y ☐n

☐ Archery
☐ Biking
☐ Birding
☐ Boating
☐ Camping
☐ Caving
☐ Geocaching
☐ Fishing
☐ Hiking
☐ Horseback Riding
☐ Hunting
☐ Off-Roading
☐ Paddle Boarding
☐ Photography
☐ Picnicking
☐ Rock Climbing
☐ Shooting Range
☐ Snowshoeing
☐ Stargazing
☐ Swimming
☐ Tennis
☐ Walking
☐ Wildlife Watching
☐ ____
☐ ____
☐ ____
☐ ____
☐ ____

Traveled by:

☐ ☐ ☐ ☐ ☐ ☐ ☐ ☐ ☐ ☐ ☐ ☐

Add your favorite ticket stub, postcard, photo, stamp or drawing here

N W E S NOT ALL THOSE WHO WANDER ARE LOST

Washington Oaks Gardens State Park

County: Flagler
6400 N. Oceanshore Blvd., Palm Coast FL 32137 | 386-446-6780

Website: https://www.floridastateparks.org/parks-and-trails/washington-oaks-gardens-state-park
Email: FSP.Feedback@FloridaDEP.gov

Water Body: Atlantic Ocean

Size: 21 acres
Established: 1964

Park has formal gardens, citrus groves and house

Star Rating ☆☆☆☆☆

What souvenir did you bring home?... Decal Magnet
My favorite thing about this place is...

Why I went ...
Who I went with ...
When I went ...

What I did...
What I saw...

What I learned...

An unforgettable moment...

A laughable moment...

A surprising moment...

An unforeseeable moment...

My List

- ☐
- ☐
- ☐
- ☐
- ☐
- ☐
- ☐
- ☐
- ☐
- ☐
- ☐
- ☐

Snapped a selfie | Location...

Took a park sign selfie? - Y | N

The weather was ...

Plan Your Trip:

☐ Trip Plan Completed

☐ Day Trip ☐ Overnight Stay

Reservations required: ☐y ☐n

Date reservations made: ______

Refund Policy: ☐y ☐n Site/Room #: ______

Confirmation #: ______

Miles to travel: ______

Time traveling: ______

Dog friendly?: ☐y ☐n

Destination Information:

Places we discovered along the way

Places to stop and see along the way

Would you go again?: ☐y ☐n Open all year?: ☐y ☐n

Activities Accomplished:

☐ Archery	☐ Fishing	☐ Picnicking	☐ Walking
☐ Biking	☐ Hiking	☐ Rock Climbing	☐ Wildlife Watching
☐ Birding	☐ Horseback Riding	☐ Shooting Range	☐ ______
☐ Boating	☐ Hunting	☐ Snowshoeing	☐ ______
☐ Camping	☐ Off-Roading	☐ Stargazing	☐ ______
☐ Caving	☐ Paddle Boarding	☐ Swimming	☐ ______
☐ Geocaching	☐ Photography	☐ Tennis	☐ ______

Traveled by:

☐ ☐ ☐ ☐ ☐ ☐ ☐ ☐ ☐ ☐ ☐ ☐

Add your favorite ticket stub, postcard, photo, stamp or drawing here

N E S W NOT ALL THOSE WHO WANDER ARE LOST

Weeki Wachee Springs

County: Hernando
6131 Commercial Way, Weeki Wachee FL 34606 | 352-610-5660

Website: https://weekiwachee.com
Email: FSP.Feedback@FloridaDEP.gov

Water Body: Weeki Wachee River

Size: 538 acres
Established: 2008

The headspring area features underwater performances by female dancers in mermaid costumes

Star Rating ☆☆☆☆☆

What souvenir did you bring home?... Decal Magnet

My favorite thing about this place is...

Why I went ...

Who I went with ...

When I went ...

What I did...

What I saw...

What I learned...

An unforgettable moment...

A laughable moment...

A surprising moment...

An unforeseeable moment...

Snapped a selfie | Location...

Took a park sign selfie? - Y | N

The weather was ...

My List

- ☐
- ☐
- ☐
- ☐
- ☐
- ☐
- ☐
- ☐
- ☐
- ☐
- ☐
- ☐

Plan Your Trip:

☐ Trip Plan Completed

☐ Day Trip ☐ Overnight Stay

Reservations required: ☐y ☐n

Date reservations made: ______

Refund Policy: ☐y ☐n Site/Room #: ______

Confirmation #: ______

Miles to travel: ______

Time traveling: ______

Dog friendly?: ☐y ☐n

Destination Information:

______

______

Places we discovered along the way

______

______

______

Places to stop and see along the way

______

______

Would you go again?: ☐y ☐n

Open all year?: ☐y ☐n

Activities Accomplished:

- ☐ Archery
- ☐ Biking
- ☐ Birding
- ☐ Boating
- ☐ Camping
- ☐ Caving
- ☐ Geocaching
- ☐ Fishing
- ☐ Hiking
- ☐ Horseback Riding
- ☐ Hunting
- ☐ Off-Roading
- ☐ Paddle Boarding
- ☐ Photography
- ☐ Picnicking
- ☐ Rock Climbing
- ☐ Shooting Range
- ☐ Snowshoeing
- ☐ Stargazing
- ☐ Swimming
- ☐ Tennis
- ☐ Walking
- ☐ Wildlife Watching
- ☐ ______
- ☐ ______
- ☐ ______
- ☐ ______
- ☐ ______

Traveled by:

☐ ☐ ☐ ☐ ☐ ☐ ☐ ☐ ☐ ☐ ☐ ☐

Add your favorite ticket stub, postcard, photo, stamp or drawing here

N E S W
NOT ALL THOSE WHO WANDER ARE LOST

Wekiwa Springs State Park

County: Orange
1800 Wekiwa Cir., Apopka FL 32712 | 407-553-4383

Website: https://www.floridastateparks.org/parks-and-trails/wekiwa-springs-state-park
Email: FSP.Feedback@FloridaDEP.gov

Water Body: Wekiva River

Size: 7,723 acres
Established: 1969

42 million gallons 159 million liters of 72 ¬∞F 22 ¬∞C water outflow daily

Star Rating ☆☆☆☆☆

What souvenir did you bring home?... Decal Magnet

My favorite thing about this place is...

Why I went ...

Who I went with ...

When I went ...

What I did...

What I saw...

What I learned...

An unforgettable moment...

A laughable moment...

A surprising moment...

An unforeseeable moment...

My List

- ☐
- ☐
- ☐
- ☐
- ☐
- ☐
- ☐
- ☐
- ☐
- ☐
- ☐
- ☐

Snapped a selfie | Location...

Took a park sign selfie? - Y | N

The weather was ...      

PLAN YOUR TRIP:

☐ Trip Plan Completed

☐ Day Trip ☐ Overnight Stay

Reservations required: ☐y ☐n

Date reservations made: ____

Refund Policy: ☐y ☐n Site/Room #: ____

Confirmation #: ____

Miles to travel: ____

Time traveling: ____

Dog friendly?: ☐y ☐n

DESTINATION INFORMATION:

____

____

PLACES WE DISCOVERED ALONG THE WAY

____

____

____

PLACES TO STOP AND SEE ALONG THE WAY

____

____

Would you go again?: ☐y ☐n Open all year?: ☐y ☐n

Activities Accomplished:

- ☐ Archery
- ☐ Biking
- ☐ Birding
- ☐ Boating
- ☐ Camping
- ☐ Caving
- ☐ Geocaching
- ☐ Fishing
- ☐ Hiking
- ☐ Horseback Riding
- ☐ Hunting
- ☐ Off-Roading
- ☐ Paddle Boarding
- ☐ Photography
- ☐ Picnicking
- ☐ Rock Climbing
- ☐ Shooting Range
- ☐ Snowshoeing
- ☐ Stargazing
- ☐ Swimming
- ☐ Tennis
- ☐ Walking
- ☐ Wildlife Watching
- ☐ ____
- ☐ ____
- ☐ ____
- ☐ ____
- ☐ ____

Traveled by:

☐ ☐ ☐ ☐ ☐ ☐ ☐ ☐ ☐ ☐ ☐ ☐

Add your favorite ticket stub, postcard, photo, stamp or drawing here

N NOT ALL THOSE WHO WANDER ARE LOST E S W

Werner-Boyce Salt Springs State Park

County: Pasco
8737 U.S. Highway 19 North, Port Richey FL 34668 | 727-816-1890

Website: https://www.floridastateparks.org/parks-and-trails/werner-boyce-salt-springs-state-park
Email: FSP.Feedback@FloridaDEP.gov

Water Body: Gulf of Mexico

Size: 3,400 acres
Established: 2001

Named for the Werner-Boyce Preserve purchased by Pasco County in 1994; undeveloped

Star Rating ☆☆☆☆☆

What souvenir did you bring home?... Decal Magnet

My favorite thing about this place is...

Why I went ...

Who I went with ...

When I went ...

What I did...

What I saw...

What I learned...

An unforgettable moment...

A laughable moment...

A surprising moment...

An unforeseeable moment...

My List

- ☐
- ☐
- ☐
- ☐
- ☐
- ☐
- ☐
- ☐
- ☐
- ☐
- ☐
- ☐

Snapped a selfie | Location...

Took a park sign selfie? - Y | N

The weather was ...

Plan Your Trip:

☐ Trip Plan Completed

☐ Day Trip ☐ Overnight Stay

Reservations required: ☐y ☐n

Date reservations made: ______

Refund Policy: ☐y ☐n Site/Room #: ______

Confirmation #: ______

Miles to travel: ______

Time traveling: ______

Dog friendly?: ☐y ☐n

Destination Information:

______

______

Places we discovered along the way

______

______

______

Places to stop and see along the way

______

______

Activities Accomplished:

Would you go again?: ☐y ☐n

Open all year?: ☐y ☐n

- ☐ Archery
- ☐ Biking
- ☐ Birding
- ☐ Boating
- ☐ Camping
- ☐ Caving
- ☐ Geocaching
- ☐ Fishing
- ☐ Hiking
- ☐ Horseback Riding
- ☐ Hunting
- ☐ Off-Roading
- ☐ Paddle Boarding
- ☐ Photography
- ☐ Picnicking
- ☐ Rock Climbing
- ☐ Shooting Range
- ☐ Snowshoeing
- ☐ Stargazing
- ☐ Swimming
- ☐ Tennis
- ☐ Walking
- ☐ Wildlife Watching
- ☐ ______
- ☐ ______
- ☐ ______
- ☐ ______
- ☐ ______

Traveled by:

☐ ☐ ☐ ☐ ☐ ☐ ☐ ☐ ☐ ☐ ☐ ☐

Add your favorite ticket stub, postcard, photo, stamp or drawing here

N E S W NOT ALL THOSE WHO WANDER ARE LOST

Wes Skiles Peacock Springs State Park

County: Suwannee
18532 180th Street, Live Oak FL 32060 | 386-776-2194

Website: https://www.floridastateparks.org/parks-and-trails/wes-skiles-peacock-springs-state-park
Email: FSP.Feedback@FloridaDEP.gov

Water Body: Suwannee River

Size: 733 acres
Established: 1986

28,000 feet 8,534 m of explored passageways make it one of the largest locations for cave diving in the U.S.

Star Rating ☆☆☆☆☆

What souvenir did you bring home?... Decal Magnet

My favorite thing about this place is...

Why I went ...

Who I went with ...

When I went ...

What I did...

What I saw...

What I learned...

An unforgettable moment...

A laughable moment...

A surprising moment...

An unforeseeable moment...

My List

- ☐
- ☐
- ☐
- ☐
- ☐
- ☐
- ☐
- ☐
- ☐
- ☐
- ☐
- ☐

Snapped a selfie | Location...

Took a park sign selfie? - y | n

The weather was ...

Plan Your Trip:

☐ Trip Plan Completed

☐ Day Trip ☐ Overnight Stay

Reservations required: ☐y ☐n

Date reservations made: ______

Refund Policy: ☐y ☐n Site/Room #: ______

Confirmation #: ______

Miles to travel: ______

Time traveling: ______

Dog friendly?: ☐y ☐n

Destination Information:

______

______

Places we discovered along the way

______

______

______

Places to stop and see along the way

______

______

Would you go again?: ☐y ☐n

Open all year?: ☐y ☐n

Activities Accomplished:

☐ Archery
☐ Biking
☐ Birding
☐ Boating
☐ Camping
☐ Caving
☐ Geocaching
☐ Fishing
☐ Hiking
☐ Horseback Riding
☐ Hunting
☐ Off-Roading
☐ Paddle Boarding
☐ Photography
☐ Picnicking
☐ Rock Climbing
☐ Shooting Range
☐ Snowshoeing
☐ Stargazing
☐ Swimming
☐ Tennis
☐ Walking
☐ Wildlife Watching
☐ ______
☐ ______
☐ ______
☐ ______
☐ ______

Traveled by:

☐ ☐ ☐ ☐ ☐ ☐ ☐ ☐ ☐ ☐ ☐ ☐

Add your favorite ticket stub, postcard, photo, stamp or drawing here

N E S W
NOT ALL THOSE WHO WANDER ARE LOST

Windley Key Fossil Reef Geological State Park

County: Monroe
84900 Overseas Highway, Islamorada FL 33036 | 305-664-2540

Website: https://www.floridastateparks.org/WindleyKey
Email: FSP.Feedback@FloridaDEP.gov

Water Body: Atlantic Ocean

Size: 32 acres
Established: 1986

Quarry provided Keystone limestone for the Overseas Railroad in 1908

Star Rating ☆☆☆☆☆

What souvenir did you bring home?... Decal Magnet

My favorite thing about this place is...

Why I went ...

Who I went with ...

When I went ...

What I did...

What I saw...

What I learned...

An unforgettable moment...

A laughable moment...

A surprising moment...

An unforeseeable moment...

Snapped a selfie | Location...

Took a park sign selfie? - Y | N

The weather was ...

My List

- ☐
- ☐
- ☐
- ☐
- ☐
- ☐
- ☐
- ☐
- ☐
- ☐
- ☐
- ☐

Plan Your Trip:

☐ Trip Plan Completed

☐ Day Trip ☐ Overnight Stay

Reservations required: ☐y ☐n

Date reservations made: ____________

Refund Policy: ☐y ☐n Site/Room #: ____

Confirmation #: ____________

Miles to travel: ____________

Time traveling: ____________

Dog friendly?: ☐y ☐n

Destination Information:

____

____

Places we discovered along the way

____

____

____

Places to stop and see along the way

____

____

Activities Accomplished:

Would you go again?: ☐y ☐n Open all year?: ☐y ☐n

- ☐ Archery
- ☐ Biking
- ☐ Birding
- ☐ Boating
- ☐ Camping
- ☐ Caving
- ☐ Geocaching
- ☐ Fishing
- ☐ Hiking
- ☐ Horseback Riding
- ☐ Hunting
- ☐ Off-Roading
- ☐ Paddle Boarding
- ☐ Photography
- ☐ Picnicking
- ☐ Rock Climbing
- ☐ Shooting Range
- ☐ Snowshoeing
- ☐ Stargazing
- ☐ Swimming
- ☐ Tennis
- ☐ Walking
- ☐ Wildlife Watching
- ☐ ____________
- ☐ ____________
- ☐ ____________
- ☐ ____________
- ☐ ____________

Traveled by:

☐ ☐ ☐ ☐ ☐ ☐ ☐ ☐ ☐ ☐ ☐ ☐

Add your favorite ticket stub, postcard, photo, stamp or drawing here

N W E S
NOT ALL THOSE WHO WANDER ARE LOST

Ybor City Museum State Park

County: Hillsborough
1818 E. Ninth Ave., Tampa FL 33605 | 813-247-6323

Website: https://www.floridastateparks.org/parks-and-trails/ybor-city-museum-state-park
Email: FSP.Feedback@FloridaDEP.gov

Water Body: none

Size: 1 acre
Established: 1976

Shows the history of Tampa's cigar industry and Latin influence

Star Rating ☆☆☆☆☆

What souvenir did you bring home?... Decal Magnet

My favorite thing about this place is...

Why I went ...

Who I went with ...

When I went ...

What I did...

What I saw...

What I learned...

An unforgettable moment...

A laughable moment...

A surprising moment...

An unforeseeable moment...

My List

- ☐
- ☐
- ☐
- ☐
- ☐
- ☐
- ☐
- ☐
- ☐
- ☐
- ☐
- ☐

Snapped a selfie | Location...

Took a park sign selfie? - Y | N

The weather was ...

Plan Your Trip:

☐ Trip Plan Completed

☐ Day Trip ☐ Overnight Stay

Reservations required: ☐y ☐n

Date reservations made: ______

Refund Policy: ☐y ☐n Site/Room #: ______

Confirmation #: ______

Miles to travel: ______

Time traveling: ______

Dog friendly?: ☐y ☐n

Destination Information:

______

______

Places we discovered along the way

______

______

______

Places to stop and see along the way

______

______

Would you go again?: ☐y ☐n

Open all year?: ☐y ☐n

Activities Accomplished:

- ☐ Archery
- ☐ Biking
- ☐ Birding
- ☐ Boating
- ☐ Camping
- ☐ Caving
- ☐ Geocaching
- ☐ Fishing
- ☐ Hiking
- ☐ Horseback Riding
- ☐ Hunting
- ☐ Off-Roading
- ☐ Paddle Boarding
- ☐ Photography
- ☐ Picnicking
- ☐ Rock Climbing
- ☐ Shooting Range
- ☐ Snowshoeing
- ☐ Stargazing
- ☐ Swimming
- ☐ Tennis
- ☐ Walking
- ☐ Wildlife Watching
- ☐ ______
- ☐ ______
- ☐ ______
- ☐ ______
- ☐ ______

Traveled by:

☐ ☐ ☐ ☐ ☐ ☐ ☐ ☐ ☐ ☐ ☐ ☐

Add your favorite ticket stub, postcard, photo, stamp or drawing here

N E S W
NOT ALL THOSE WHO WANDER ARE LOST

Yellow Bluff Fort Historic State Park

County: Duval
New Berlin Road, Jacksonville, FL 32226 | 904-251-2320

Website: **https://www.floridastateparks.org/parks-and-trails/yellow-bluff-fort-historic-state-park**
Email: **FSP.Feedback@FloridaDEP.gov**

Water Body: Atlantic Ocean

Size: 1,600 acres
Established: 1949

Confederate camp constructed during the American Civil War

Star Rating ☆☆☆☆☆

What souvenir did you bring home?... Decal Magnet

My favorite thing about this place is...

Why I went ...

Who I went with ...

When I went ...

What I did...

What I saw...

What I learned...

An unforgettable moment...

A laughable moment...

A surprising moment...

An unforeseeable moment...

My List

- ☐
- ☐
- ☐
- ☐
- ☐
- ☐
- ☐
- ☐
- ☐
- ☐
- ☐
- ☐

Snapped a selfie | Location...

Took a park sign selfie? - Y | N

The weather was ...

Plan Your Trip:

☐ Trip Plan Completed

☐ Day Trip ☐ Overnight Stay

Reservations required: ☐y ☐n

Date reservations made: ______

Refund Policy: ☐y ☐n Site/Room #: ______

Confirmation #: ______

Miles to travel: ______

Time traveling: ______

Dog friendly?: ☐y ☐n

Destination Information:

Places we discovered along the way

Places to stop and see along the way

Would you go again?: ☐y ☐n Open all year?: ☐y ☐n

Activities Accomplished:

☐ Archery
☐ Biking
☐ Birding
☐ Boating
☐ Camping
☐ Caving
☐ Geocaching
☐ Fishing
☐ Hiking
☐ Horseback Riding
☐ Hunting
☐ Off-Roading
☐ Paddle Boarding
☐ Photography
☐ Picnicking
☐ Rock Climbing
☐ Shooting Range
☐ Snowshoeing
☐ Stargazing
☐ Swimming
☐ Tennis
☐ Walking
☐ Wildlife Watching
☐ ______
☐ ______
☐ ______
☐ ______
☐ ______

Traveled by:

☐ ☐ ☐ ☐ ☐ ☐ ☐ ☐ ☐ ☐ ☐ ☐

Add your favorite ticket stub, postcard, photo, stamp or drawing here

N E S W NOT ALL THOSE WHO WANDER ARE LOST

YELLOW RIVER MARSH PRESERVE STATE PARK

County: Santa Rosa

Dickerson City Road at Garcon Point Rd (CR-191), Milton FL 32583 | 850-983-5363

Website: https://www.floridastateparks.org/parks-and-trails/yellow-river-marsh-preserve-state-park
Email: FSP.Feedback@FloridaDEP.gov

Water Body: Yellow River

Size: 11,000 acres
Established: 2000

One of Florida's last remaining tracts of wet prairie; no recreation facilities

Star Rating ☆☆☆☆☆

What souvenir did you bring home?... Decal Magnet ________

My favorite thing about this place is... ________

____

Why I went ... ________

Who I went with ... ________

When I went ... ________

____

What I did... ________

What I saw... ________

____

____

What I learned... ________

____

____

An unforgettable moment... ________

____

____

____

A laughable moment... ________

____

____

A surprising moment... ________

____

____

____

An unforeseeable moment... ________

____

____

Snapped a selfie | Location... ________

Took a park sign selfie? - Y | N

The weather was ...

MY LIST

- ☐ ________
- ☐ ________
- ☐ ________
- ☐ ________
- ☐ ________
- ☐ ________
- ☐ ________
- ☐ ________
- ☐ ________
- ☐ ________
- ☐ ________
- ☐ ________

PLAN YOUR TRIP:

☐ Trip Plan Completed

☐ Day Trip ☐ Overnight Stay

Reservations required: ☐y ☐n

Date reservations made: ______

Refund Policy: ☐y ☐n Site/Room #: ______

Confirmation #: ______

Miles to travel: ______

Time traveling: ______

Dog friendly?: ☐y ☐n

DESTINATION INFORMATION:

______

______

PLACES WE DISCOVERED ALONG THE WAY

______

______

______

PLACES TO STOP AND SEE ALONG THE WAY

______

______

Activities Accomplished:

Would you go again?: ☐y ☐n Open all year?: ☐y ☐n

- ☐ Archery
- ☐ Biking
- ☐ Birding
- ☐ Boating
- ☐ Camping
- ☐ Caving
- ☐ Geocaching
- ☐ Fishing
- ☐ Hiking
- ☐ Horseback Riding
- ☐ Hunting
- ☐ Off-Roading
- ☐ Paddle Boarding
- ☐ Photography
- ☐ Picnicking
- ☐ Rock Climbing
- ☐ Shooting Range
- ☐ Snowshoeing
- ☐ Stargazing
- ☐ Swimming
- ☐ Tennis
- ☐ Walking
- ☐ Wildlife Watching
- ☐ ______
- ☐ ______
- ☐ ______
- ☐ ______
- ☐ ______

Traveled by:

☐ ☐ ☐ ☐ ☐ ☐ ☐ ☐ ☐ ☐ ☐ ☐

Add your favorite ticket stub, postcard, photo, stamp or drawing here

Yulee Sugar Mill Ruins Historic State Park

County: Citrus
State Road 490, Homosassa FL 34446 | 352-795-3817

Website: https://www.floridastateparks.org/parks-and-trails/yulee-sugar-mill-ruins-historic-state-park
Email: FSP.Feedback@FloridaDEP.gov

Water Body: Homosassa River

Size: 6 acres
Established: 1953

Senator David Levy Yulee built the mill on his 5,100-acre 2,064 ha plantation, Margarita, in 1851

Star Rating ☆☆☆☆☆

What souvenir did you bring home?... Decal Magnet

My favorite thing about this place is...

Why I went ...

Who I went with ...

When I went ...

What I did...

What I saw...

What I learned...

An unforgettable moment...

A laughable moment...

A surprising moment...

An unforeseeable moment...

Snapped a selfie | Location...

Took a park sign selfie? - Y | N

The weather was ... °F

My List

- ☐
- ☐
- ☐
- ☐
- ☐
- ☐
- ☐
- ☐
- ☐
- ☐
- ☐
- ☐

Plan Your Trip:

☐ Trip Plan Completed

☐ Day Trip ☐ Overnight Stay

Reservations required: ☐y ☐n

Date reservations made: ____________

Refund Policy: ☐y ☐n Site/Room #: ______

Confirmation #: ____________

Miles to travel: ____________

Time traveling: ____________

Dog friendly?: ☐y ☐n

Destination Information:

Places we discovered along the way

Places to stop and see along the way

Would you go again?: ☐y ☐n

Open all year?: ☐y ☐n

Activities Accomplished:

- ☐ Archery
- ☐ Biking
- ☐ Birding
- ☐ Boating
- ☐ Camping
- ☐ Caving
- ☐ Geocaching
- ☐ Fishing
- ☐ Hiking
- ☐ Horseback Riding
- ☐ Hunting
- ☐ Off-Roading
- ☐ Paddle Boarding
- ☐ Photography
- ☐ Picnicking
- ☐ Rock Climbing
- ☐ Shooting Range
- ☐ Snowshoeing
- ☐ Stargazing
- ☐ Swimming
- ☐ Tennis
- ☐ Walking
- ☐ Wildlife Watching
- ☐ ____________
- ☐ ____________
- ☐ ____________
- ☐ ____________
- ☐ ____________

Traveled by:

☐ ☐ ☐ ☐ ☐ ☐ ☐ ☐ ☐ ☐ ☐ ☐

Add your favorite ticket stub, postcard, photo, stamp or drawing here

N E S W NOT ALL THOSE WHO WANDER ARE LOST

Pick Your Own Place

Star Rating

☆☆☆☆☆

What souvenir did you bring home?... Decal Magnet

My favorite thing about this place is...

Why I went ...

Who I went with ...

When I went ...

What I did...

What I saw...

What I learned...

An unforgettable moment...

A laughable moment...

A surprising moment...

An unforeseeable moment...

My List

- ☐
- ☐
- ☐
- ☐
- ☐
- ☐
- ☐
- ☐
- ☐
- ☐
- ☐
- ☐

Snapped a selfie | Location...

Took a park sign selfie? - y | n

The weather was ...

PLAN YOUR TRIP:

☐ Trip Plan Completed

☐ Day Trip ☐ Overnight Stay

Reservations required: ☐y ☐n

Date reservations made: ____________

Refund Policy: ☐y ☐n Site/Room #: ____

Confirmation #: ____________

Miles to travel: ____________

Time traveling: ____________

Dog friendly?: ☐y ☐n

DESTINATION INFORMATION:

PLACES WE DISCOVERED ALONG THE WAY

PLACES TO STOP AND SEE ALONG THE WAY

Would you go again?: ☐y ☐n

Open all year?: ☐y ☐n

Activities Accomplished:

- ☐ Archery
- ☐ Biking
- ☐ Birding
- ☐ Boating
- ☐ Camping
- ☐ Caving
- ☐ Geocaching
- ☐ Fishing
- ☐ Hiking
- ☐ Horseback Riding
- ☐ Hunting
- ☐ Off-Roading
- ☐ Paddle Boarding
- ☐ Photography
- ☐ Picnicking
- ☐ Rock Climbing
- ☐ Shooting Range
- ☐ Snowshoeing
- ☐ Stargazing
- ☐ Swimming
- ☐ Tennis
- ☐ Walking
- ☐ Wildlife Watching
- ☐ ____________
- ☐ ____________
- ☐ ____________
- ☐ ____________
- ☐ ____________

Traveled by:

☐ ☐ ☐ ☐ ☐ ☐ ☐ ☐ ☐ ☐ ☐ ☐

Add your favorite ticket stub, postcard, photo, stamp or drawing here

NOT ALL THOSE WHO WANDER ARE LOST

Pick Your Own Place

Star Rating ☆☆☆☆☆

What souvenir did you bring home?... Decal Magnet

My favorite thing about this place is...

Why I went ...

Who I went with ...

When I went ...

What I did...

What I saw...

What I learned...

An unforgettable moment...

A laughable moment...

A surprising moment...

An unforeseeable moment...

My List

- ☐
- ☐
- ☐
- ☐
- ☐
- ☐
- ☐
- ☐
- ☐
- ☐
- ☐
- ☐

Snapped a selfie | Location...

Took a park sign selfie? - Y | N

The weather was ...

Plan Your Trip:

☐ Trip Plan Completed

☐ Day Trip ☐ Overnight Stay

Reservations required: ☐y ☐n

Date reservations made: ____

Refund Policy: ☐y ☐n Site/Room #: ____

Confirmation #: ____

Miles to travel: ____

Time traveling: ____

Dog friendly?: ☐y ☐n

Destination Information:

____

____

Places we discovered along the way

____

____

____

Places to stop and see along the way

____

____

Activities Accomplished:

Would you go again?: ☐y ☐n

Open all year?: ☐y ☐n

- ☐ Archery
- ☐ Biking
- ☐ Birding
- ☐ Boating
- ☐ Camping
- ☐ Caving
- ☐ Geocaching
- ☐ Fishing
- ☐ Hiking
- ☐ Horseback Riding
- ☐ Hunting
- ☐ Off-Roading
- ☐ Paddle Boarding
- ☐ Photography
- ☐ Picnicking
- ☐ Rock Climbing
- ☐ Shooting Range
- ☐ Snowshoeing
- ☐ Stargazing
- ☐ Swimming
- ☐ Tennis
- ☐ Walking
- ☐ Wildlife Watching
- ☐ ____
- ☐ ____
- ☐ ____
- ☐ ____
- ☐ ____

Traveled by:

☐ ☐ ☐ ☐ ☐ ☐ ☐ ☐ ☐ ☐ ☐ ☐

Add your favorite ticket stub, postcard, photo, stamp or drawing here

N W E S NOT ALL THOSE WHO WANDER ARE LOST

PICK YOUR OWN PLACE

Star Rating ☆☆☆☆☆

What souvenir did you bring home?... Decal Magnet

My favorite thing about this place is...

Why I went ...

Who I went with ...

When I went ...

What I did...

What I saw...

What I learned...

An unforgettable moment...

A laughable moment...

A surprising moment...

An unforeseeable moment...

MY LIST

- ☐
- ☐
- ☐
- ☐
- ☐
- ☐
- ☐
- ☐
- ☐
- ☐
- ☐
- ☐

Snapped a selfie | Location...

Took a park sign selfie? - y | n

The weather was ...

Plan Your Trip:

☐ Trip Plan Completed

☐ Day Trip ☐ Overnight Stay

Reservations required: ☐y ☐n

Date reservations made: ____________

Refund Policy: ☐y ☐n Site/Room #: ______

Confirmation #: ____________

Miles to travel: ____________

Time traveling: ____________

Dog friendly?: ☐y ☐n

Destination Information:

Places we discovered along the way

Places to stop and see along the way

Would you go again?: ☐y ☐n

Open all year?: ☐y ☐n

Activities Accomplished:

☐ Archery
☐ Biking
☐ Birding
☐ Boating
☐ Camping
☐ Caving
☐ Geocaching
☐ Fishing
☐ Hiking
☐ Horseback Riding
☐ Hunting
☐ Off-Roading
☐ Paddle Boarding
☐ Photography
☐ Picnicking
☐ Rock Climbing
☐ Shooting Range
☐ Snowshoeing
☐ Stargazing
☐ Swimming
☐ Tennis
☐ Walking
☐ Wildlife Watching
☐ ____________
☐ ____________
☐ ____________
☐ ____________
☐ ____________

Traveled by:

☐ ☐ ☐ ☐ ☐ ☐ ☐ ☐ ☐ ☐ ☐ ☐

Add your favorite ticket stub, postcard, photo, stamp or drawing here

N E S W
NOT ALL THOSE WHO WANDER ARE LOST

Pick Your Own Place

Star Rating

☆☆☆☆☆

What souvenir did you bring home?... Decal Magnet

My favorite thing about this place is...

Why I went ...

Who I went with ...

When I went ...

What I did...

What I saw...

What I learned...

An unforgettable moment...

A laughable moment...

A surprising moment...

An unforeseeable moment...

My List

- ☐
- ☐
- ☐
- ☐
- ☐
- ☐
- ☐
- ☐
- ☐
- ☐
- ☐
- ☐

Snapped a selfie | Location...

Took a park sign selfie? - y | n

The weather was ...

Plan Your Trip:

☐ Trip Plan Completed

☐ Day Trip ☐ Overnight Stay

Reservations required: ☐y ☐n

Date reservations made: ______

Refund Policy: ☐y ☐n Site/Room #: ______

Confirmation #: ______

Miles to travel: ______

Time traveling: ______

Dog friendly?: ☐y ☐n

Destination Information:

______

______

Places we discovered along the way

______

______

______

Places to stop and see along the way

______

______

Would you go again?: ☐y ☐n

Open all year?: ☐y ☐n

Activities Accomplished:

- ☐ Archery
- ☐ Biking
- ☐ Birding
- ☐ Boating
- ☐ Camping
- ☐ Caving
- ☐ Geocaching
- ☐ Fishing
- ☐ Hiking
- ☐ Horseback Riding
- ☐ Hunting
- ☐ Off-Roading
- ☐ Paddle Boarding
- ☐ Photography
- ☐ Picnicking
- ☐ Rock Climbing
- ☐ Shooting Range
- ☐ Snowshoeing
- ☐ Stargazing
- ☐ Swimming
- ☐ Tennis
- ☐ Walking
- ☐ Wildlife Watching
- ☐ ______
- ☐ ______
- ☐ ______
- ☐ ______
- ☐ ______

Traveled by:

☐ ☐ ☐ ☐ ☐ ☐ ☐ ☐ ☐ ☐ ☐ ☐

Add your favorite ticket stub, postcard, photo, stamp or drawing here

N W E S NOT ALL THOSE WHO WANDER ARE LOST

Pick Your Own Place

Star Rating ☆☆☆☆☆

What souvenir did you bring home?... Decal Magnet

My favorite thing about this place is...

Why I went ...

Who I went with ...

When I went ...

What I did...

What I saw...

What I learned...

An unforgettable moment...

A laughable moment...

A surprising moment...

An unforeseeable moment...

My List

- ☐
- ☐
- ☐
- ☐
- ☐
- ☐
- ☐
- ☐
- ☐
- ☐
- ☐
- ☐

Snapped a selfie | Location...

Took a park sign selfie? - Y | N

The weather was ...